A WAR GUEST
IN CANADA

Darling Phil

Alec's arranged
v such a help to
We're all in the
same cabin
a lovely one —
Post going
Love Lil

Cunard White Star
"Britannic"
Sat: July 20ᵗʰ.

ar Mother,

When we arrived at Liverpool we waited
an hour in the dockyard. Then we had
t a full <u>three</u> hours showing up our
sports and proving we had not got jewell
signing embarkation cards and showi
passports at the immigration offices, and
of all showing passports to censors. My
ra was taken away and the film taken aw
ilm is being sent to you. When at last w
n board and into our cabin we found
age had been mixed up. We got some pe
the Holms's in our cabin too. The s
d us to find it Paul doing most work an
st we found all the cases mine being also

Studies in Childhood and Family in Canada

A broad-ranging series that publishes scholarship from various disciplines, approaches and perspectives relevant to the concepts and relations of childhood and family in Canada. Our interests also include, but are not limited to, interdisciplinary approaches and theoretical investigations of gender, race, sexuality, geography, language, and culture within these categories of experience, historical and contemporary. We welcome proposals and manuscripts from Canadian authors.

For further information, please contact the Series Editor, Professor Cynthia Comacchio, History Department, Wilfrid Laurier University.

Studies in
Childhood and Family
in Canada

A WAR GUEST IN CANADA

W.A.B. Douglas

Foreword by Cynthia Comacchio
Introduction by Roger Sarty

 WILFRID LAURIER
UNIVERSITY PRESS

Wilfrid Laurier University Press acknowledges the support of the Canada Council for the Arts for our publishing program. We acknowledge the financial support of the Government of Canada through the Canada Book Fund for our publishing activities. Funding provided by the Government of Ontario and the Ontario Arts Council. This work was supported by the Research Support Fund.

Library and Archives Canada Cataloguing in Publication

Title: A war guest in Canada / W.A.B. Douglas ; foreword by Cynthia Comacchio ; introduction by Roger Sarty.
Names: Douglas, W. A. B. (William Alexander Binny), 1929– author. | Comacchio, Cynthia R., 1957– writer of foreword. | Sarty, Roger, 1952– writer of introduction.
Series: Studies in childhood and family in Canada.
Description: Series statement: Studies in childhood and family in Canada | Includes bibliographical references.
Identifiers: Canadiana (print) 20230159974 | Canadiana (ebook) 20230160018 | ISBN 9781771123686 (softcover) | ISBN 9781771123693 (PDF) | ISBN 9781771123709 (EPUB)
Subjects: LCSH: Douglas, W. A. B. (William Alexander Binny), 1929-—Correspondence. | LCSH: World War, 1939-1945—Personal narratives, British. | LCSH: World War, 1939-1945—Children—Canada—Correspondence. | LCSH: World War, 1939-1945—Children—Great Britain—Correspondence. | LCSH: World War, 1939-1945—Evacuation of civilians—Great Britain. | LCSH: World War, 1939-1945—Evacuation of civilians—Canada. | LCSH: Children and war—Canada. | CSH: Canada—Social life and customs—1918-1945.
Classification: LCC D810.C4 D68 2023 | DDC 940.53/161—dc23
--

Cover design by Lara Minja. Interior design by Blakeley and Blakeley.

The photo on the front cover shows, from left to right, Alec Douglas, David Fry, Susan Fry, and Jeremy Fry at the Farm near Nobleton, ON, in 1943. The farm, nicknamed Moocowsgarden by Jeremy, is first mentioned on page 63, in the 17 August 1940 letter. Image courtesy of the author.

© 2023 Wilfrid Laurier University Press
Waterloo, Ontario, Canada
www.wlupress.wlu.ca

This book is printed on FSC® certified paper. It contains recycled materials and other controlled sources, is processed chlorine-free, and is manufactured using biogas energy. Printed in Canada

Wilfrid Laurier University Press is located on the Haldimand Tract, part of the traditional territories of the Haudenosaunee, Anishnaabe, and Neutral Peoples. This land is part of the Dish with One Spoon Treaty between the Haudenosaunee and Anishnaabe Peoples and symbolizes the agreement to share, to protect our resources, and not to engage in conflict. We are grateful to the Indigenous Peoples who continue to care for and remain interconnected with this land. Through the work we publish in partnership with our authors, we seek to honour our local and larger community relationships, and to engage with the diversity of collective knowledge integral to responsible scholarly and cultural exchange.

CONTENTS

Contents

FOREWORD
CYNTHIA COMACCHIO

Alec Douglas was a ten-year-old scholarship student at Christ's Hospital preparatory school in West Sussex, England, when the Second World War commenced in September of 1939. In that year, hundreds of thousands of British children were evacuated from cities, ports, and industrial centres likely to be targeted for Nazi aerial bombardment. His mother briefly considered sending him to family in Australia to keep him safe. The larger plan to evacuate British children was aborted when the Battle of the Atlantic began in earnest very soon after the war started. Young Alec would nonetheless make his cross-Atlantic journey in July 1940, though to a different commonwealth. After sailing as part of a convoy to New York, he was welcomed into a Canadian foster family in Toronto. He returned to England in 1943, later resettling in Canada as a young naval officer. Did his early ocean-faring experiences shape his chosen career path? That is a story best left to him to tell, which he does with aplomb in the pages that follow.

If Douglas's adult life was adventurous, he had already packed in some unique, even historic, adventures by the age of thirteen, as recounted in these pages. My purpose here is to draw from my own area of interest and scholarship, that of children's history, to contextualize what was undoubtedly—after the early and tragic loss of his father—his most formative childhood experience. The evacuation and resettlement of child refugees between the ages of five and fifteen—with a few even younger and a few more verging on eighteen years old—distinguished a cohort within the generation growing up and coming of age during the war, the larger defining experience of them all.[1] Although new historical accounts of the evacuation are becoming available, the scholarly literature on the Canadian aspects of the "guest children" experience is, on the whole, still scant.[2] And as Alec's memoirs testify, this story deserves to be better known.

It is generally acknowledged that the Second World War finished the Great Depression. What is less widely noted is that these historic world events also shortened childhood. As in the First World War, Canadian children were fortunate to be spared the brutalities of growing up in a constant state of siege and deprivation. They were nonetheless affected by the war's demands on the key adults in their lives. Many mothers took on full-time labour and shift work, or spent hours away from home in volunteer activities. Those with enlisted fathers suddenly found themselves in single-parent families. Children of Japanese heritage quickly discovered the meaning of public suspicion and racist animosity. Many of those children in particular endured the bitter loss of home and community as they were classified as enemy aliens, "evacuated," and incarcerated in internment camps for the protection of "Canadians." By the actions of racism and war—both adult creations—they lost any prospect of childhood shelter in a dangerous adult world. Although the war, coming on the heels of the long economic crisis of the 1930s, brought better material conditions than most children had known during that dark decade, the price was a share in adult concerns about the menacing international situation.

Many Canadian and British children were quickly made aware of what war in the Atlantic meant: only a few hours after Britain's declaration of war against Germany on September 3, 1939, a German U-boat attacked the British passenger ship SS *Athenia*, travelling from Liverpool to New York. The war's first known

Canadian civilian casualty was ten-year-old Margaret Hayworth of Hamilton, Ontario, who had been visiting her Scottish grandparents with her mother and younger sister. They were on board the *Athenia* precisely because Margaret's mother had moved up their date of departure for fear of being stranded overseas if war broke out. Fully three-quarters of the passengers were women and children fleeing the United Kingdom, and several British children on the voyage also perished.[3]

If the prospect of an Atlantic crossing in wartime was fraught for all who attempted it, it was all the more so for the young. Margaret Hayworth was hit by flying debris and died five days later on the rescue ship. Her five-year-old sister, Jacqueline, survived the sinking but was mistakenly sent back to her maternal relatives in Scotland by rescuers and only returned to Canada several months later, long after Margaret's funeral. As her experience shows, separation from parents and family were frequent outcomes of attack at sea. Jacqueline Hayworth was fortunate to have been carrying identifying information at a time when reuniting unidentified children with their kin was challenging, if not impossible, at least until after the war was over. Those who survived often found themselves suddenly orphaned, or presumed orphaned, and could well spend their childhood years in institutions or foster homes, potentially losing any sense of their own identity or any memory of their parents and siblings.

On the whole, Canadian children were not directly affected by a war far from their own shores. From the start of the conflict, however, they regularly heard and saw enough to be aware of what "the war to save the world for democracy" demanded of all Canadians, regardless of age. As during the Great War, barely a generation before, duty and sacrifice and home-front support became their rallying cry, in school, in church, at home, in their extracurricular activities, and in their after-school clubs.[4] One man who grew up during that time captured the sense that many children likely had about social expectations that they "do their bit": "We were steeped in propaganda up to here," he recalled. "They seemed to direct an awful lot of it at the kids ..."[5]

Consequently, plans that were set in motion overseas to evacuate British children—the plans that would so profoundly affect young Alec Douglas—were met with enthusiasm by Canadian organizations, especially those representing various national, local, and cultural women's groups, and also by the children who were going to be instrumental in making the little "guests" comfortable for the duration. Some of the plans had been drawn up even before official declarations of war. As Nazi forces trampled central Europe in the late 1930s, the British government encouraged parents in the areas likely to be targeted by Nazi bombs to arrange for their children to be sent to the nearby countryside, usually to stay with kin or family friends. Lists of families willing to take in children were also made up, though some children boarded with strangers, not always happily. Other parents—perhaps better off, more anxious, or able to rely on distant family and friends—looked further afield, hoping to send their children to safe havens in the various nations attached to or allied with the United Kingdom.

Canadians quickly demonstrated their eagerness to offer the little refugees temporary sanctuary if war broke out. Already by May of 1938, the National Council of Women was compiling lists of potential sponsors; by early September of 1939, the group had received 100,000 offers from across Canada.[6] In Ontario, the premier, the press, the churches, and the schools were avid supporters of the "guest children" program, as it came to be known. Canadian socialite and philanthropist Lady Flora Eaton offered her estate in King City, Ontario, as a temporary home for child evacuees.[7] Her invitation included the young princesses Elizabeth and Margaret, but the royal family was determined to remain in London for the sake of civilian morale. Evacuating children from cities and other vulnerable areas, however, became an urgent war duty for the British that was supported by Canadian civilians.

Many Canadians had become familiar with, or at least knew about, what the mass arrival of unescorted British children entailed, thanks to the child immigration schemes that had operated, virtually without pause, from the Victorian years until the Great Depression. While the transatlantic movements of these "home children" were always, and increasingly, problematic, the evacuation of "guest children" from England to Canada seems to have been uniformly endorsed by both countries. Unlike the "waifs and strays" of earlier waves—the neglected, abandoned or at least semi-orphaned and generally deprived child immigrants who were frequently exploited for their labour rather than being enfolded into families—the young war evacuees were selected according to rigorous class and race-defined criteria. The first arrivals who came by private means, some with their mothers or other adult escorts, especially fit the prevalent Canadian image of the ideal immigrant, a construction that endured despite the rising xenophobia and anti-Semitism that were setting Europe on fire. That immigrant was white, English-speaking, mostly Protestant, and of British birth and heritage. Among the first 6,000 or so child evacuees—the numbers are challenging to fix because of the private arrangements made for many—few, if any, were other than solidly middle class. They were at once ideal immigrants and ideal children of the sort Canadians wanted their own to be.[8]

In any case, the arrangements made were meant to be "for the duration" emergency measures that might net Canada some worthy future citizens if any of the children opted to stay. Unlike the home children who had come before, these little immigrants would continue to have some semblance of their former lives: they would live as family members, not servants, and they would go to school, not be sent out to earn their keep. In no way could they be confused with the "pauper children" of earlier transatlantic child migration programs. In an editorial titled "Our Duty to British Children," the *Globe and Mail* declared that Canada would happily provide sanctuary for "as many British boys and girls as we can make room for."[9] The period's influential child experts were also remarkably reassuring about the evacuation's effects for the children involved. Dr. William Blatz, Director of the Child Studies Institute at the University of Toronto, concluded in 1940 that "[i]f this social pilgrimage is carried on reasonably, calmly and efficiently, then no harm will follow," based on his own experiences with children in both Canada and England, where he had been placed in charge of the wartime day nurseries. But he did warn about the importance of avoiding "confusion and undue emotional excitement," which could render the experience of being removed from family and home and shipped far away to live with strangers "more harmful than bombing," indicating these were the crucial factors in determining its effect.[10]

Blatz and his mostly like-minded colleagues, both in Canada and abroad, seem to have neglected what else could induce evacuation-induced trauma: the tender age and sensibilities of the children, as well as their experiences of being removed from their home, parents, family, school—in sum, from their only known world. It is difficult for historians, untrained in psychiatry, to estimate rates of trauma resulting from events in the past. Trauma is a psychological classification, although it is often used synonymously with "effect" or "impact." Recent studies of the long-term impact of the evacuation, informed by developmental neuroscience, suggest that these were far more serious than child psychologists of the time believed.[11]

In June of 1940, as France fell, the British government established the Children's Overseas Reception Board (CORB) to ensure that children whose families could not afford their passage were also given an opportunity to leave. The CORB ultimately received 211,448 applications, representing as many as half of all eligible British children in the category of five- to fifteen-year-olds. In the face of this organized state effort, the Canadian government began to voice some trepidation, emphasizing that only "suitable" children be selected. Unlike the earliest evacuees, these newer refugees were more likely to be comprised of lower-class and less "refined" types, including those from racial and religious minorities.[12] Thus the meaning of "suitable" was self-evident.

Young Alec Douglas was eminently suitable, as a student at a prestigious private school. His widowed mother, however, although of the right race, religion, and "station," was unable to evacuate with him, despite a Toronto friend's invitation to them both, as she was working as a fashion designer and buyer at an exclusive London department store. Initially, Phyllis Douglas did not want to participate in "any" government scheme, but rapidly escalating danger on the high seas was starting to imperil the evacuation convoys. Disaster finally came in September of 1940, when the SS *City of Benares* was torpedoed and seventy-seven of the ninety children aboard, and six of their escorts, were lost.[13] By June of 1940, however, Phyllis Douglas's anxiety to see her only son to safety led to complicated but successful arrangements for him to travel with wealthy friends and to be delivered to Toronto. On 20 July 1940, Alec departed, after hasty preparations with his mother's friends on the MV *Britannic*, as he well remembers. His mother bade him an emotional farewell, but Alec believes he was "too excited to be sad, and too callow!" His guardians on the ship later wrote to his mother that he "seemed very thrilled" on the entire journey.

At least as their own memories serve, some of the child evacuees who left Britain, whether by private or state means, were just as excited as Alec was about the prospect of an ocean voyage and the adventure they assumed awaited them in Canada and elsewhere on "the other side." Journalist Michael Henderson was eight years old and his brother six when they sailed from Glasgow to Boston via Halifax in 1940 In Henderson's view, they had been "oblivious to the dangers we had come through ... it was a sense of adventure that prevailed." Patricia Backlar arrived in August 1940 after a harrowing ten days in a convoy travelling under strict black-out conditions because of German submarines. Backlar felt that "coming into Halifax was like coming into fairyland ... the nicest part of all was to see the millions of unshielded harbour lights that night."[14] Cheering crowds met the children at Pier 21 in Halifax, and at every train station as they were dispersed across the country.

In the end, approximately 1,535 children in the CORB program, along with another 1,654 privately sponsored children, made the journey to Canada safely before the mission was forcibly terminated due to the dangers of overseas travel. Of these nearly 3,200 children, 607 passed their sojourn in Ontario. Thousands of Canadian families that had prepared to receive child evacuees were disappointed, as undoubtedly were the British families who had tried unsuccessfully to secure their children's safe removal. Canadian children, meanwhile, were carefully primed about their patriotic duty and the special needs of their British refugee peers, and were prepared to look upon the new arrivals with considerable sympathy as well as typical childhood curiosity. Writer Jean Little remembers how she would "stare sideways" at one of the girls in her Guelph schoolroom, wondering at her evident self-possession and calm with her parents so far away and in such a perilous situation. Little believes that her writerly empathy was sparked by these youthful reflections about these children when she herself "couldn't imagine living separated from my mother," and she worried obsessively about her father who, though enlisted, was stationed at Canadian training camps.[15] For writer Budge Wilson, whose Halifax elementary school "seemed to be full of them," the guest children were "a crucial element of my journey through and out of childhood." Like Little, she sensed that they felt "strange" because of their accents, the clothes they wore, their choices in food, their "British" demeanour. Moreover, the evacuees' own strongly defined class position "at home" made them uncomfortable even within their refugee group, where children of different class, cultural, and regional identities were suddenly mixing as they never had before. She and her friends, Wilson concluded, had "a love-hate relationship" with the guest children, at once admiring them and trying to imitate their accents and manners and also resenting them for the "specialness" granted by their very presence in Canada.[16]

Although the guest children—even the name allotted them suggested a happy, and temporary, status—were by and large warmly welcomed and cared for, their abrupt separation from parents and community was unquestionably traumatic for them in varying degrees. Official home inspections were conducted by a number of local child welfare agencies but instability in placement was not uncommon. Like the home children before them, some war guests were relocated several times during their stay, sometimes due to the illness, death, or relocation of host parents, and sometimes to their hosts' inability to cope with a child's behavioural issues triggered or exacerbated by their experiences.

The Sharp brothers, Bill, Christopher, and Tom, started their Canadian adventure in what appeared an ideal situation. Through private arrangements made by their mother, Margaret Sharp, and her distant cousin in Canada, Marie Curtis Peterkin Williamson, they were sent in 1940 to board with the Williamson family in their comfortable Toronto neighbourhood. John Williamson, a senior actuary with the Canada Life Assurance Company, had been sent to work at their London office for several months in 1923. It was at this time that Marie Williamson had met the Sharps, along with the boys' maternal grandparents. Back in Toronto, Marie kept up an occasional correspondence with her London cousins. As war threatened in 1938, the Williamsons were approached about giving refuge to the boys and their mother, although Margaret later decided to remain in England with her widowed mother.[17]

Marie Williamson was a 42-year-old mother of two school-aged children when the boys arrived in 1940. She suffered from continuing health issues that made raising five children, three of whom were strangers to her, a considerable strain. The two older boys were soon sent separately to other family friends: Bill remained in Toronto with the Ratcliffe family, while Christopher went to his godfather's family in Washington. Tom and Christopher were reunited and sent together back to England in June of 1944. Tom was then thirteen years old and Christopher fifteen.

Biology and environment ensured that these were not the same children who had departed in 1940. Their adjustment to "home" in England was challenging; Tom and Christopher had spent their formative years in very different environments with very different foster families. Furthermore, their parents had divorced and their father was remarried and had a new son. England itself had also greatly changed since their evacuation, and, unlike North America, would long afterwards feel the war's effects. Their forced childhood separation, not surprisingly, had lifelong repercussions. The brothers never redeveloped any fraternal closeness despite remaining in England, nor did they ever reinstate anything but a long-distance relationship with Bill.[18] Eighteen years old when his brothers departed from Canada, Bill Sharp opted to attend the University of Toronto, despite his father's pleas that he enrol at one of the elite British universities. After obtaining a BA and MA in mathematics at Toronto and a PhD from Princeton, he joined the faculty at the University of Toronto as a theoretical physicist.[19]

A number of those who came of age in Canada chose to remain, while others, like Teddie Davy, despite being well-treated in the Halifax home of RCAF chaplain Reverend Walter Dunlap chose to return home early. At age fifteen, Davy worked his passage home as a cabin boy on a Norwegian cargo ship when the Dunlaps were transferred to Montreal in 1943.[20] Yet he found it difficult to "settle" in England and returned to Canada as a permanent immigrant in 1948.[21]

By early 1946, 1,326 of the 1,535 children who had taken part in the CORB program had been repatriated.[22] Some were haunted by a sense that they had been unwanted by their parents and had consequently been sent to Canada to live among strangers. There were also foreseeable difficulties of adaptation once they did return to homes and families that, for the younger children, were perhaps only a vague memory. They had bonded with their Canadian "parents" and siblings, had started school in Canada and made fond friends. Many "felt" more Canadian than British. Some had known material comforts they would never again enjoy in their working-class families of origin. Some resented the more obvious and rigid British class hierarchy that curtailed their education and work prospects. Of course, host families were also torn about relinquishing their "guests," who had become regular family members and participants in their everyday lives, and thereby integral to their circles of kin, church, and community.[23] Alec Douglas appears to have been one of the more fortunate, or the more resilient: his experience with his foster family, as he details it here, was a positive experience for him during early adolescence, a critical time in individual self-formation.

From what their own memories reveal, what the official records demonstrate, and what historians have so far put together, the unquestionably difficult child evacuation—for parents, siblings, foster families, and above all for the guest children themselves— had relatively few dramatic outcomes. We can't exactly generalize from Alec Douglas's warm memories of his own situation, but what we know supports an argument for its relative commonality. Certainly the young British refugees fared much better than other European children in far more pressing need of refuge, especially Jewish children. Only about one per cent of the Jewish children in Europe at the war's beginning survived to the end.[24] During the eight months of the ferocious Nazi Blitzkrieg, an estimated 43,000 civilians were killed, countless thousands were severely injured and often permanently disabled, while about 70,000 homes were destroyed. By the time the war ended in May of 1945, the total of civilian deaths, injuries, and displacement is believed to be at least twice those numbers.

Although Canada provided safe haven for only a few of the original 50,000 predicted to come, the 3,200 or so "guest children" experienced a mercifully different war. Despite their separation from home and family, the war in Canada must have felt like peace. I'm sure that Alec Douglas would agree.

Notes

1 Although they were undoubtedly emotionally affected and even traumatized by their separation from family and home, the experiences of the British guest children clearly do not compare directly to those of the estimated one million child-victims of the Holocaust; see, for example Ben Lappin, *The Redeemed Children: The Story of the Rescue of War Orphans by the Jewish Community of Canada* (Toronto: University of Toronto Press, 1963); S. Gigliotti, and M. Tempian, eds., *The Young Victims of the Nazi Regime: Migration, the Holocaust, and Postwar Displacement* (London, U.K.: Bloomsbury Academic, 2016).

2 Recent examples include Carlton Jackson, *Who Will Take Our Children?: The British Evacuation Program of World War II* (Jefferson, N.C.: McFarland, 2008); Claire Halstead, "'Dangers Behind, Pleasures Ahead': British-Canadian Identity and the Evacuation of British Children to Canada during the Second World War," *British Journal of Canadian Studies* 24, no. 7 (2014): 163–79; Helen Brown, "Negotiating Space, Time, and Identity: The Hutton-Pellett Letters and a British Child's Wartime Evacuation to Canada," in *Letters Across Borders: The Epistolary Practices of International Migrants*, ed. Bruce Elliott, David Gerber and Suzanne Sinke (New York: Palgrave Macmillan, 2006), 223–47; Claire Halstead, "'Dear Mummy and Daddy': Reading Wartime Letters from British Children Evacuated to Canada During the Second World War," in *Children, Childhood and Youth in the British World*, ed. Shirleene Robinson and Simon Sleight (London, U.K.: Palgrave Macmillan, 2016), 92–108; R.J. Barman, *Safe Haven: The Wartime Letters of Ben Barman and Margaret Penrose, 1940–1943* (Montreal and Kingston: McGill-Queen's University Press, 2018). Older books include Geoffrey Bilson, *The Guest Children: The Story of the British Child Evacuees Sent to Canada During World War II* (Saskatoon: Fifth House, 1988) and Ben Wicks, *The Day They Took the Children* (Toronto: Stoddart, 1989).

3 "Hamilton Girl, Age 10, Nazi Torpedo Victim, Dies on Rescue Ship," *Globe and Mail*, 10 September 1939. There were 1,400 passengers on board; 117 passengers and crew were killed. See *Dictionary of Canadian Biography Online*, s.v. "Hayworth, Margaret Janet," by Jonathan Vance, accessed 30 October 2022, http://www.biographi.ca/en/bio/hayworth_margaret_janet_16E.html

4 Home front efforts are discussed in Norah Lewis, "Isn't This a Terrible War?": The Attitudes of Children to Two World Wars," *Historical Studies in Education* 7, no. 2 (1995): 193–215; Jeff Keshen, *Saints, Sinners, and Soldiers Canada's Second World War*, 2nd ed. (Vancouver: UBC Press, 2004); Cynthia Comacchio, "'To Hold on High the Torch of Liberty': Canadian Youth and the Second World War," in *Canada and the Second World War: Essays in Honour of Terry Copp*, ed. Geoffrey Hayes, Michael Bechthold, and Matt Symes (Waterloo, ON: Wilfrid Laurier University Press, 2012), 33–65.

5 Cited in Barry Broadfoot, ed. *Six War Years, 1939–1945: Memories of Canadians at Home and Abroad*, 3rd ed. (Don Mills, ON: PaperJacks, 1980), 124. Broadfoot includes neither dates nor names for the oral histories in this collection.

6 Jonathan Vance, ""Forward," in *Just a Larger Family: Letters of Marie Williamson from the Canadian Home Front, 1940–1944*, ed. Mary F. Williamson and Tom Sharp (Waterloo, ON: Wilfrid Laurier University Press, 2011), xxvi. Mary F. Williamson, is the daughter of Marie and John Williamson, and Tom Sharp is the youngest of the three boys taken in by the Williamsons. They also contributed the introduction and biographical notes; the epilogue is written by Mary Sharp, wife of Tom.

7 Lady Eaton (1880–1970) was the wife of department store president Sir John Craig Eaton. See Flora McCrea Eaton, *Memory's Wall: The Autobiography of Flora McCrea Eaton* (Toronto: Clarke, Irwin & Co., 1956).

8 Estimates suggest that a further 260 children disembarked in Canada in 1941, and another 120 in 1942 (see Halstead, "'Dangers Behind, Pleasures Ahead,'" 163–79). 1,306 British children went to Australia, 470 to New Zealand, 1,473 to South Africa, and 2,928 to the United States; see also J. Mann, *Out of Harm's Way* (London: Headline Book Publishing, 1998), 11.

9 "Our Duty to British Children," *Globe and Mail*, 8 July 1939.

10 W.E. Blatz, *Hostages to Peace: Parents and the Children of Democracy* (New York: W. Morrow and Co., 1940), 201–2. Dr. William E. Blatz (1895–1964) was director of the University of Toronto's Institute of Child Study and the leading child psychologist in Canada at the time

11 Psychologists who have examined case histories from the Second World War have uncovered its deep legacy in the individual psyche and its lifelong effects; see, for example, Peter Heinl, *Splintered Innocence: An Intuitive Approach to Treating War Trauma* (New York: Routledge, 2013); James S.M. Rusby and Fiona Tasker, "Childhood Temporary Separation: Long-Term Effects of the British Evacuation of Children during World War 2 on Older Adults' Attachment Styles," *Attachment and Human Development* 10, no. 2 (2008): 208–10. Using historical evidence and contemporary trauma theory, psychologists Rusby and Tasker interviewed 900 respondents evacuated from Kent to rural districts, though not overseas. They found a significant harmful impact on attachment in adult relationships and on fearfulness. Rusby and Tasker's focus on attachment was also informed by the post-war findings of Dr. John Bowlby (1907–90), the British child psychologist who introduced the highly influential attachment theory. Bowlby also believed the repercussions of early childhood separation from parents, especially mothers, were highly detrimental to adult functioning. See especially *Attachment and Loss*, vol. 1, *Attachment* (London: Hogarth Press, 1969) and vol. 2, *Separation: Anxiety and Anger* (London: Hogarth Press, 1973).

12 "1580 Children Arrive on Battle-Grey Liners," *Globe and Mail*, 30 July 1940.

13 Keshen, *Saints, Sinners, and Soldiers*, 197–98; Vance, "Forward," in Williamson and Sharp, eds. *Just A Larger Family*, xvii; Halstead, "'Dangers Behind, Pleasures Ahead,'" 164.

14 Michael Henderson, "Across the Atlantic to Safety," *The Chronicle Herald/The Novascotian*, 5 September 2010. English journalist/broadcaster/author Henderson published a book about the boys' experiences, *"See You After the Duration"—The Story of British Evacuees to North America in World War II* (Richmond, VA: Publish America Paperback, 2004), forward by historian Sir Martin Gilbert. He and his brother Gerald spent five years in Milton, Massachusetts. Many of the chapters and other related essays can be found on his webpage, https://www.michaelhenderson.org.uk

15 Jean Little, "I Sat in Loew's Theatre ..." in *Too Young to Fight: Memories from Our Youth During World War II*, ed. Priscilla Galloway (Toronto: Stoddart, 1999), 88–89.

16 Budge Wilson, "To Live in Halifax," in Galloway, ed, *Too Young to Fight*, 179–81.

17 Williamson and Sharp, "introduction," *Just a Larger Family*, 2-4; 6; 14. See also their "Biographical Notes," especially "Williamson, Marie Curtis nee Peterkin, (1898-1969)", 25; "Sharp, Margaret, nee Tout (1896-1987)", 22-23; "Sharp, William Douglas (1894, 1955)", 23.

18 Vance, "Foreword," in Williamson, *Just a Larger Family*, 14-15; Sharp, "Epilogue," 331.

19 Sharp, "Epilogue," in Williamson, 237.

20 John D. Reid, "WW2 British Child Evacuees to Canada," accessed 1 November 2022, http://www.johndreid.com/ww2-british-child-evacuees-to-canada/. Dr. John D. Reid is an Ottawa-based local historian with a particular interest in the child evacuees.

21 Reid, "WW2 British Child Evacuees to Canada."

22 "War Guest Children Now Britain Bound," *Toronto Daily Star*, 5 July 1945.

23 Keshen, *Saints, Sinners, and Soldiers*, 200–202.

24 The classic reference regarding the official Canadian position on Jewish refugees is Irving Abella and Harold Troper, *None Is Too Many: Canada and the Jews of Europe* (Toronto: Lester & Orpen Dennys, 1982; Toronto: University of Toronto Press, 2012). Canada admitted only 5,000 to 8,000 Jews in the years from 1933 to 1945, the worst record of any large non-European country. See also Adara Goldberg, *Canadian Encyclopedia*, s.v. "Canada and the Holocaust" by Adara Goldberg, accessed 1 November 2022. https://www.thecanadianencyclopedia.ca/en/article/holocaust. Among the 170,000 postwar Jewish refugees, 4,000 were children, and none were younger than fifteen.

INTRODUCTION
THE CAREERS OF W.A.B. DOUGLAS: SAILOR AND HISTORIAN
ROGER SARTY

"I came here [Canada] long before you arrived." This was Alec[1] Douglas's response (as best I can recall) to my teasing about his English accent sometime in the early 1980s. As I later learned, he had in fact come to Canada twice: first as a "war guest" from 1940 to 1943, and then permanently in 1947. That is the story told in the letters reproduced here. Alec himself maintains that these experiences profoundly influenced his later life, which is the subject of this introduction.

In 1950, at the beginning of Alec's final year at the University of Toronto, he enrolled as a regular officer in the Royal Canadian Navy. During the 1960s, while still serving in the navy, he reinvented himself as a historian and was posted to the Directorate of History at Canadian Forces Headquarters in Ottawa, the office that carried out historical research and publishing for the Department of National Defence (DND) and the armed services. In 1973 he retired from the navy to become the civilian director of history, one of the most prominent historical positions in the Government of Canada. While there, he promoted Canadian naval and air force history, fields that had previously barely existed, and pioneered international research that shed new light on the world wars of the twentieth century. He supervised the production of five substantial volumes of official military history, and was principal author of three of them. He also regularly wrote—and continues to write—for both academic and general interest publications. Long an adjunct professor at Carleton University in Ottawa, where he supervised graduate students, he was also a visiting professor at Duke University in Durham, North Carolina, from 1988 to 1989 and from 2001 to 2002.[2]

Wordsworth's poetic line "The child is father of the man" has become hackneyed since first published in 1807, perhaps because of its insight. Certainly Alec's childhood letters are evidence that his interest in the navy and, ultimately, historical studies, was kindled by his experience of the Second World War's Battle of the Atlantic. In 1940, he had crossed from England to New York in a convoy on a passenger ship, and returned by convoy to England in 1943, but this time on a British warship. (Fortunately, neither convoy came under enemy attack.)

The letters also reveal personal qualities of Alec's that would serve him well. Even before his evacuation, there had been a good deal in his early life that could have set him back. Born in Salisbury, Southern Rhodesia (now Harare, Zimbabwe) in 1929, Alec was three when his mother, Phyllis, took him home to England to protect him from the malaria that ran rampant in the area (and that she was already afflicted with). Alec never got to know his father, Hector, who stayed behind in Rhodesia at his job as a dam engineer. Hector Douglas died when Alec was six of blackwater fever, a rare and dangerous complication of malaria. Alec was raised in London by his mother, who had to work full-time to support herself and her son. In 1940, at the age of eleven, he was suddenly removed from his boarding school south of London and sent to Canada to live with a family he only slightly knew, and immediately had to adjust to an education system quite different from the one in the United Kingdom. His mother remarried while he was gone, to a Canadian Army officer serving overseas, and so when Alec returned to London at the age of fourteen, he had to adjust to a new stepfather while readjusting to the British education system, for which he was not well prepared after his time in Canada. Nevertheless, the letters—Alec's own and those about him by his foster mother in Toronto—show no hint of distress or discouragement. Rather the reverse: he was apparently cheerful, optimistic, and made the best of whatever was thrown at him.

Alec, when he began his studies at the University of Toronto in 1947, also enrolled in the Royal Canadian Navy's University Naval Training Division to help cover the cost of his education. Under that program he became a member of the naval reserve, with pay for sixty hours of training through the school year, and for fourteen weeks of full-time training during the summer. He was obliged, after graduation, only to continue in the naval reserve. The experience, however, led him to make a career choice by enrolling as an officer in the regular navy in September of 1950, the beginning of his final year at university. The timing was fortuitous, as the Canadian armed forces had just embarked upon a period of unheralded growth in size and professionalism. The Royal Canadian Navy (RCN) had barely existed prior to the Second World War and then expanded thirty-fold, with more than 90,000 personnel and 250 ocean-going warships, to counter the German submarine assault on Allied shipping. Although greatly reduced after the war, the service was able to retain the most capable of its new warships. The deepening of the Cold War in 1948 and 1949 saw the creation of the North Atlantic Treaty Organization (NATO), with Canada as a founding member; the outbreak of the Korean War in 1950 then triggered full-scale rearmament among the Western powers. Canada built up a substantial regular armed forces for the first time in its history. The navy grew and, by the early 1960s, had some 21,000 full-time personnel and sixty seagoing warships, including twenty Canadian-designed and -built destroyers that were among the most capable and innovative vessels of their type in the world. Alec served on many of the warships of the new fleet, including two of the state-of-the-art destroyers.

Alec was part of the first generation of young personnel in a more consciously national navy. Canada's tiny pre-1939 service had depended heavily on the British Royal Navy, and continued to rely on the Royal Navy's expertise during the Second World War. In the late 1940s, the RCN had begun to operate more closely with the U.S. Navy, which by then had replaced the Royal Navy as the strongest in the world. Still, the RCN continued to turn to the Royal Navy for assistance in training its people. Alec did two tours in the United Kingdom: the first in 1953 for the courses that qualified him for the rank of lieutenant; and then in 1958, when he took the challenging "long" course for his specialization as a navigator. He was, nevertheless, building his career in a service that had established its own traditions during the hard-fought Battle of the Atlantic. In 1953, Alec gained first-hand experience of those traditions on the frigate HCMS *Swansea*, herself a distinguished war veteran having participated in the destruction of four German U-boats.

Almost immediately after joining we sailed for Exercise Mariner [a major NATO transatlantic exercise] in the teeth of a gale and I suffered the miseries of seasickness for several days. When a seaman took pity on me and helped to clean up my upchuck, the first lieutenant passed by and immediately stopped my leave for the next period ashore because I was not cleaning it up entirely by myself.

Swansea was not in very good condition: in bad weather the sea poured in through a seam on the ship's side and our mess was usually awash with sea water. However, we were young and flexible and managed to survive these conditions. I stood as second officer of the watch. ... Swansea had an open bridge (she would go in for conversion to the Prestonian Class, with enclosed bridge, at the end of her commission in 1956). By the end of

4

each watch I remember being soaked to the skin with
no adequate facilities for drying our weather jackets and
oilskins. ...

Perhaps this was an unconventional way to prepare a
junior officer for sub-lieutenants' courses. However, those
in Naval Service headquarters[3] who controlled our destiny,
no doubt themselves veterans of small ship time in the
Second World War, evidently knew exactly what they were
doing. Two weeks on the North Atlantic in a rather tired
old frigate probably stood me in better stead than months
in a well-equipped destroyer carrying out glamorous roles
in more exotic climes![4]

The positive spin Alec put on a trying ordeal echoed the tone
of his childhood letters, and it was a quality regularly in evidence.[5]
Alec has tended to see opportunities rather than roadblocks
throughout his life, and opportunities outside the normal sort
of military career became available in the 1950s and 1960s with
the expansion of the Canadian defence establishment. Equally
important, he somewhat unwittingly prepared himself to grasp
those opportunities by returning to academic studies in history
on his own time when he was in his early thirties. Although he
had majored in history at the University of Toronto and studied
with some of the top historians in the country, the subject had
not excited him—in part, as he later reflected, because there were
no courses in military history. From 1958 to 1960, following his
navigation course in the United Kingdom, he had rewarding
naval postings as the navigation and operations officer on HMCS
Ottawa and then HMCS *Kootenay*, two of the newest destroyers.
He also passed the rigorous qualifying examinations for command
of a destroyer. Setting his sights on wider professional horizons,
he asked to attend the staff course where mid-career officers
study higher level operations and the relationship of armed forces

to national policies and international relations. Instead, he was posted in Halifax as assistant staff officer (navigation) on the staff of Flag Officer Atlantic Coast, a routine job that involved adjusting the compasses of warships as they swung around their moorings in Bedford Basin, and sailing on the work-up cruises of newly refitted ships to ensure their navigation equipment was working properly.

To stave off boredom, he enrolled in a history M.A. program at Dalhousie University. He combined his earlier historical training with his service experience to complete a 199-page thesis, "Halifax as an Element of Sea Power, 1749 to 1766," in 1962. Much as Halifax has always been a "navy town," this was the first focused study on the Royal Navy's role in the founding and early development of the city. It was not only substantial, but well researched and argued. Under the guidance of Dalhousie historians P.B. Waite (who had served in the RCN during the war, and had done research on the military and naval aspects of Canadian confederation), Guy MacLean (who worked in military history and history of the British Empire), and C. Bruce Fergusson, the archivist of Nova Scotia, Alec digested the major works in British empire naval history, along collections of naval and military documents held by the Public Archives of Nova Scotia and the Public Archives of Canada.

Alec was drawn to his subject by C.P. Stacey's article "Halifax as an International Strategic Factor, 1749–1949," written on the occasion of the city's bicentennial in 1949.[6] The article, still the best overview on the subject available, demonstrated how little serious research had been done on Halifax's military history. Stacey, one of the first Canadian academics to specialize in military history, was the author of the official history of the Canadian Army in the Second World War. In the process of writing that multi-volume history, he turned the army's historical section in Ottawa into a top-flight research institution before he retired in 1959, at the rank of colonel, to take up a professorship at the University of Toronto.[7] Stacey was a Toronto native and graduate of the university, and he had given a lecture there on the army's historical program during Alec's time as an undergraduate. Alec recalled that he had not found Stacey's talk inspiring; an irony in view of the influence Stacey would have on Alec's later career.

Alec was still working on his thesis in the evenings and on the weekends when, in 1961, he was promoted to lieutenant commander and posted as the senior navigator and operations officer for the Seventh Escort Squadron, comprising five recently modernized anti-submarine frigates. His new post put him in a key position when the squadron conducted sweeps in company with naval and RCAF maritime patrol aircraft in search of Soviet submarines off Nova Scotia during the Cuban Missile Crisis of October 1962. This was the closest the West and the Soviet bloc came to war. The United States Navy, which needed all its available ships for patrols in southern waters to intercept Soviet freighters delivering missiles to Cuba, requested Canadian forces to make an all-out effort in northern waters through which Soviet submarines were transiting to support the buildup in Cuba. Although the crisis was peacefully resolved through personal negotiations by telephone between U.S. President John F. Kennedy and Soviet premier Nikita Khrushchev, the extensive patrols mounted by the Canadian forces on short notice demonstrated the capabilities reached by the RCN and the maritime air group of the Royal Canadian Air Force (RCAF) since the expansion of the armed services began in the early 1950s.

In 1964, Alec's career significantly changed direction once again when he was posted to the Royal Military College of Canada (RMC) in Kingston as the naval staff officer and an associate professor of military studies. His job was to attend to the welfare and discipline of the naval cadets in the tri-service college and also, together with the army and air force staff officers, teach military subjects to all the cadets, including history. Alec was uniquely qualified as the only executive officer in the navy who possessed a post-graduate history degree.

Alec enjoyed the convivial company of his military and academic colleagues at the college, and the regular contact with cadets in both their course work and busy schedule of sports and other extra-curricular activities. Kingston, moreover, was home of the few academics in Canada, other than C.P. Stacey, who focused on military history. Alec made a particular connection with R.A. Preston and D.M. Schurman at RMC, and with Sydney F. Wise at Queen's University, just across the harbour, who had started his own career teaching military history at RMC. Alec soon joined them in the annual spring tours of American Civil War battlefields organized by Jay Luvaas, a military historian at Duke University, where Preston had recently been a visiting professor. Luvaas, considered to be one of the fathers of the post-1945 revival of battlefield studies as a part of military education, had considerable stature. The "Army of the Cussawago," as the group termed itself, included notable scholars as well as influential officers from the U.S. armed forces, which had long recognized the importance of academic historical studies for professional development and "lessons learned" for policy making, administration, and operations. For Alec, a keen traveller who palpably enjoys meeting new people and learning of their experiences and interests—traits that also run through his childhood letters—these excursions were high points.[8] He is no less happy while attending academic conferences, fully engaged and often one of the first in the audience to encourage presenters, especially young academics, with positive comments and questions.[9] In later years, when Alec bore heavy responsibilities, he would return from professional travel (and, no less, local academic conferences), refreshed and recharged, regaling staff with what he had learned and, not infrequently, with sketches of interesting or quirky people he had met. Up to the present day, he has retained a gift for not just seeming, but actually being, more interested in what others have to say than in expounding on his own wisdom.

At RMC, Alec also had a chance to continue his own formal education in history. The college, which had become an accredited degree-granting institution only in 1959, was anxious to continue to improve its academic program. It offered its first-ever graduate course in the 1965–66 school year. History 500 was taught by Brian Tunstall, the prominent naval historian from the London School of Economics, who had a visiting appointment at RMC. Alec seized this remarkable opportunity, his superiors agreeing— as in the case of his M.A. program at Dalhousie—that he could on condition he did the course on his own time.

He did still more, developing one of the chapters of his M.A. thesis for publication. "The Sea Militia of Nova Scotia, 1749– 1755: A Comment on Naval Policy" appeared in the *Canadian Historical Review*, the top Canadian academic history journal, in March 1966. The publication was a major achievement in establishing professional credentials. In hindsight, the subtitle "A Comment on Naval Policy" was significant. The chapter on which the article was based was key to the central argument of the thesis, which was that the Royal Navy had no interest in Halifax when the city was founded by the British government in 1749. The city, as a centre of settlement, existed to counter the continued domination of mainland Nova Scotia by a largely French population, despite the fact possession of the region had passed from France to Britain in 1713. Consequently, the civilian administration at Halifax had armed and crewed its own small vessels. This "Sea Militia" was so successful in supporting operations against growing French military efforts in the region that the Royal Navy was ultimately drawn, in 1755 and after, into what was becoming a significant theatre of conflict between the two European powers. In retrospect, Alec's thesis, and the article, were the first efforts in studying Canada's own naval history as distinct from that of Britain, central as the role of the Royal Navy was in Canadian history right down to the era of the world wars of the twentieth century. In the meantime, although Alec enjoyed the RMC appointment, he wondered about the future.[10]

It was a fair concern, as the 1960s were a time of considerable change within the Canadian military. From 1964 to 1968, Canada's military—and the navy especially—was in the midst of upheaval as the result of the integration, and then full unification, of all three branches led by Paul Hellyer, minister of national defence in the Liberal government of Lester Pearson. As it turned out, those upheavals opened new opportunities. One of Hellyer's first initiatives in integrating the three service headquarters in Ottawa was to combine the Army Historical Section with the much smaller historical sections of the air force and the navy into a single "Directorate of History." C.P. Stacey, who had had more than his fill of government bureaucracy when he left the army in 1959, reluctantly answered Hellyer's personal appeal in 1965 and agreed to take leave from the University of Toronto to create the new organization. He made it clear he would not stay longer than a year, and one of his principal concerns was to find a suitable new director.

Stacey had considerable prestige in the DND because of his success in pushing through to completion four substantial volumes of the official history of the Canadian Army in the Second War. The books both met high professional standards— academic as well as military—and were very well received by the public, and it was known that the achievement was largely the result of Stacey's strong academic background. Stacey had completed his Ph.D. in 1933, taught at Princeton University, and published two books by the time he entered the army in 1940. He had been recruited specifically as a historical officer, the only capacity in which he served until his retirement from the army in 1959. The senior authorities at defence headquarters agreed that the permanent director who would take over from Stacey should be selected primarily for academic credentials. They also agreed that the position should continue to be, as it had become with Stacey's return, a civilian one—although, ideally, the successful candidate should have military experience.[11] The logical candidate was Lieutenant Colonel D.J. Goodspeed, the most gifted of the serving officers posted to the historical section ("genuinely brilliant," Stacey later wrote). In 1965, Stacey established the new appointment of "senior historian" for Goodspeed, which came with the responsibility for training the other historical staff members and editing their work. Goodspeed was not interested in leading the new directorate, however, and had already been planning to retire from the army within a few years to pursue a career outside of government.[12]

Stacey's next choice to recruit was Sydney Wise from Queen's, who took over as director of history in September 1966.[13] Wise had served in the RCAF during the war, and was excited that the directorate's new major project was to be the official history of the RCAF, which had originally been cancelled in 1948 due to budget cuts. As soon as he accepted the job in the spring of 1966, Wise suggested that Alec should also come to the directorate in a position as a historian. Wise, whose main interests were in late eighteenth- and early nineteenth-century Canadian history, had read Alec's M.A. thesis, and been impressed. In the same year, Wise also urged Alec to do a Ph.D.,[14] and then arranged for him to work under the supervision of George A. Rawlyk, a specialist in eighteenth-century Nova Scotia, at Queen's. Alec's proposed thesis was an expansion of his M.A., examining the role of the Royal Navy in the development of the whole of Nova Scotia (which then included what is now the province of New Brunswick) in the period from 1713 to 1766.

Wise discussed the possibility of Alec coming to the directorate with Stacey, who agreed. Alec was one of the very few officers in the armed forces with a graduate history degree, and would be a likely candidate to succeed Lt. Col. Goodspeed as senior historian when the latter retired.[15] The military bureaucracy that arranges for the posting and promotion of officers is reputed to be a byzantine empire into which people from outside the personnel administration world venture at their peril. Stacey, however, had unusual influence, with direct access right up to the minister if need be, and Wise, also a tenacious administrator, got a personal assurance of similar access from the deputy minister of national defence, Elgin Armstrong.[16] Alec was posted to a military position at the directorate as a historian early in the summer of 1967.

One of the directorate's mandates was to produce reports on recent operations, and Alec's first assignment was on recent UN peacekeeping activities by Canadians along the Egyptian–Israeli border. In May 1967, the large Canadian air force and army logistics contingent in the area, which were part of the United Nations Emergency Force monitoring the Egyptian–Israeli border in the Sinai and the Gaza Strip, had to be hurriedly withdrawn from the region as a result of demands from Egyptian president Gamal Abdel Nasser. The 1967 withdrawal marked an ignominious end to the UN's first major peacekeeping effort, which had begun in 1956 during the Suez Crisis, and had been engineered by Canada's then foreign minister, Lester Pearson. Only Egypt, however, and not Israel, had agreed to the presence of the UN peacekeepers, who patrolled the border but were based on the Egyptian side. In the lead-up to the Six-Day War in June 1967 between Israel and the Arab States, UN peacekeepers faced pressure from Egyptian forces building up in the area. This was just days before the Israelis launched a pre-emptive strike, starting the war, which resulted in casualties to other UN national contingents that had not evacuated as quickly as the Canadians. Alec's report, based on then-current classified defence department files, ran to 175 legal-length pages. It concluded with a searching analysis of the problems caused by the imperfect agreement for the UN intervention in the Sinai (the best that could be achieved during the crisis of 1956), and the flaws the 1967 emergency had revealed in the ability of the United Nations to control complex military operations at a long distance;

a difficulty reflected in the ponderous communications between the United Nations and the Canadian government and its armed forces. Alec also commented bluntly on the shortcomings of the newly integrated Canadian Forces organization, as well as noting what had worked.[17]

In the spring of 1968, Alec joined the directorate's major project: the official history of the RCAF.[18] Substantial work had started only when Wise became director in the fall of 1966, and there were significant hurdles. One was the eternal struggle, which Stacey had faced in completing the army histories, of finding historical staff able to carry out research to academic standards and then bringing that staff up to speed on the history of military aviation, which had never been a subject of serious study in Canada. Only two of the researchers who had been in the small historical section of the RCAF ultimately carried on in the new directorate. The RCAF section had done planning for an official history, prepared preliminary studies, and done yeoman's work preserving records, but the records had never been catalogued. There had been no sustained effort to find out which files had been preserved at the Public Archives, let alone discover what was available in the vast records, located in the U.K., of the British flying services in which Canadians had served.[19] Wise (like Goodspeed and Stacey) was something of a fanatic, even by professional historical standards, in searching out the full documentary record. Unusually for a historian at that time, Wise had a degree in library science, and he was equally fanatical about fully and completely indexing all materials to ensure they were readily accessible, and properly and thoroughly used, by all the research staff. This foundational work in finding and organizing the documentary record was central to Alec's early training at the directorate. Soon he took a leadership role in both archival research and in ensuring that materials were promptly integrated into the directorate catalogues: a commitment and special interest that would continue throughout his career.[20]

The big intellectual challenge in front of the directorate was to make sense of the Canadian story in the air war of 1914–18. While Canada had played a large part, it was in the form of diverse contributions to the British flying services. These were the army's Royal Flying Corps and the navy's Royal Naval Air Service, which in April of 1918, were combined into a new independent armed service: the Royal Air Force. At no time during the war was there a settled Canadian government policy towards aviation. Rather, individual Canadians enlisted in the British flying services, and the Canadian government ultimately assisted in recruiting, along with organizing a large training organization throughout Ontario in response to British requests and which was under the direction of the British Royal Flying Corps. Altogether, more than 22,000 Canadians served in the British air services overseas and with the training scheme in Ontario during the First World War.[21]

The proposal that Stacey distilled from the air historical section's original plan suggested a "relatively small" first volume covering the First World War within perhaps 180 pages, with another 125 pages spent on the 1920s and 1930s. This book would set the stage for two larger volumes on the Second World War, one covering activities and operations in Canada, and the other dealing with the air force overseas.[22] It became evident, however, as the staff worked on the first chapters, that a compressed account could not do justice to the large, and virtually unknown, Canadian contribution to Allied aviation in the First World War as revealed by the rich sources turning up in the archives. By the spring of 1969, Wise and Goodspeed—the latter a specialist on the First World War—decided that the first volume of the RCAF history would be entirely devoted to the First World War, and be substantial; the published volume in fact would be 791 pages in length, and a major international contribution that placed the Canadian story in the context of important new research on the air war of 1914–18.[23]

In the meantime, Alec's initial assignments in 1968 and 1969 allowed him to further his own studies in naval history. First, he wrote a working paper, "Canadians Who Served in the Royal Naval Air Service, 1914–18." In the fall of 1969, he prepared a draft chapter, "The Admiralty and the Air," which traced the development of the Royal Naval Air Service in 1914 and 1915, and concluded with the arrival of the first Canadian aircrew in front-line units at the end of 1915. At the beginning of 1970, he shifted his focus onto the Royal Flying Corps, and worked on documenting the first effort to provide large-scale air support of the Allied land forces at the Battle of the Somme in 1916. This broadening of Alec's experience in the project was good preparation for when he became senior historian in June of 1970, along with a promotion in naval rank to commander, following Goodspeed's retirement from the army.

Alec's new responsibilities included the supervision of eight or nine historians, working closely with them in drafting the outlines for their assignments, regularly reviewing their progress, and leading detailed review of chapter drafts by the whole team when they were completed. (Wise had brought the academic practice of holding seminars in which the author of a new draft presented the work to the whole group, each of whom then passed written comments to the senior historian, who synthesized the memos with his own comments for the director.) One of Alec's key commitments as senior historian was to help new members of the team come up to speed with the project, ensuring they had a good handle on the published literature and were thoroughly conversant with the growing body of research files, including the directorate's own considerable holdings from the old air force historical section and a growing mass of material copied from the Public Archives of Canada and at the U.K's Public Records Office and Ministry of Defence.

During the whole time Alec was senior historian in Ottawa, he was also plugging away on his Ph.D. dissertation, working again mainly in the evenings and on the weekends thanks to the forbearance of his wife, Jane Ann, and daughter, Mary Susan.

He kept his hand in publishing outside the directorate, writing a series of articles on eighteenth-century naval figures for the *Dictionary of Canadian Biography*, a major new national project at the time. In 1971 Alec was a presenter, along with leading Canadian and American historians of the sea, at a conference held at the University of Maine. The event was also the initial organizing meeting of the North American Society for Oceanic History (NASOH), of which Alec served as a vice president later in the 1970s. In the early 1980s, as work on oceanic history progressed in Canada, Alec took a leading part in creating the Canadian Nautical Research Society, a sister organization closely affiliated with NASOH.[24]

Alec completed his Ph.D. dissertation in 1973, at the time of an unanticipated upheaval in the directorate as Sydney Wise left his leadership position to take up a full professorship at Carleton University. Alec then became Director of History, retiring from the navy as he did so to become a civilian executive in the public service. With the new post came large additional demands, as the director is the main line of communication with senior authorities, other offices, and the public. Alec had to coordinate and approve all correspondence, and personally negotiate many items of business, notably the frequently fraught matters of staffing and budget. C.P. Stacey, to preserve his time and energy (and that of his research staff) for working on the official histories, had established small administrative and inquiries sections: the latter to deal with the large volume of questions the historical services received from other parts of the department and government, the armed forces, and the public. Stacey and Wise found the position's obligations exhausting and frustrating, which were part of the reason for their departures to university positions.[25] Alec, with a few rare exceptions, appeared to enjoy the challenge of being director and the chance to work with a wide variety of military and civilian personnel of diverse backgrounds, which always interested him. That winning manner with people may well have figured in Wise's recognition of Alec's potential for leadership in the directorate.[26] A striking feature of Alec's childhood letters is his evident cheerful willingness to deal with things as they are and get on with whatever is required. Of course, naval officers are quick to point out that their training for living and working in the perilous environment of the sea make them uniquely adaptable and competent ("fitted to rule the world" is the saying). Alec is no exception, but usually declared this self-evident truth with a wink, to indicate the intention to annoy air force and army compatriots. He did, nevertheless, seem to slip easily into a leadership style much like the model of a ship's captain. He was collegial with the section heads whom he trusted to run internal operations, and took upon himself full responsibility for dealing with the larger world of the defence department and other branches of the government. When occasionally necessary, he fiercely protected "his" people against intrusions by outside authorities.

Alec consciously walked in the footsteps of his predecessors.[27] At the core of Stacey's leadership was the ambition to make the army's Historical Section and then the tri-service Directorate of History prominent scholarly institutes to promote wider interest in military history in Canada, and recognition in other countries of Canada's significance as a military power. The connections with the universities that he had always cultivated through assistance to professors and students interested in military studies, and his own academic publishing and service on graduate theses committees, became especially important in building the new directorate in the late 1960s. The key to the success of the army's pre-1965 Historical Section had been several military officers gifted in historical work whom Stacey had recruited during the war and then, at the end of the conflict, arranged to be permanently assigned to the Historical Section; they were assisted by officers on standard military three-year appointments. By 1965, however, the last of the core historical officers had retired or, as in the case of Lt. Col. Goodspeed, would do so shortly, and the reductions in strength of the armed forces in the late 1960s meant it would be exceedingly difficult to find and develop replacements. In establishing the new directorate, therefore, Stacey reduced the number of positions for military officers on three-year appointments, and created additional positions for civilians with academic qualifications, as had been done in the selection of Wise as his successor. Most of the civilian historical staff hired in the late 1960s and after by Wise, and then Alec, had Ph.D.s in hand or in progress, several in military or related fields. Some also had professional experience, such as university teaching. At the same time, almost all of the military officers posted were now enrolled in, or had completed, M.A. programs. Stacey and Wise had, as in Alec's case, encouraged both civilian and military members of the directorate who were interested in further graduate studies, and academic publishing. One of the notable legacies of Alec's longer time at the helm was the result of his consistent efforts to make sure the members of the staff with academic ambitions had the same opportunities Stacey and Wise had opened for him. This movement towards greater professionalism among the history directorate staff was part of a larger trend within the civil service. Alec played a leadership role, as Wise had done, in working with the heads of the Public Archives, the National Library, the historical branch of Parks Canada, and the historical section at the Department of External Affairs, to persuade the Public Service Commission of Canada to assure opportunities for research staff to participate in academic conferences and publishing, and recognition through promotion for distinguished research work.

One of the early issues to arise on Alec's watch as director was that of official bilingualism. A leading priority for the administrations of Prime Minister Pierre Trudeau (1968–79, 1980–84) was to ensure fuller bilingualism in the civil service and military. Previously, all work in the directorate and its predecessor organizations had been in English, with translators producing French editions of the completed books. Alec established the section historique, which ran parallel in organization to the official histories section, although it only contained two or three historical staff due to government restraints on budget and personnel. One of them was Major Jean Pariseau, a francophone raised in Alberta who was fluently bilingual and served in a western regiment (the Princess Patricia's Canadian Light Infantry). He had worked on the air force history in English before retiring from the army in 1973, and had been able to complete an M.A. in history. He came back to the directorate in 1974 as a civilian, in the position of historien-en-chef, to lead projects of special interest to French Canadians and carried out by francophone personnel. At the same time, he carried on to complete a Ph.D.[28]

When Wise left in 1973, work was underway on the last of the draft chapters for the expanded First World War air force volume. During this final phase of basic research and writing, Alec shifted his work focus again, to the chapters on the development of strategic bombing in the last years of the war—which would become the main role of the British Commonwealth air forces in the Second World War.[29] Much remained to be done to trim and reshape the long, detailed draft chapters into a cohesive book.[30] Wise, as the principal author of the volume, carried on, working through Alec who coordinated support from the directorate in research, map-making, the production of an index, and other production details. Much of the later editorial assistance was provided by Brereton Greenhous, who had arrived at the directorate from a teaching position at Lakehead University in 1971, and succeeded Alec as senior historian. Wise was a perfectionist, however, and that fact, combined with the demands of his university career, meant that the publication of this distinguished book, *Canadian Airmen and the First World War: The Official History of the Royal Canadian Air Force*, vol. I, was delayed until 1980.[31]

Work on volumes two and three of the history, however, did not wait while volume one moved slowly forward. From 1970 to 1973, while still senior historian, Alec pressed forward on volumes two and three, reassigning members of the historical team as they completed their drafts for the first volume. When he became director in 1973, the main effort shifted to volume two, of which he was the principal author. Norman Hillmer, who succeeded Greenhous as senior historian at the beginning of 1981, took on the role of senior editor, as Goodspeed, Alec, and Greenhous had done for volume one. *The Creation of a National Air Force: The Official History of the Royal Canadian Air Force*, vol. II, was published in 1986. It was as large as the first volume, and comprised four substantial parts. The first, covering the period 1919 to 1939, included a chapter on the founding of the RCAF in the early 1920s; two on the RCAF's commitment to civil operations in support of other federal departments and provincial governments ("bush pilots in uniform") down to the mid-1930s; and one on the service's reorganization as a military air force in the last years before the Second World War. The second part, also of four chapters, covered the British Commonwealth Air Training Plan, initiated by Britain in 1939, but then built and run largely by the RCAF. This massive program, with training airfields and schools across the country and hundreds of training aircraft produced in Canadian factories, ultimately produced more than 130,000 aircrew—some 73,000 of them Canadians—for the Commonwealth air forces. The third part treated, in three chapters, the RCAF's large effort to defend Canada and its ocean frontiers between 1939 and 1945. Both military and civilian officials had, since the latter part of the First World War, realized that aviation was particularly well-suited to the defence of the country's far-flung territory and coastlines. During the Second World War, the main home defence organizations, Eastern Air Command (eastern Quebec, Newfoundland and Labrador, and the Maritime provinces) and Western Air Command (British Columbia), were expanded to include, at peak strength, thirty-four bomber reconnaissance and fighter squadrons, and were operating a total of some five hundred aircraft from a dozen air stations on each coast. The final and longest part of the book (six chapters) was devoted to the important and virtually unknown role Eastern Air Command played in the defence of Allied shipping against German naval attack—and especially against the U-boat offensive in the central and western Atlantic during the years from 1941 to 1945.

The RCAF project moved into the era of the Second World War just when the national archives of Canada, Britain, and the U.S. were beginning to organize enormous collections of records in their possession that had been relegated to long-term storage, and to open large blocks of that material for research. Alec was among the first Canadian historians to undertake and promote work in the newly accessible archives; in 1977, he and Greenhous published *Out of the Shadows: Canada in the Second World War*, a pioneering survey of the entire Canadian war effort that drew on archives-based research by academic authors that was then beginning to appear.[32] As a former naval officer, Alec immediately grasped the special significance of the many files now available on the development of electronic detection equipment, including radar, for the war against the German submarine fleet, and on the struggle between the Germans and Allies to gain an edge in operational intelligence for the more effective employment of their naval and maritime air forces. Here were vital new insights into how the Atlantic war was actually fought, allowing much better analysis of when and why the balance shifted back and forth between the Axis and Allied forces. Equally important were newly opened materials on higher policy that showed precisely how relations between Canada, Britain, and the United States— the dominant Allied powers in the Battle of the Atlantic—had evolved during the course of that struggle. They also showed how the Canadian government had come to support an all-out national effort in the Atlantic, and demand a share in directing the Allied forces.[33]

How much there was to learn about Canada's part in the Battle of the Atlantic was highlighted dramatically in 1981, when the discovery of the remains of a German automatic weather station at the northern tip of Labrador hit the front pages of the daily press. The first information about the station had come to Alec from Franz Selinger, a retired German engineer, who had located records while researching stations placed in the Arctic during the war by German forces to provide information on weather fronts from the west that was essential to forecasts for planning military operations in northern Europe. Copies of German U-boat logs recently acquired by the Directorate of History confirmed that the German submarine *U-537* brought the station ashore, in October of 1943, and that the submarine, after leaving the coast, had been so severely shaken by a near-miss attack by an RCAF aircraft that it laid low and did not strike at shipping. Alec got in touch with the Canadian Coast Guard, whose director of fleet operations, Jim Clarke, then arranged for Alec and Selinger to travel to the site. They left on the icebreaker CCGS *Louis S. St-Laurent*, which by good fortune was scheduled to carry out survey work in the area in July 1981. As the *St-Laurent* neared the coast, Alec, Selinger, and Clarke, flying in the ship's helicopter, located the rusted drums that had held the instruments and battery-driven radio transmitter. The helicopter crew lifted the drums back to the ship for delivery to the Canadian War Museum. [34]

Under Alec's advocacy, the directorate's research into the role the RCAF's Eastern Air Command played in the protection of supply lines to Europe during the Second World War became the leading edge of a fresh examination of the whole of the Battle of the Atlantic. What can only be described as a passion grew out of Alec's commitment to Canadian maritime history—the influence of the seas on Canada's development, and Canada's international influence as a maritime nation. In the 1970s, he facilitated research by Commander Wilfred Lund for an M.A. thesis that shed new light on how the Canadian forces convinced the Allied high command to give Canada control over Allied convoy operations north of New York, and south and west of Greenland, in April

1943.[35] Alec also became a co-supervisor of Marc Milner's Ph.D. thesis at the University of New Brunswick, which used newly opened archives to show the enormous difficulties the RCN experienced in its rapid expansion to assist the hard-pressed British and U.S. navies in the Atlantic battle—not least the sharp Allied criticism that came when the hastily built vessels and newly recruited crews did not initially perform to the high professional standards of those long-established services.[36] At the same time, Alec worked with the foremost German researcher on the German navy, Jürgen Rohwer, to produce two pathbreaking articles on four of the most important convoy battles of the war. These articles combined detailed work utilizing the full operational records of the U-boats and Allied forces, both air and sea, and featured information from newly released intelligence records—most notably, the first releases by the British government of "Ultra Top Secret" decryptions of German radio traffic.[37] Only in 1975 did the British reveal the success of Allied codebreakers in "breaking" German radio messages "scrambled" by electrical-mechanical Enigma equipment. One of the dramatic revelations was the British-led break in 1941, and then on a more sustained basis from 1943 to 1945, into the signals with which German U-boat headquarters directed submarines against Allied convoys and other shipping. The Ultra files, which were gradually opened for research, beginning in the late 1970s, also showed that in 1943 the Allies discovered that German success to that time had come in significant measure from their ability to decrypt Allied convoy signals.

For some time, Alec had been on a mission. He wanted the Department of National Defence to sponsor a new history of the navy in the Second World that would be produced in tandem with the RCAF volumes.[38] The RCN, like the RCAF, had established an official history program during the Second World War that was shut down in the defence budget cut of 1948. The RCN team under the direction of Gilbert N. Tucker, a Canadian academic who had been teaching at Yale University in the United States, had completed two volumes. The first covered the history of the navy from its founding in 1910 to the outbreak of the Second World War; the second examined activities on shore during the Second World War. The latter, still an indispensable work, dealt with such topics as procurement of warships, the development of bases, and the recruitment and training of personnel. Tucker, however, refused to push on with the planned third volume, covering operations at sea, until the team had access to German naval records and highly classified materials on intelligence. Instead, the navy had Lieutenant Commander Joseph Schull, an accomplished playwright and author who was serving as a public information officer, write *The Far Distant Ships*. Published in 1950, the book was a lively work that covered all the main operations, but was based solely on the Canadian and Allied documents the naval historians had been able to assemble during the war.[39]

As he began work on the Battle of the Atlantic for the RCAF history in the 1970s, Alec realized that the newly available archives included the precise material that Tucker had demanded, but had not been able to gain access to, prior to the cuts in 1948. Equally important was that the newly available materials showed how the Canadian contribution, both the RCN and RCAF, had been more substantial and vital than existing accounts suggested. Because of the truncation of the Canadian naval official history and the cancellation of the air force program, scholars and popular authors depended mainly on the more substantial British and American official histories of operations in the Atlantic that were published in the 1950s, with the result that the Canadian contribution was greatly understated or ignored.[40]

Alec knew one way to gain support for the new naval history was to make it the most "public" of the DND official histories. From his earliest promotional efforts in the mid 1970s, he sought to involve anyone with a serious interest in Canadian maritime history, including the staffs of museums and archives, university faculty and students, serving members of the armed forces, retired personnel, and veterans. Harnessing that public interest was a means of winning support from the senior levels at DND for a new project when the established priority was for the air force volumes. At the same time, Alec wanted to stimulate research that could assist with the project, as with his work with Lund and Milner. There was no chance of acquiring more than one or two additional historical positions at the directorate, and it was impractical to re-assign people now fully trained in air history and committed to the air force volumes. Alec also saw the opportunity for making the little-studied history of the navy a focal point in the emerging academic fields in Canada of maritime history and the history of the Second World War. The involvement of the wider naval community was particularly important, as one of the key purposes of an official history is to build the corporate knowledge and culture of armed forces, and building that knowledge was a pressing issue in the 1970s and 1980s. The navy had had particular difficulties in adjusting to the unification of the military in 1968, in the midst of budget cuts that severely disrupted urgently needed modernization of the fleet. It had endured hard times in the past, however, and there was much to be learned from earlier experiences. "History ... is a two-way street," Alec explained in one of his several talks on the need by the armed forces for active participation in historical studies:

> The historian can learn as much from the sailor as the sailor from the historian. Historians can help sailors to develop a clear perspective on the past and assist policy-makers in building new policies on the rock of fact (or as close to "fact" as responsible historians are able to come) rather than the sand of myth.... And when historians expose themselves to the dynamic of people immersed in the daily activities of the naval profession, they invariably return to the documents with important new

insights. A partnership is possible, and failure to cultivate it is plainly a dereliction of duty.[41]

An early opportunity to bring the naval and academic communities together came from Professor James Boutilier, a historian at Royal Roads Military College (the former Royal Canadian Naval College) in Esquimalt, B.C., who organized a conference on Canadian naval history in March of 1980. Alec presented on the Battle of the Atlantic, as did Rohwer, Milner, and Lund, along with British author Patrick Beesley, a veteran of the Admiralty's wartime U-boat tracking room who published the first substantial study of the role of Ultra intelligence in maritime operations. More generally the conference revealed a wealth of interest and knowledge on the whole history of the RCN, including a paper by Rear Admiral Nigel D. Brodeur on his grandfather, Louis-Phillipe Brodeur, a member of Sir Wilfrid Laurier's cabinet who played a leading role in founding the navy and then served, from 1910 to 1911, as the first minister of the Naval Service. Rear Admiral Hugh Francis Pullen (ret.), who had already published studies of Nova Scotia's maritime history, presented a paper on the service in the 1920s and 1930s based on his own memories.[42] Alec took the lead in organizing with the navy further Fleet Historical Conferences, which especially featured work by members of the armed forces and by university academics engaged in maritime history projects. In 1989, Alec assisted the Royal Australian Navy in setting up a similar conference in Sydney, Australia, to help stimulate their own historical program. Four Canadian speakers attended, presenting papers that compared the development of the two dominion navies.[43] Alec also encouraged presentations at international maritime and military history conferences by Canadian presenters, especially in Britain and the United States, where the fiftieth anniversary of the Second World War stimulated interest in fresh analysis of the Battle of the Atlantic.

The conference presentations and publications by the directorate's few permanent staff, those on short-term engagements, and the wider communities that responded to Alec's encouragement proved still more important than originally foreseen because of challenges posed by resources. The Department of National Defence ultimately authorized a single volume from the Directorate of History on the navy's operations during the Second World War, and work began at the end of 1985[44] as *Creation of a National Air Force* was readied for publication. Most of the directorate's staff moved on to volume three of the air force history, under the leadership of Greenhous and Stephen Harris.[45] The naval work, aside from that done by Alec and two staff members, was undertaken by military or civilian personnel (mostly graduate students) on short-term contracts. In fiscal year 1989–90, the department approved expansion of the project to include multiple volumes that would cover the whole history of the navy, and allowed extension of some of the short-term contracts to five-year terms.[46] In the years from 1993 to 1996, however, the soaring national debt led the government to impose deep cuts on the defence department. In the case of the directorate, the cuts reduced the staff from something over thirty people to only ten. That left just two naval historians, one of whom could only devote part of their time to the project because of other, administrative, responsibilities.

Alec retired in 1994, after overseeing the publication of volume three of the RCAF history, on the overseas effort from 1939 to 1945,[47] and arranging for the production of an official history of Canada's participation in the Persian Gulf War of 1991.[48] His successor as director, Serge Bernier,[49] gave full support to the naval project within the limits of the directorate's greatly diminished resources. He arranged for Alec to continue work on contract, while reassigning to the naval project two of the RCAF historians, William Johnston and William Rawling; in 1998,

Bernier was then able to bring back on staff the most experienced of the naval historians lost in the cuts, Michael Whitby, who then led the project's completion. Priority was given to coverage of the Second World War, which had grown to two large volumes; those were published in 2002 and 2007.[50]

The two-volume *Official Operational History of the Royal Canadian Navy in the Second World War* was a benchmark in the renaissance of Canadian naval history and in international studies of the naval war of 1939–45, in which Alec played a central role for more than thirty years. The bibliography for the volumes listed 132 "narratives" (drafts for chapters or parts of chapters) and technical studies produced by the Directorate of History's permanent staff, and the many civilian and military personnel on short-term engagements. The bibliography also contained some eighteen books and fifty-six articles that had been published by these writers and by military personnel and university academics who had collaborated in the project with Alec's encouragement and assistance. In the words of one of Alec's American graduate students from his first appointment at Duke University in the late 1980s, "the commitment" to mentorship is one [of his] greatest gifts to all who worked with him. A quiet generosity of time, energy, and [in] guidance ... that Alec shared with graduate students, young scholars, and seasoned professionals throughout his career."[51]

Academic and popular publications inspired by Alec's efforts have continued to appear. Another benchmark was the prominent historical projects in the celebration of the navy's centennial in 2010. These included two popular illustrated volumes, the first introduced by Alec, with chapters by the academic and naval authors whom he had encouraged and mentored.[52] There was also an international conference that same year; the ninth in the series of navy-sponsored historical conferences since 1980, in which Alec had played such a prominent role. Notable among the speakers were British, Australian, and American historians with whom Alec had worked both on the official histories and within his leadership role in maritime history societies.[53] The centennial year also saw the publication of another volume of the series Alec had established in 1989–90, on the origins and early history of the navy.[54] Alec himself undertook a new, related project on the life of Admiral Sir Charles Kingsmill, the founding director of the Canadian navy from 1910 to 1921.[55] This line of inquiry was inspired by his meeting Michael and Patti Kingsmill, the admiral's grandchildren, with whom Alec, typically, instantly had a good rapport. They provided fresh insights into the history of the family and provided valuable papers on the admiral's career not available in official records. Based on this work, Alec prepared an article on Kingsmill for the *Dictionary of Canadian Biography*, his seventeenth for the series. It was published online in December 2022, some months after Alec's ninety-second birthday.[56]

Notes

1 I met Alec in 1981 when I went to work for him in Ottawa. Those were different times, when juniors rarely referred to their seniors by first name (and Alec himself was a year older than my own father: a fact that he asked me not to bring up). Within a few weeks of my arrival, another senior member noted that I had just referred to the director, no less, by his first name. They laughed, I think, because I had been so formal until that time. I was shocked at my slip at first, but then realized I had been the odd one out. Alec encouraged collegiality, and so he has been "Alec" ever since.

2 This account draws on an interview with Alec on April 24, 2007, when he visited Wilfrid Laurier University in Waterloo, Ontario, and two memoir pieces: Pat Barnhouse, Fred Herrndorf, and Bill Mercer, "A promise to join the Navy ... From the London Blitz to a career in the RCN to Chief Historian for Canada's Department of National Defence, an interview with historian Cdr (Ret'd) Dr. W.A.B. (Alec) Douglas," 18 June 2016 (in press for the NOAC [Ottawa Branch] series *Salty Dips*) and W.A.B. Douglas, "RMC's First History Postgraduates," unpublished text for W.A.B. Douglas, "War Studies at 50: Memories of a First Student," The Ronald Graham Haycock Lecture in War Studies, The War Studies Programme of the Royal Military College of Canada, 13 January 2016, author's files.

3 The headquarters of the Department of National Defence in Ottawa included headquarters for each of the three armed services: army, navy, and air force.

4 W.A.B. Douglas, "Getting Sea Legs," *Argonauta* (Winter 2016): 4–5.

5 I'm grateful to Michel Farache, Alec's son-in-law, who developed this point at some length when I discussed this project with him in Toronto on 4 February 2022. One of my relatives had a similarly unpleasant training cruise on an unimproved frigate in the early 1950s, and the experience simply angered him as an example of shameful neglect of the living conditions for personnel.

6 C.P. Stacey, "Halifax as an International Strategic Factor," *Canadian Historical Association Annual Report* (1949): 46–56; Douglas interview, 24 April 2007.

7 On the development of military history studies in Canada, and particularly the role of Stacey and the official histories program, see Tim Cook, *Clio's Warriors: Canadian Historians and the Writing of the World Wars* (Vancouver: UBC Press, 2006), and Roger Sarty, "The Origins of Academic Military History in Canada, 1940–1967," *Canadian Military History* 23, no. 2 (Spring 2014): 79–118. Alec periodically published overviews of the field: see, for example, W.A.B. Douglas, "Why Does Canada Have Armed Forces," *International Journal* 30, no. 2 (Spring 1975): 259–83; and, for an American readership, W.A.B. Douglas, "Marching to Different Drums: Canadian Military History," *The Journal of Military History* 56, no. 2 (April 1992): 245–60.

8 Interview with Syd and Verna Wise at their home on Lisgar Street, Ottawa, 28 November 2005, and with Verna Wise at the same location, in late June or early July of 2008. In the first interview, Syd asked Verna to join us at various times to refresh his memory or offer her memories. When I visited in 2008 after Syd's passing, she again showed her close interest in his career and her clear memory.

9 The author joined Alec on professional trips at various times from May 1981 (a conference at Halifax and tour of historic military sites in Nova Scotia) to June 2008 (a conference at Reykjavik and tour of Second World War sites in Iceland where Canadian forces served). He matched the energy and enthusiasm of colleagues more than twenty years younger, not least in Iceland, when, as I now realize, he was seventy-nine: something that scarcely occurred to any of his companions at the time as he strode easily on those long legs over the rough terrain.

10 Douglas to Wise, 28 June 1966, file "Douglas, W.A.B.," Carleton University Archives, S.F. Wise papers, box A-164.

11 Sarty, "The Origins of Academic Military History," 114.

12 Goodspeed had served in the artillery during the war, and then attended Queen's University where he achieved the then almost unheard record of an A standing in every course before joining the regular army: see [Goodspeed,] "Short Biography," [1966], "9-4-5 Personal Files—Col.

Goodspeed," Carleton University Archives, S.F. Wise papers, box A-145; C.P. Stacey, *A Date With History: Memoirs of a Canadian Historian* (Ottawa: Deneau, 1983), 255 (quoted); Wise to Preston, 25 May 1966, file "S.F. Wise," Duke University Archives, R.A. Preston papers, box 4.

13 On Wise's career, especially his time at the directorate of history, see W.A.B. Douglas, "Sydney F. Wise, 1924–2007: A Personal Recollection," *Canadian Military History* 16, no. 3 (Summer 2007): 75–80. The piece shows Wise's influence on Alec's subsequent leadership of the directorate.

14 Douglas to Wise, 6 October 1966, file "Douglas, W.A.B.," Carleton University Archives, S.F. Wise papers, box A164: this document gives Alec's "initial thoughts on a thesis"; see also same to same, 27 September 1966, which reports on preliminary work for a nineteenth-century topic.

15 Stacey to Wise, 7 September, 1966, Wise to Stacey, 10 September 1966, Stacey to Wise, 24 September 1966, file "DND D.Hist 1966–67," University of Toronto Archives, C.P. Stacey papers, B90-0020, box 41.

16 Wise to Preston, 25 May 1966; see also Wise to Preston, 10 May 1966, file "S.F. Wise," Duke University Archives, R.A. Preston papers, box 4.

17 W.A.B. Douglas, *The Withdrawal of UNEF from Egypt, May–June 1967: Canadian Aspects* (Report No. 16, Directorate of History, Canadian Forces Headquarters, 1 April 1968).

18 The main published account of the work of the directorate during the late 1960s to 1990s, with good coverage of Alec's role, is in Tim Cook, *Clio's Warriors*, chapter 6.

19 Hugh Halliday, "The Air Historian, Part II," *The Canadian Air Force Journal* 4, no. 4 (Fall 2011): 27–29.

20 Alec's informal report on his research trip to England in the summer of 1973 shows his intense focus and the pleasure he took in the work: Douglas to Wise, 7 August 1973, file "4-1-7 vol 3 RCAF history—Planning ... 1971–1973," Carleton University Archives, S.F. Wise papers, box A-117.

21 For examples of Alec's important role in addressing this issue, see Douglas to Wise, 22 July 1970, file "4-1-7 vol I RCAF History—Planning ... 1969–1970," and senior historian (Douglas) to director, 13 November 1970, file "4-1-7 vol 2 RCAF History—Planning ... 1967–1971," Carleton University Archives, S.F. Wise papers, box A-117.

22 Stacey, "History of the Royal Canadian Air Force Tentative Outline Plan," 12 July 1965, file "RCAF History Planning 1963–1966," Carleton University Archives, S.F. Wise papers, box A-117.

23 "R.C.A.F. History. Planning Discussion Director-Senior Historian 12 June 1969," file "4-1-7 vol I RCAF History—Planning ... 1969–1970," Carleton University Archives, S.F. Wise papers, box A-117.

24 W.A.B. Douglas, "The Ocean in Nineteenth Century Canadian History," *University of Maine 1971 Seminar in Maritime and Regional Studies Proceedings*, ed. Clark G. Reynolds and William J. McAndrew (Orono, ME: University of Maine at Orono Printing Office, 1972), 123–34; Alec Douglas, "Of Ships and Sealing Wax," *The Northern Mariner/Le marin du nord* XXVI, no. 3 (July 2016): 247–58.

25 Wise reported that, in his first eleven months, he had been able to devote only thirty percent of his time to the RCAF history: see Wise, "Progress Report on R.C.A.F. History," [26 July 1967], file "4-1-7 vol 2 RCAF History—Planning ... 1967–1971," Carleton University Archives, S.F. Wise papers, box A-117. Stacey's office diaries for 1950–58 suggest he was able to commit about the same proportion of his working days to the army official history volumes: see University of Toronto Archives, C.P. Stacey papers, B90-0020, boxes 18–20.

26 Verna Wise, interview by Roger Sarty, late June or early July, 2008.

27 I am grateful to Owen Cooke and Norman Hillmer for responding to questions and sharing their memories, which include both Wise's and Alec's times as director. Owen, who had graduate degrees in library science as well as history, joined the directorate in 1971. After drafting a study for the First World War volume, he became an archival officer and, later, the senior archival officer. Norman, who had studied under C.P. Stacey at the University of Toronto, joined in 1972 while completing his Ph.D. at Cambridge University. He was senior historian from 1981 to 1990, when he left to became a professor at Carleton University.

28 Serge Bernier and Jean Pariseau, *French Canadians and Bilingualism in the Canadian Armed Forces*, vol. II, *1969–1987: Official Languages: National Defence's Response to the Federal Policy* (Ottawa: Minister of Supply and Services, 1994), 189.

29 Douglas to director and senior historian, 28 November 1972, file "4-1-7 vol. 3, RCAF History— Planning Discussions—Chapter Briefings 1971–1973," Carleton University Archives, S.F. Wise papers, box A-117.

30 "First Draft Chapters Completed—MS Pages … [22 February 1972]"; Goodspeed to Wise, 24 April 1973, ibid.

31 File "6-1 RCAF History—Dir. Of History Contract 1974–1980," Carleton University Archives, S.F. Wise papers, box A-135; see Greenhous to Wise, 12 February 1979, for an example of the exacting editorial work that was done; even at that late state, editors were fine-tuning the balance between coverage of the Canadian aspects of the story and the essential context on the history of the British air services.

32 W.A.B. Douglas and Brereton Greenhous, *Out of the Shadows: Canada in the Second World War* (Toronto: Oxford University Press, 1977). See also their academic literature review, "Canada and the Second World War: The State of Clio's Art," *Military* Affairs 42, no. 1 (February 1978): 24–28. Among the most important early research cited was work by J.L. Granatstein. Granatstein as a young army officer in the 1960s, and with Stacey's encouragement had gone on to complete a Ph.D. before becoming a professor at York University.

33 For a detailed account that shows Alec at work in the early 1980s, leading the search for and analysis of intelligence and other technical sources, see Roger Sarty, "Adventures in Government History," *Canadian Military History* 21, no. 1 (Winter 2021): 64–78.

34 Don Butler, "Labrador was 'base' for Nazis," *Ottawa Citizen*, 1 August 1981, 1, 57; W.A.B. Douglas, "The Nazi Weather Station in Labrador," *Canadian Geographic* 101, no. 6 (1981): 42–46.

35 Wilfred G.D. Lund, "Command Relationships in the North West Atlantic 1939–45: The Royal Canadian Navy's Perspective" (M.A. thesis, Queen's University, 1972).

36 Marc Milner, "No Higher Purpose: The Royal Canadian Navy's Mid-Atlantic War 1939–1944" (Ph.D. dissertation, University of New Brunswick, 1983). Marc joined the directorate in 1982. He contributed to the Battle of the Atlantic chapters in the RCAF history and carried out planning for the new naval official history before taking up a professorship at the University of New Brunswick in 1986. While at the directorate he was able to publish his thesis as *North Atlantic Run: The Royal Canadian Navy and the Battle for the Convoys* (Toronto: University of Toronto Press, 1985), which became a key source for the new naval official history. This was one of many examples of Alec's encouragement of professional development by staff, which both advanced directorate projects and raised the profile of military history in the universities and among the reading public.

37 "'The Most Thankless Task' Revisited: Convoys, Escorts, and Radio Intelligence in the Western Atlantic, 1941–43," in *RCN in Retrospect, 1910–1968*, ed. James A. Boutilier (Vancouver: University of British Columbia Press, 1982), 187–234; "Canada and the Wolf Packs, September 1943," in *The RCN in Transition*, ed. W.A.B. Douglas (Vancouver: University of British Columbia Press, 1988), 159–86.

38 One of Alec's earliest and most important academic pieces, which showed the need to reconceptualize the understanding of the navy's development in the Second World War, resulted from his work in the archives in the mid-1970s: see W.A.B. Douglas, "Conflict and Innovation in the Royal Canadian Navy, 1939-1945," in *Naval Warfare in the Twentieth Century 1900–1945: Essays in Honour of Arthur Marder*, ed. Gerald Jordan (London: Croom Helm, 1977), 210–32. The piece was foundational in later planning for the new official history of the RCN.

39 Gilbert N. Tucker, *The Naval Service of Canada: Its Official History*, vol. II: *Activities on Shore During the Second World War* (Ottawa: King's Printer, 1952); Joseph Schull, *The Far Distant Ships: An Official Account of Canadian Naval Operations in the Second World War* (Ottawa: King's Printer, 1950).

40 Samuel Eliot Morison, *The Battle of the Atlantic, September 1939–May 1943: History of United States Naval Operations in World War II*, vol. I (Boston: Little, Brown and Company, 1947) and *The Atlantic Battle Won, May 1943–May 1945: History of United States Naval Operations in World War II*, vol. X (Boston: Little, Brown and Company, 1956); S.W. Roskill, *The War at Sea, 1939–1945* (History of the Second World War, United Kingdom Military Series), 3 vols. in 4 parts (London: Her Majesty's Stationary Officer, 1954–61).

41 W.A.B. Douglas, "The Prospects for Naval History," *The Northern Mariner/Le marin du nord*, I, no. 4 (October 1991): 19.

42 Both papers were published in Boutilier, *RCN in Retrospect, 1910–1968*.

43 The papers were published in T.R. Frame, J.V.P. Goldrick and P.D. Jones, *Reflections on the Royal Australian Navy* (Kenthurst, NSW: Kangaroo Press, 1991).

44 "Minutes of the first meeting of the naval operations in the Second World War team, 5 December 1985," 9 December 1985, 1325–27 (DHIST), copy in author's files.

45 Stephen Harris taught at the Canadian Forces College in Toronto, and completed a Ph.D. at Duke University before joining the directorate in 1980; he became chief historian in the reorganized Directorate of History and Heritage in 1997, and was acting director from 2007 to 2022.

46 Douglas to chief of the defence staff, "Official History of the Royal Canadian Navy," 14 September 1989 (copy in author's files) lays out the expanded project.

47 Brereton Greenhous, Stephen J. Harris, William C. Johnston, and William G.P. Rawling, *The Official History of the Royal Canadian Air Force*, vol. III, *The Crucible of War, 1939–1945* (Toronto: University of Toronto Press in cooperation with the Department of National Defence, 1994).

48 Major Jean H. Morin and Lieutenant-Commander Richard H. Gimblett, *Operation Friction: The Canadian Forces in the Persian Gulf* (Toronto: Dundurn Press in cooperation with the Department of National Defence, 1997). Alec arranged for Jean, a member of the section historique, to be deployed with the force as historical officer and for Richard, who served on one of the warships and had earlier in his career done an M.A. in history, to be posted to the directorate on his return from the Gulf to work on the history. Richard was able during his time at the directorate to also complete a Ph.D. From 2006 to 2018, after he had retired from the forces, Richard became the navy's first command historian, on the staff of the Chief of the Maritime Staff at National Defence Headquarters in Ottawa. This position was created as a result of Alec's advocacy of the assignment of a historian to the command staffs of each of the armed services on the model of U.S. practice of having historians permanently assigned to major commands to coordinate the creation and retention of complete records.

49 Serge joined the directorate as an army officer in 1980, completed a Ph.D. (Université de Strasbourg, France), and in 1988 succeeded Jean Pariseau as historien-en-chef.

50 W.A.B. Douglas, Roger Sarty, and Michael Whitby, *The Official Operational History of the Royal Canadian Navy in the Second World War, 1939–1943*, vol. II, part 1: *No Higher Purpose* and *The Official Operational History of the Royal Canadian Navy in the Second World War, 1943–1945*, vol. II, part 2: *A Blue Water Navy* (St. Catharines, ON: Vanwell Publishing in cooperation with the Department of National Defence, 2002–2007).

51 Elizabeth Elliot-Meisel, professor of history, Creighton University, Omaha, Nebraska, to author, 15 April 2022.

52 Richard H. Gimblett, ed., *The Naval Service of Canada 1910–2010: The Centennial Story* (Toronto: Dundurn Press in co-operation with the Department of National Defence, 2009); Richard H. Gimblett and Michael L. Hadley, eds., *Citizen Sailors: Chronicle of Canada's Naval Reserve 1910–2010* (Toronto: Dundurn Press in co-operation with the Department of National Defence, 2010).

53 Richard H. Gimblett, ed., *From Empire to In(ter)dependence: The Canadian Navy and the Commonwealth Experience, 1910–2010*, Proceedings of the Canadian Navy Centennial/Ninth Maritime Command History Converence, May 5–6, 2010; the papers were jointly published

in *The Northern Mariner/Le marin du nord* XXIV, nos. 3 and 4 (July and October 2014) and in *Canadian Military History* 23, nos. 3 and 4 (Summer and Autumn 2014).

54 William Johnston, William G.P. Rawling, Richard H. Gimblett, and John MacFarlane, *Official History of the Royal Canadian Navy, 1867–1939*, vol. I, *The Seabound Coast* (Toronto: Dundurn Press in co-operation with the Department of National Defence, 2010).

55 W.A.B. Douglas, "A bloody war and a sickly season. The remarkable career of Admiral Sir Charles Edmund Kingsmill, RN," *The Northern Mariner/Le marin du nord* XXIV, no. 1 (January 2014): 41–63.

56 *Dictionary of Canadian Biography, s.v.* "Kingsmill, Sir Charles Edmund," by W.A.B. Douglas, accessed February 26, 2022, http://www.biographi.ca/en/bio/kingsmill_charles_edmund_16E. html.

A WAR GUEST
IN CANADA

Parentheses within Alec's letters were in the original text. Square brackets denote editorial additions; text in *italics* within square brackets were added by Alec Douglas.

Footnotes in *italics* are written by Alec Douglas.

CHAPTER 1
1935 TO JULY 1940:
FROM ENGLAND TO CANADA

Growing up in England in the 1930s was fun.

Looking back, it is clear that all too often there was more hardship than fun in a society where class distinction and unemployment prevailed, but youngsters surrounded by loving family had the world at their feet, whether they knew it or not. Phyllis Douglas and her mother, Nellie Fernie, provided a secure and loving home for me when my father, Hector Douglas, died in Southern Rhodesia in 1935, when I was six years old, and there were strong family ties within both the Fernie and Douglas families. My father's employers, the British South Africa Company, did not provide the family with a pension, however, and my mother depended solely on her job in sales and fashion to make ends meet. From the mid-1930s, she brought me up, and sent me to kindergarten and prep school. Eventually she managed to have me sponsored by a Governor of Christ's Hospital[1] (also known as the Bluecoat School for the colour of the uniform), in Horsham, West Sussex, which she had come to know about when she was a girl in Sussex during the First World War. My Governor was Sir George Jessel of the British South Africa Company,[2] whom my mother

---

1 The Governor of Christ's Hospital was a charitable school founded in 1553 by Henry VIII and Edward VI.

2 *Christ's Hospital identified my Governor by name but his position with the British South Africa Company could not be confirmed. Upon further research, I believe my governor was Sir George Jessel (1891–1977), a London financier and decorated veteran of the First World War. He was*

Fig. 1: Phyllis Douglas and Alec at his school, Christ's Hospital, 1939.

had approached because the company had not provided her with a pension. Her letter to Sir George puts the situation in context:

> I have received the 1937 list of Governors with Presentations for Christ's Hospital & am writing to ask if you will consider giving it to my son. My husband, who was employed by the British South Africa Company, died very suddenly nearly two years ago & left his affairs in such an unsettled state that when they were cleared up it appears that we were penniless. My son's name is William Alexander Binny Douglas and he was born on June 4, 1929, in Salisbury, S. Rhodesia. His father's name was Hector James Binny Douglas and my name is Phyllis Douglas. I have no private income & earn just enough to live on & keep up appearances—on which my job depends to a great extent.
>
> I would be glad to bring my boy to see you if you are kind enough to give me an interview.

The interview with this gentleman took place and was memorable. He sat me at his desk and told me to write a description of him. In this composition I wrote that he had a very red neck, which fortunately made him laugh, and he sponsored me as a "presentation" boy in 1938. By 1939 I was a *bona fide* "Housey"[3] boy, enjoying the benefits and travails common to my fellow boarding

---

the grandson of the distinguished lawyer and Master of the Rolls Sir George Jessel, PC, FRS (1824–83), who had been chair of the board of the Imperial Continental Gas Association, which his grandfather had helped found in 1824. My Governor was appointed to the board in 1924 and became chair in 1947. Presumably, as a leading businessman in England, he was a member of the board of directors of the British South Africa Company, one of the financial contributors who sustained the school; he thus represented the company as one of the "governors" of the school. He was able to nominate boys for admission, and was thus termed a Governor with Presentation, that is the ability to "present" a prospective student. See *The Times* (London), 23 August 1977, 12 and 29 August 1977, 10; N.K. Hill, "The History of the Imperial Continental Gas Association 1824–1900" (Ph.D. Thesis, Faculty of Economics, University of London, 1950), 198. "Christ's Hospital," Encyclopedia Britannica, 11th edition (Cambridge: Cambridge University Press, 1911), vol. 6, 296.

3 Housey was what we called Christ's Hospital, my school in England.

school students. The picture taken in September 1939 illustrates the happy outcome of these events.

The war had brought changes to school routine. A circular dated 14 October 1939 explained:

VISITS OF PARENTS AND FRIENDS IN WAR TIME

The possibility of air raid warnings and the complications of school activities owing to the black-out have compelled the Council to curtail the visits of parents and friends of boys to the school. The following regulations have been made:

1. The visits of parents may only take place on Saturdays. It cannot be promised that boys will be set free from houses or school activities, nor will they be free as a rule before 1:00 p.m.

2. No boy will be allowed to receive more than two visits, whether from parents or others, during the current term.

3. Visitor are advised to bring their respirators and must undertake to obey implicitly the instructions of Air Raid Wardens in case a warning is given during their visit.

4. Until further notice no boys may be taken outside the school without special permission.

5. Children under 16 years of age may not visit the school without special permission.

6. Cars of visitors may not be parked in the Avenue, but must be driven into the car park. This is a permanent regulation.

H.L.O. Flecker
14th October 1939
Headmaster

Fig. 2: Best friends Phyllis Fernie (later Gilling) and Mavis Smith (later Fry), c. 1918.

Later that year, my mother asked me if I would like to go to Australia while the war was on. She was, in typical fashion, being very proactive about my welfare. It sounded wonderful, and I said I would love to go, but the scheme she was looking into never came to fruition. It was in 1940, as the Battle of Britain started to take shape, that Mavis Fry, Mother's old and (I believe) best school friend—who was also my godmother—wrote and invited us to come and stay with her family in Forest Hill Village, a neighbourhood in what was then the northern part of Toronto. My reaction to that suggestion was ecstatic—Canada was the land of cowboys and Indians, of the Rocky Mountains and Grey Owl, a very cornucopia of new adventures—and there was no hesitation in my answer to Mother's "Would you like to go?": it was "Yes, please!"

The prospect was delightful, yet the concerns of a ten-year-old were necessarily more immediate and mundane. Four letters, from me to Mother, survive from the summer of 1940 that I spent at school, where I had been placed in Preparatory B (one of the two preparatory houses at Christ's Hospital). The housemaster, Mr. Willink, had served in the Mediterranean during the First World War, and used to keep us entertained with slide shows of photographs he had taken in Mesopotamia. He and his assistant housemasters went out of their way to spark our interest, reading to us every evening after we went to bed from an extraordinary variety of books. We were very well looked after both by the teaching staff and the house matron, a no-nonsense lady who was quick to notice when any of us needed extra care.

My letters home were invariably cheerful. Of those that have survived, one talks of birthday presents and whole holidays being cancelled; another is about an air raid that lasted twenty minutes and learning to swim the crawl (three strokes!). In them, I mentioned Speech Day, and buying marmalade from the tuck shop because my chocolate spread had run out. The third mentions our four-hour stint in the tube, which is what we called the underground passage that passed between the school buildings, while a German aircraft could be heard droning overhead. I also mention more regular activities: "We had some biscuits at dawn. On Wednesday we had a whole holiday, staying in bed practically all morning ..." and on the following Saturday, "we played the Abbey School ... and won by 20 runs." Whether I played in the match, I do not know—probably not! The letter also contains a code that I had made up. The last letter, on 14 July, reports on exam results, a house cricket match, and a match against Mrs. Willink's team. (The ladies won.) By this time, my mother had told the school of her intention to send me to Canada and, on 27 June 1940, the Clerk of Christ's Hospital sent her a form letter that deserves recording:

Dear Sir or Madam,

In reply to your enquiry, I beg to inform you that the question of sending children overseas is one that must be dealt with by individual parents.

The Hospital would be most unwilling to oppose the Government Scheme in any way; but it is felt that the Hospital should not take any steps collectively in a matter which is plainly the responsibility of parents. If you wish your child to participate in the Government Scheme, the Hospital would be unable to make any financial grant towards the cost, and you will understand that it is not at present possible to express any opinion as to the chance of his or her return to the School.

Yours faithfully

George A.T. Allan,
Clerk.

It should be mentioned that the Westminster Cathedral Choir School had been evacuated to Christ's Hospital, and added

Fig. 3: Portrait of Phyllis Fernie, the author's mother's, c.1926. The piece was painted at her mother's (Mumsmum's) insistence when the family was on holiday in Belgium.

a lovely sound to our chapel services. We were not, in other words, believed to be in a danger zone, and the veiled threat of Mr. Allan's last paragraph was not to be taken lightly.

That said, Mother had no intention of participating in the Government Scheme, and she was not to be put off by a bureaucratic form letter that was so careful not to make a commitment of any sort. Mavis Fry's invitation had been for us both, but Mother could hardly afford to give up her job as a fashion buyer and designer at Walpole's, an exclusive department store in the west end of London. She only wanted to ensure that I would not be in England if and, as seemed all too likely at that moment, when the Germans invaded. The difficulty was to find a way of getting me to Canada. In the end, as will be seen, she managed to solve this problem through the help of a friend, Lilian Kingston. Lilian, the daughter of wealthy British magnate Sir John Power, had just married a Canadian, Dr. Paul Kingston, who did not meet the medical standards for military service and was returning with her to live in Canada. Mother arranged to take me with them, and after two days of intense activity—as I recalled in a letter to my mother of 22 June 1942 ("30 minutes to pack everything at school and then only a day to get all the stuff sorted and repacked properly")—managed to be ready for the voyage. We were to sail on the MV *Britannic* of the Cunard-White Star Line, and had to leave London for Liverpool on 20 July 1940.

When the train left King's Cross station, it was a poignant moment. Mother did not really know if she would ever see me again, and she was in tears as she waved goodbye. I was too excited to be sad, and too callow!

As the Kingstons and I headed for Liverpool, Mother sent two telegrams. One was to our old friend Mildred Dilling, a distinguished harpist (she had apparently taught "Harpo" Marx to play the harp) who lived in New York:

ALEC SAILED EN ROUTE MAVIS FRY LAST CUNARD DEPARTURE
ONLY AVAILABLE BERTH WITH LILIAN AND PAUL KINGSTON.
CALLING NEW YORK. TRY CONTACT BOAT ARRIVAL. LOVE
DOUGLAS.

The other was to Mavis Fry:

ALEC JUBILANT SAILED LAST CUNARD DEPARTURE WITH PAUL
KINGSTON BRINGING HIM TORONTO FROM NEW YORK. THEY
WILL COMMUNICATE ARRIVAL SHORTLY. LOVE DOUGLAS.

We spent the next three days waiting to sail—"that was a gyp really," I said in a letter written to Mother two years later, "fancy spending three days in port!"

I was able to get off a short letter to my mother as we joined the ship:

Cunard White Star
Britannic

Sat. July 20th

Dear Mother

I've just got on board and have been waiting at least three hours at the passport office etc. It's a lovely ship and we have got a super cabin. I'm in top bunk and am with the Kingstons.

Love from Alec

Later that day I began the first of many letters that would be written over the next three years to describe my life as a war guest. Dr. and Mrs. Kingston probably encouraged me to keep a daily record of our passage to New York, but it was not an unwelcome task. There was so much to share with my mother, because we had always been exceptionally close (my father had died in 1935, when I was six). She had always listened to what I had to say, so she could see the world unfolding to her son through his eyes, and in the unaffected language of an eleven-year-old boy. Because this was the first letter I had written during the passage to New York, it is reproduced in full except for a page or two at the end that were lost.

Sat. July 20th

Dear Mother

When we arrived at Liverpool we waited half an hour in the dockyard. Then we had to wait a full three hours showing up our passports and proving we had not got jewelry, signing embarkation cards and showing our passports at the immigration offices, and last of all, showing passports to censors. My camera was taken away. The film is being sent to you. When at last we got on board and into our cabin we found our luggage had been mixed up. We got some other peoples' luggage in our cabin too. The steward helped us to find our own suitcases, Paul doing most of the work, and at last we found all the cases, mine being last. My trunk did not appear though. I went to bed at 9:10.

Sun. July 21st

We were still in harbour when we woke up and it was drizzling. I went on deck at 8:15 and found ten steamers and four tugs. I tested my binoculars and I could see past the river mouth. We started at 9:45 but only for the river mouth. I saw two fast destroyers a bit later on, and saw bluejackets[4] on their decks. We had a lifeboat drill on Sunday and Saturday. I made friends with a boy called Timothy Forsyth too. He is very nice and knows about 100 people already. He is only eight and behaves

---

4 General term for sailors in the British Royal Navy.

*like a boy of twelve. He is not a whiner either. I went to bed at
twenty-five to nine. My trunk had not appeared then.*

Mon. July 22nd

*We started in the night with a convoy of two destroyers. There
were three ships with us too. A little after breakfast we sighted
two convoys joining up. There were thirty-two ships in them.
We passed the northern tip of Ireland at about 9:30 a.m. The
swimming pool was in use too. My binoculars are very good
because I saw the thin line of land about 150 miles away through
them.* [This would have been a unique case of super refraction!]
*What was so wonderful was that the latest newspaper was
hanging up in the cabin class. The ship started to roll in the
middle of lunch and made me feel quite dizzy. Lilian had to
go and lie down. I had roast turkey for supper and it tasted
delicious. I went to bed at 8:45 that night and found my trunk.*

Tues. July 23rd

*The ship was rolling a lot when I woke up and I nearly fell over
directly I reached the floor. The steward told me a convoy of
forty-nine ships had passed us earlier in the morning. Lilian
was feeling better and ate her lunch in peace. I saw a school of
porpoises just after breakfast. Timothy sighted a tidal wave in
the distance as well as a convoy. After lunch a storm arose and
the wind was about 20 m.p.h. We had two films in technicolor
too. I found out that I was not scolded if I trespassed into
the first class but I was if I went to third. I played a game of
shuffleboard with Timothy and lost. Shuffleboard is rather a
good game. You use sticks like this* [crude sketch] *and with them
you push discs onto a square like this:* [another sketch] *and you
have to push your disc and get it in a square till you get fifty.
There is quoits too. I have never played it but it is just the same
as on land.... After that we had supper. I had a bath before. It is
a very funny arrangement. First you have a fresh-water shower,*

*then you soap yourself then you wash it off with sea water and
then you dry. I had to have a shower twice to soap properly. For
supper I had Hors Deuvres [d'oeuvres], brochette a la turque
and chocolate with whipped cream on top. I was in bed by 8:45
and Lilian got me up at 8:50 because there was a battle cruiser
patrolling near us. I had to put trousers on over my pajamas
and a wind sheeter over my jacket. I rolled my pajama trousers
up over my shorts and wore my deck shoes without any socks.
I don't think you would of done it. I noticed before that some
of the waves were over 15 ft high. Paul was not feeling very well
and as he was never seasick we thought it was the food.*

Wed. July 24th

*I woke up at 6 o'clock, and, thinking it was 12:30, went to sleep
again. I got up at 8:35. I had some porridge and buckwheat
cakes for breakfast, then I went up and played with Timothy.
We had just been playing a game of touch wood when I sighted
smoke on the horizon. I brought up my field glasses and saw
there was a convoy. It was too far away to see properly, so we
went up to the sports deck which is really only meant for the
cabin class. First we had a game of shuffleboard then we played
deck tennis, then we stopped. The convoy was just beside us.
There was an armed merchant cruiser and three destroyers,
in fact there were sixty-nine ships. They were going to England
so they probably were carrying guns and food for the troops.
When Timothy had left for lunch I played deck tennis with
another nice boy who had been to S. Africa. Soon I left for lunch
a quarter of an hour late. (I am always served quicker if I am
late.) After lunch I came and wrote my letter up to date. I wrote
the rest just before bedtime. I went and had tea at 4 o'clock and
made friends with a boy called Adrian Garret. He showed me
the way to the third-class ping pong room and it was terrible.
It was almost like a prisoner's hold in Napoleon's time. Then
we went on deck which was good fun and squeezed through to*

the first class and went on the boat deck. Adrian took one of the quoits for deck tennis down to the tourist class. There we had a game with a girl and a boy. Me and the other boy, whose name is Faber and has the cabin next to ours, were the best so we had a finishing match. We were very even but finally he won. Then I had supper and had roast duckling in the process. I was in bed by 8:45. There was horse racing for the grown-ups which was very dull so I did not stay up for it.

Thurs. July 25th

I got up at 8 o'clock and went on deck but there was nothing to be seen so I went down to C deck and looked to see what was on. There was a film called Bulldog Sees It Through[5] *on....
The breakfast bell went then so I went in and had an ordinary breakfast then after tried to get the games steward to put the net up for deck tennis but he would not till after lunch. Then I went to the film. It was a very exciting war film. A lot of sabotage and stuff. There were German parachute troops coming down and bombing the Houses of Parliament etc. After that I played deck tennis and was twenty minutes late for lunch. I played deck tennis after lunch and came down at 6 o'clock to write my letter. I started counting how many words I had done but got tired of it by 7:50. Then I just read. I was in bed by 8:45.*

Fri. July 26th

I woke up at 6 o'clock and got up at 8:30. Then I went on deck and found it was a lovely day though it was windy. I had a very large breakfast and then I was told to change my name on the labels to Kingston and the steward supplied me with a round label with an initial in the middle of it, then I wrote my letter. I went out after that and found it was very foggy. You could not see more than 100 yds. I looked around a bit and found a boy called Christopher Layton who was very nice. We had a game of

---

5 British film from 1940, directed by Harold Huth and starring Jack Buchanan and Greta Gynt.

quoits and then lolled about in a warm part of the deck. I found out from the steward that we were on the Grand Banks, which was the most foggy place in the world almost. We were about 200 miles from Newfoundland and saw a fishing boat nearby. Unluckily I only caught a glimpse of it. I had lunch then I went to have an hour's rest. I went out on deck after that and looked for Timothy. I found him alright only he had to look after two little girls. I tried to find someone else but couldn't so I had some tea. I did not do anything till 7 o'clock when I had a bath then I had dinner then I wrote my letter. I got in bed by 9 o'clock.

Sat. July 27th

I got up at 8:45 to find that the porthole in the passage was open. I went on [deck] just before breakfast. I had a large breakfast and swayed when I got up. There was an American woman who was quite drunk, and in the middle of breakfast shouted "help" and started singing. She was given some water to drink and that soothed her. I had a quiet morning. I had a large lunch with two meat courses. After lunch I had some games of deck tennis, winning two and losing one. I did not have any tea and played a game of deck tennis with a friend and two very nice Siamese girls. I forgot to tell you that we had a film in the morning called Star Dust. *It was a very good film about Hollywood. I had a bath at 7 o'clock and was five minutes late for dinner. After dinner I wrote my letter for the day. (I was wearing my new shoes for dinner). I was in bed by 8:45.*

Sun. July 28th

I woke up at 5:30 a.m. and tried to get to sleep again but it was no use. Lilian was awake because the people next door were making such a noise. I asked her whether I could get up soon but she said not till half past seven. I played Patience till then and then got up. I looked to see what kind of a day it was and found it marvelous. There was only the slightest ripple on the sea and

a small swell. I went out on deck and was really surprised to see
a school of <u>WHALES!</u> They were about 200 yds to the stern. One
came right out of the water on its belly. Some of the stewards
said it reminded them of the Pacific, "Wot with wiles and calm
dies." We sighted a fishing fleet later on, of about thirteen boats.
Me and Michael Faber went to the bows to see if we could see
better, and we certainly could. After that we had breakfast and
I had five courses. After that I made friends with a Canadian
steward. He lived in London [Ontario], 121 miles from Forest
Hill Village [Toronto]. He went to school in Toronto too. After a
bit of talking he said he was going to "feed the lions." By that he
meant he was going to give the petty officers their lunch. I found
that we were going to sight land at 1 p.m. Whether it was true
or not I don't know. I decided to go swimming at 11 o'clock but
found out I had grown out of it. Then I wrote my letter for the
day. My trunk was taken at noon. It started being foggy at 12:30
again. The foghorn was blown every minute. I had lunch and
did not have any tea. I did not do much till after dinner except
play deck tennis with two very nice Siamese girls. After dinner
we had a concert. The first turn was Bazzoni, a famous violinist
playing a few tunes. The last one was "Ave Maria" by Schubert.
Do you know it? Then came Noel Coward singing a few songs ...

[The last few pages of this letter are missing.]

That casual reference to a live performance by the great Noel
Coward probably does not reflect the excitement of an eleven-
year-old boy at being exposed to the great and famous, but it does
perhaps show my determination to be accepted as a seasoned
traveller!

For some reason, perhaps because we were told not to say
anything about it, the letter fails to mention that the three ships
with us in our original convoy were Canadian Pacific "Duchess"

liners, heading for Canada to return as troop ships, and that flying boats had accompanied us out of harbour as far as Northern Ireland. This was a thrilling sight. Nor does the letter note that a member of the crew told me that, although warships were not in sight all the time, they were providing distant cover. The "battle cruiser" mentioned by the crew member was actually the light cruiser HMS *Glasgow*, if my memory is correct. Lilian Kingston also added some details in a letter to my mother, dated 27 July:

Your ewe lamb is being an angel—"He keeps me young!" Everyone thinks he is my son & say I wear well! I don't know whether you or I should be insulted? One or the other—I feel I must add a bit to the wonderful serial letter which he's writing—

(a) He's left out an hour's rest a day!

(b) I hadn't the heart to prevent the dinners he puts down—they don't seem to hurt him—he's an Hors d'oeuvres King & had it for every meal! He had to go to bed rather late to fit the feed in but he has rested & doesn't seem too tired. It was very sad having his film removed[6]—could you send the photos on to him. I'm afraid I haven't played with him much as I've been keeping the feet up most of the time: but the ship is swarming with children & he plays all over the ship with them—Timothy the big friend is a nice little boy.

Oh dear it was all such a wrench. I still don't think back at all. Thank goodness we had Alec otherwise I would have wept buckets. He's made one lovely remark: "What is the name of that other rich woman who lives at Lymington?" (This after we'd been talking about Mummie [Lilian's mother]!) He's a great respect for wealth it seems! It's priceless.

Darling Phil I wish you were with us though I expect you're

---

6 *The film was to be removed by customs before departure, but this never happened.*

right. Do write and tell me just what Walpole's offered you—you remember you were never alone when telephoning.

We get to New York tomorrow night & disembark Monday. I do hope we'll see Mildred alright. I must stop. Alec will write a few words from New York itself. Goodbye darling. He seems quite happy & is always talking about "my mother."

Lots of love
Lil & Paul

The ship arrived in New York on 29 July, and we disembarked the next day. Although Mother had sent Mildred Dilling word of our passage, Mildred was away on tour and could not meet us. But after Paul Kingston phoned Mildred's number, her secretary—Miss Macdonald—did come, took us to Mildred's wonderful apartment on East 52nd Street and insisted we stay there. "We did most gratefully," Lilian Kingston reported, "as the heat was most appalling—damp & misty & hotter than I ever felt."[7] Despite being dressed in grey flannel shorts, long socks and a jacket, with a shirt and tie (normal wear for an English eleven-year-old in 1940), I do not seem to have noticed the heat, being much too interested in the elevated trains, Broadway and Fifth Avenue. The Kingstons found the New York experience to be somewhat traumatic, however: it was not only the heat, but the shock of discovering that their pounds were worth only about two dollars, instead of the five dollars they had always received in the past. They barely had enough to pay the train fare for the three of us to get to Toronto.

---

7   Lilian Kingston to Phyllis Douglas, 11 August 1940, reproduced on pages 55–57.

CHAPTER 2
AUGUST 1940: ARRIVAL IN TORONTO

Our train ride to Toronto appears to have been uneventful. What sticks in my mind, even today, is my first taste of Coca-Cola, offered to me upon our arrival late on the evening of 31 July at the Fry house on 3 Ava Crescent in Forest Hill Village. Pure nectar!

Lilian Kingston, now staying with friends on Riverside Drive in Toronto, wrote on 11 August to my mother about the trip to North America:

My dearest Phil

Well here we are all complete and Alec handed over! He was sweet & we did love having him. I hope he enjoyed the journey, he seemed very thrilled. We haven't seen him since we arrived since the Fry's have all gone off to Muskoka. It's a lake & the holiday place, about 125 miles from here. I expect they're having a gorgeous time—it's v. hot here & v. quiet as everyone is away. I'm greatly looking forward to meeting Mavis properly— it's a bit lonely here, or will be once Paul starts work. Most of his friends seem to have moved since he was here last & so far he hasn't got in touch with many. His sister Mary & her husband Frank are perfectly sweet & I think she & I will be real friends. I'm so glad. ... She & Frank had to go off on their holiday the Saturday after we got here—so we've had their flat to ourselves

*for the last week. They hated to go but had to take their holiday
now as they'd already had to put it off once ...*

*Paul seems to have heard of several jobs which pay fairly well
& has put in for one or two. The rents here are higher than
London, though you get heating and water thrown in. We've
spent all week looking at flats & it's a terrible job. All the
bedrooms are* minute, *would never hold our furniture. Toronto
is a* huge *place. All the houses have little green unfenced lawns
in front of them & little gardens and garages behind & the city
stretches about twelve miles east & west & five north from the
lake. It's not a very pretty place but I haven't penetrated half
yet as we've no car & it takes ¾ hr from here to the main street
[Yonge Street] & the town stretches equally far the other side.
We're right on the edge here & almost in the country. Yesterday
we went past the Forest Hill school where I expect Alec will go.
It's a lovely new-looking building & very large.*

*We were v. sad not to see Mildred in N.Y. Her secretary Miss
McDonald came and met us—we telephoned from the dock
about 12 on the Monday. She took us to Mildred's flat & fed
us & then we went "downtown" on an elevated train (for Alec's
benefit) & then walked up Broadway & along Fifth Avenue &
home. It was lovely seeing so much of N.Y. in such a short time.
Miss McDonald insisted we should stay the night in the flat &
we did most gratefully as the heat was quite appalling—damp
& misty & hotter than I have ever felt. Miss McD. said she &
Mildred were expecting Alec to stay even if you didn't. So I
murmured about the intermittent home business & that you
simply couldn't get your permit through in time to come. I also
wrote Mildred & explained. She still seems to hope you may get
out, though I told her you couldn't without Alec: & all seems to
be well. She doesn't seem annoyed.*

Well darling write & tell me all your news—it was just ghastly leaving—I could never do it again— it's just hateful to leave you all just now—but still I suppose it was meant. Do tell me about Walpole's & all—I'm so vague about what really happened.

Write soon & lots & lots of love to you—I'm sure Alec will love it here, it's a lovely airy place.

All my love dear
Lil

....

My mother was enormously relieved at the news of our safe arrival. On 27 August, she wrote to Mavis Fry:

Mavis darling

I haven't time before the post to write you a real letter so I am slipping this into Alec's to thank you for your lovely long letter & to thank you again for your goodness to him. All these lovely things you are doing for him & the happy home life more than makes up for sending him away. I have never felt so clearly before that I am doing the right thing as I do now. Your letter came just as the Blitzkrieg got going, and the contrast in the life out there with what it is now in England is like looking into another world. It's alright for grown-ups in England and we are not fussing but you can imagine how much piece of mind I would have had if Alec had been in England now—probably down in Cornwall or in Hampshire—not with me. It would have been awful.

I do hope you see something of the Kingstons—Lilian will miss her mother & sister dreadfully but being English & reserved won't say anything—you know!

Darling—don't worry too much about things in England. Nothing is as bad as you probably read in the papers. There have been one or two bombs on London & more in the

*country—but if one is careful & keeps indoors there is about the
same chance of being hit as by a thunderbolt. Everyone is very
cheerful & though sleepy. It's amazing how quickly people will
adapt themselves to anything! Bless you—*

My love
Phil

In the meantime, the Fry family—Aunt Mavis and Uncle Harold[1];
David, three months younger than I; his younger sister Susan,
about eight; and Jeremy, about three years old—were taking
me into their bosom. Their home, 3 Ava Crescent in Forest Hill
Village, was a large and smiling mock Tudor home, roughly
divided into two parts. The front door opened onto the first
part of the house, with a spacious hall leading to the living room
and dining room on the ground floor. Both rooms were big and
comfortable, furnished in traditional English style. A refectory
table in the dining room could seat probably up to a dozen people
at a time, and the big fireplace in the living room was designed
to hold substantial three-foot logs. On this side of the house, a
handsome staircase (our Christmas portrait in 1940 was taken on
it) stretched upstairs to reach a very big master bedroom, complete
with en suite and separate dressing rooms for Aunt Mavis and
Uncle Harold. Entrance to the second part of the house, clearly
divided from the front, went directly through the back door into
the kitchen, and was where the servants' and children's domains
lay. On the second floor were the nursery, Nurse's bedroom, and
three bedrooms for David (with bunk beds), Susan, and Jeremy. I
stayed with David, in the upper bunk. There was a small, fenced-

---

1 Harold Fry (1891–1964) was born in Collingwood, Ontario, and worked in financial securities
his whole career. He founded the investment firm Fry and Company in Toronto in 1936, and
was active in the company until his death. He was considerably older than his English wife,
Mavis Florence Smith (1908–69); they were married in London, U.K., in 1928. *The Canadian
Who's Who, Vol. IX: 1961–1963* (Toronto: Trans-Canada Press, 1963), 385; *The Times*
(London), 27 August 1928, 1; *Globe and Mail*, 27 October 1964, 40 and 21 October 1969, 48.

in front garden with a jungle gym for Jeremy to play in, and a pretty backyard in the centre of which was an "umbrella tree,"[2] something that particularly delighted me.

Nurse Ruby Clarke, from Arnprior, Ontario, who had previously worked for a family in Montreal, was a huge influence in our upbringing. When we provoked her, she sometimes compared David and I unfavourably to the "fine boys" under her previous charge. How we disliked those boys, whom we never met! She imbued us with her strict Ottawa Valley values and her intense Canadian patriotism. Next to Syl Apps of the Toronto Maple Leafs, her greatest heroes were our troops overseas, who were going to win the war for England. From time to time there was also a cook in residence, but neither Aunt Mavis nor Nurse, whose word carried great weight, seemed to be able to find satisfactory cooks. They came and went.

Getting into the swing of things in this the new situation was delightfully easy, although one or two new experiences took some getting used to. I looked with deep suspicion on peanut butter when it first appeared on the breakfast table, because of its colour, and had to be persuaded to try it. Appearances proved deceiving, and I soon learned to like the stuff. What David and I never did get used to was the practice of putting drops of cod liver oil into our porridge, cream of wheat and Red River Cereal. It totally spoiled the taste, and we actually looked forward to getting doses of sulphur and molasses, another staple medication for growing children, because the taste was so much less nauseating! In other respects, I was made to feel so much a part of the family that I immediately felt at home.

Soon after arriving, as Lilian Kingston had reported, David and I were off to Lake Muskoka to stay for several days at the cottage owned by David's Uncle Art, Harold Fry's bachelor brother, on Keewatin Island, with Aunt Edith (Harold's unmarried sister) and Grandma Fry. This was a wonderful adventure. In a

2 A type of small magnolia tree.

letter completed around 3 August that probably crossed with my mother's letter to Aunt Mavis in transit, I wrote with great enthusiasm about my new experiences with the heading "THIS IS FOR EVERYBODY WE KNOW WELL":

Dear Mother

I hope you like my letter (if you've finished reading it). Wasn't it a record.

I finished on the 29th [July] didn't I? At any rate, if I did I'll go on from 8 o'clock of the 30th. We had to get examined by the immigration officer and our landing cards getting clipped. We had to wait three hours showing our passports etc.

We searched vainly for Mildred but could not find her. So her secretary Miss McDonald came. We found out that Mildred had gone to Hollywood to broadcast there. Miss McDonald was very nice and gave us some long-wanted lunch. After that we went out and saw New York. We did lots of things and went on top of buses with open tops. They are just like the old English ones.

We passed the Empire State Building and went up to the forty-third floor on Woolworths. We started out at four and ended up at 7 p.m. but had a lovely supper and I went to bed at 9 o'clock. By the way I had a peep at the skyscrapers and saw nearly all of them illuminated. It was a great shame because Mildred thought I was going to be with her and found me lots of schools in America.

Tues. July 31st [30th]

I got up at half past seven and got ready for the train including breakfast then we took a taxi to the station and got a porter. He took our luggage for us and got us into the train barely five minutes before the train left. It was a comfort to be in the train which was air-conditioned and in the station it was at least 120 above [Fahrenheit]. At 9:00 am the train started off. We passed the Hudson and found that the lunch was very expensive so we only had one sandwich and a drink. Then I finished my letter in the smoking room. That is why it is so untidy and in black ink at the end. After that I just watched the scenery and stations. I arrived in Toronto and found Auntie Mavis, Uncle Harold and David waiting for me. First, we went and had our baggage checked. That done we got in the Studebaker and drove to Forest Hill Village. On the journey I saw a skyscraper thirty-two floors up, the biggest hotel in the British Empire.[3] When we got there [the Frys' house] *we had a drink of Coca-Cola. We got to bed at about 10 p.m.*

Wed. Aug. 1st [July 31st]

I got up at 7:30 next morning and did not do much till 11 a.m. Then we went for a visit to Sunnyside. Sunnyside is a recreation ground a little away from Toronto. Susan and Jeremy went with us too. Susan and Jeremy had vanilla and Aunt Mavis, David and me had strawberry. After that we had lunch with sausages, mashed potatoes and French beans. Of course David did not like it and only had one sausage. We had a delicious pudding, it was something with whipped cream on top. We all had an hour's rest after that. David and me had a wireless on downstairs .... We had a walk after rest and came back at about 4:30. Aunt Mavis was on the phone and when she finished we were told that we were going to Muskoka Lake on Saturday, as we had been invited by David's Aunt Edith. I was told we would stay a week then come back .... We had supper at 5 o'clock and went out to spray the garden with Uncle Harold's little sprayer. I went to bed at 7:30 p.m.

---

3 A probable reference to the Royal York Hotel, which is actually twenty-eight storeys.

Thurs. Aug. 2nd [1st]

I got up at 7:30 a.m. and had breakfast at 8 o'clock. I listened to the gramophone (Victrola in Canadian) after being persuaded by Susan. Susan is seven and Jeremy is two... Auntie Mavis took David and me "downtown" to Eaton's and Simpson's to get the same kind of clothes for me as David had. We stayed there till 1 o'clock then we went home for lunch. We had the usual wireless and rest then we went for a ride around Forest Hill Village. I did not do anything till supper and after that I listened to the gramophone. I went to bed at 7 p.m.

Fri. Aug. 3rd [2nd]

I got up at 7:30 and had breakfast at 8 a.m. Then David and me got ready for Muskoka. We found two boats and a lot of linen. We made sails for my boat with it and signal flags. We stowed a lot of pins and packed my binoculars. We did not finish everything till after 4 p.m. We had to find the rudder for David's boat, fix it on properly, hustle about looking for linen and then making mistakes on the sowing machine cutting out pieces of linen for flags then make a flag for David's boat, all this till lunch. Having to read books for an hour after lunch, cutting out the sails for my boat wrong then after twenty minutes fuss the sowing machine did not work so I took twenty minutes doing the sails by hand. Then I had to put the sails on. It was. 4 o'clock and then we had to look around for anything we had missed. Suddenly David said "We haven't got a compass." We had to ask permission from Auntie Mavis to use the phone then so we looked for her. After ten minutes we found she had gone out. We phoned without permission after that and got Uncle Harold to get us one. I shall have to finish now as it is Wednesday already.

Sat. Aug. 3rd

*I woke up very excited. Having never been to a place like this
it was much more exciting than usual. We rested till 10:30.
Then David, Aunt Mavis and Uncle Harold and me set off.
Poor Jeremy was crying like anything when we left him. Susan
was very good about it. We passed into Young [Yonge] Street
in the car and everything was usual except for driving in the
right side of the road. Lunch was short and our desserts (sweets)
cancelled. Then Aunt Mavis bought me a sun [hat] as my felt
one was no good. Then we got off again and passed the Holland
marshes [the Holland Marsh, north of Toronto]. The land there
was just like Holland and most of the people there were Dutch.
We got to Beaumaris at about 3 o'clock. Beaumaris is an island
which you cross to by bridge.[4] Dr. Routley[5] was staying there, at
least [on] Keewaydin [Keewatin] Island. Just as we started he
appeared on the scene. We all had the usual meeting, shaking
hands etc. We got into his speedboat and started off. We did not
go full speed as something was wrong with the engine. We saw
Mr. Silverwood's boat and island on the way. Mr. Silverwood
has a famous dairy.[6] We arrived there at 3:45 p.m. and had a
swim directly we got there. After that we had supper and went
to bed.*

*Well, cheerio till next week
Lots of Love from Alec*

On 17 August, we went to Harold and Mavis Fry's property north
of Toronto, located between Nobleton and Bolton: they called it

---

4 Beaumaris is a settlement on Tondern Island in Lake Muskoka, and is indeed reachable by a
    small bridge.

5 Dr. Frederic William Routley, director of the Canadian Red Cross Society.

6 Albert Edward Silverwood was the founder of Silverwood Dairy, based in London, Ontario,
    and acquired a number of smaller dairies throughout the twentieth century. Silverwood
    Dairy was acquired by Ault Foods in 1984 and the brand name slowly dwindled, disappearing
    completely by 1999.

the Farm, but Jeremy called it "Moocowsgarden." We drove up in Harold Fry's beautiful blue Studebaker Commander, a classic design of car. The letter describing this outing sets the tone for the next three years of my becoming a virtual member of the Fry family—of becoming David's "war brother," as they have since described me.

Dear Mother or if you like Darling Mother

I will start at Saturday the 17th. I was woken up at 7:30 and had breakfast at eight, at breakfast I was told that we were going to the farm. After breakfast David and me brought out his stamp collection and put on a few stamps. He has 3,552 stamps in his collection. He gave me some he did not want and that was about twenty. He has dollar- and fifty-cent stamps as well. After stamp collecting it was lunch time as we were having lunch early.

Directly after lunch we started off. Susan was saying the name of the road all the time. When we arrived there we rushed out. David and me did the carrying and then rushed down to change into our bathing trunks. David went down to cut dead trees and I amused Jeremy because I was only in the way of the others. After a bit I suggested a swim so David came down and we went to the deepest part of the stream. It was only about a foot deep but you could just do dog paddle. After that we had tea ... After tea we found a lot of scrap iron. We found all that we could find of an old cart and a lot of barbed wire. We found one of David's old boats and hid it for next time. Then we left for home, sweet home!

Sun. Aug. 18th

I got up at 8 o'clock and after breakfast went down and put the gramophone on. Then I remembered about my stamps. I stuck in a few and then went down and listened to the gramophone.

I did not go out till Auntie Mavis suggested a ride in the car. We went round the lake shore and saw the baby Queen Mary. *It had been shown at the World's Fair. It was a marvelous little thing, it was big enough to hold a full-grown man and went about 15 m.p.h. A little after that we heard a Bren gun being tested. So we're not so far from the war. After that it was lunchtime and after that I had a rest. I finished my library book then went for a walk. I had a nice tea and listened to the wireless till bed time. There was a play on called* Bartholomew Cubbins' 500 Hats.[7] *I was in bed by 8:30.*

Mon. Aug. 19th

I got up at 7:30 and had breakfast at 8 o'clock. After breakfast David went roller skating and I went with him. When we got back we waited about till lunch. After lunch I settled down to my letter and after that went to Simpson's Stores. First David and me looked at the stamps. Then we went to the third floor for some towels and flannels for me. We were just going to Eaton's when Auntie Mavis said we should have our polyphoto[8] taken. We had a little bit of shopping in Eaton's then came out. Now, after supper, I'm writing my letter and am going to bed at 8 o'clock.

Tues. Aug. 20th

I awoke at 6 o'clock to remember it was Auntie Mavis's wedding anniversary. I lay awake till 7:30 and thought and thought and thought for a present to Auntie Mavis and Uncle Harold. At last it came to me, a show, but what kind of a show, so I said to myself "a radio programme." That morning I borrowed the

---

7   *The 500 Hats of Bartholomew Cubbins* by Dr. Seuss (and still in print) was one of the first of Theodor Seuss Geisel's books to be adapted for radio, for the Columbia Workshop series on the Columbia Broadcasting System. For the original 18 August 1940 broadcast, go to https://www.youtube.com/watch?v=BRuMflemYEg.

8   A polyfoto is a sheet of 48 photos, each a half-inch by half-inch, made by Kodak Limited. Polyfoto machines provided a photographic portrait service in many department stores, and were the forerunner of the photobooth.

*typewriter and for quite a time typed out a programme. Then
I went to the shopping centre and got her a box of chocolates.
When I got home I told David to make out a treasure hunt for
the chocolates. I finished the programme and then waited for
Auntie Mavis. She found the chocolates and then told me the
Kingstons were coming to supper. I could not have it with them
but could see them.*

*I waited impatiently till it was time to fetch them. We went
to Riverside Drive (that's where they are) and found that their
house was not there so we inquired and found that there was a
continuation to Riverside Drive. We got them home and waited
till after supper then we gave the invitation and tuned in. We
started with gramophone records then I gave a speech and
then David did the news, then I came in as "Ma Jones" giving a
cooking recipe and so on till we had to go to bed at 8:30.*

Wed. Aug. 21st

*I woke up to remember we were going to a Honey Dew and going
to see a film called Convoy. It was the best film of the season.
Well—of all nasty things, David was sick at breakfast. He stayed
in bed all the time till it was time to go. We saw* Convoy[9], *which
was marvelous and another called* Blonde[10] *which was stupid.
Then we went to bed at 10 p.m.*

Thurs. Aug.22nd

*I got up at 7:30 and had breakfast at 8 o'clock. After breakfast
we went to the shopping centre and bought a few things. Then
we had lunch. After lunch we had an hour's rest trying to get to
sleep. After that we had a phone call to say we were going down
to Muskoka. Dr. Routley's brother was taking us. We started at*

---

9   British war film (1940) about a British ship saving refugee ships from U-boats, directed by Pen
Tennyson and starring Clive Brook and John Clements.

10 Possibly *Free, Blonde, and 21* (1940), an American noirish drama film directed by Ricardo
Cortez and starring Lynn Barri and Mary Beth Hughes.

5:30 and had a nice ride till we came to a country lane. Then he really started up. He got to a hill and rushed down it at 70 m.p.h. Then he started at 80 m.p.h. rushing down and up the hills. Then after a bit he slowed down and stopped beside a farm gate. He got out and opened it and then drove in. He told us this was his farm and he was just going to look over it to see if it was alright or not. All was well though so we went on stopping once at Lake Simcoe to see a New York friend. [blot of ink here with note at bottom of page: *"sorry about the ink but it's my pen."*] *At last we arrived there. We got in the boat and raced over to the island. When we got there we found Aunt Edith was ill in bed. We went over to Aunt Gertrude's (Mrs. Routley's) and got in bed there at 10 p.m.*

Fri. Aug. 23rd

I got up at 8 o'clock and had breakfast at Grandma's.[11] After breakfast we found a sail for a rowing boat and played with it at Uncle Fred's[12] Common. After that it was lunch time and we went back to Grandma's. After lunch we washed the dishes and brought up wood for the fire then had a rest. We did not do much except climb rocks for the rest of the holiday and we did not have one swim. Aunt Edith [Fry] *was in bed all the time so we were not allowed to use her boat. We left on Sunday and now it's Monday. This morning I met another English boy and David, him and me had great fun.*

Well—Lots of Love from Your Very Affectionate son—
William, Alexander, Binny Douglas

P.S. Aunt Davina's[13] letter to the September Chatelaine *is marvelous. Read it.*

---

11 *My foster father Harold Fry's mother.*

12 *Referring to Dr. Frederic William Routley, whose wife, Gertrude, was Harold Fry's sister.*

13 *Davina's stage name was Davina Craig, and she was in about forty movies between 1936 and 1940 for Twickenham Film Studios. She was a big deal in New Zealand, and became an Officer of the Order of the British Empire in 1985. She died in 2002.*

CHAPTER 3
SEPTEMBER TO OCTOBER 1940: SCHOOL!

As August came to an end we went to the Canadian National Exhibition (CNE)—as we would for the next two years as well—and our summer came to a close on Tuesday, 3 September. By that time, all the English children who had come to Forest Hill Village had been assessed for their level of schooling: something difficult to judge, as the two educational systems were very different. We seem to have been simply allocated positions at Forest Hill Village School (FHVS) according to the average age in each grade.

Darling Mother

I'm writing rather late but school has started and I'm forgetting. I'll start now.

Monday Sept. 2nd

I had come back from holiday with one of David's best friends because we started school on Tuesday. Monday was "Labour Day" so we went the day after. We are going to the village school and it is the best in the district so we are well off. It is only a day school[1] so I am lucky except for covering books and homework, etc. Well—I woke up at 7:30 and hurried up on dressing. Uncle Harold did not have to go to work so he suggested a drive. He

---

1 Unlike Christ's Hospital, Alec's boarding school in England.

whispered to us that it was really a pony ride for Susan, but ir
[it] rained so we could not. We were trying to fix a gramophone
and needed something for it but the shops were closed so we
did not do it. It was a nasty day (worst luck) so we could not
do much. How did you like the paper I sent you? It's a birthday
present. I got it at the Exhibition [the CNE, which took place*
every year at this time]. *If you look at the top left-hand corner*
[of this page] you will see Exhibition Issue written. Well—I'll
start Tuesday now as there is nothing else to say about Monday.

Tuesday Sept. 3rd

I woke up with a dreadful thought in mind. SCHOOL WAS
STARTING! *Still, it was new and exciting. We went to school*
with nothing but David's school bag. We went to an office or
more like a classroom. One of the masters filled in a registration
card for David and mine had been done so we had a half
holiday till 1:30. We started school then but nothing happened
different from in Housey except the way we were taught. We
ended at 3:30 and came home with a whole lot of books we had
to cover. We went to bed at 8 o'clock.

Wednesday Sept. 4th

[The timetable for classes is listed in the letter, showing times
and classrooms, but without much helpful information about
subjects being taught] *There are 1400 boys at this school* [Aunt
Mavis added a note: *"Really 700—the school consists of two*
schools, Prep and High, they are in the Prep"]. *Gym is generally*
games outside. David and me are both in Grade 7. Our form
master, Mr. Perry, is very nice, everybody likes him, and he had
two snakes only today they escaped and Mr. Perry had to kill
them or they would have been too dangerous.

Well, I wish I could think of something to tell but I'll wait a
bit and think of something. Oh yes, of course, I wanted to give

Gordon my love [Gordon Wheatley, whose mother was a dear and close friend of my mother in Cornwall] *and please tell me what part of London you are, SW, S, ENW, NWEN or what.*

Well lots and lots of love from your most affectionate Alec

There is a revealing postscript to this letter by Aunt Mavis: "This was all ready to send days ago & I found it in his pocket. Posted? Oh yes! These boys! He's awfully well & grown inches *both* directions I'm sure! Oh darling—I worry about you all so: what hell! Thank goodness the children are happy & care-free—I know you'd be happy to see them. Alec seems to be getting on well at school— I'll know more later!"

The school, as I explained to my mother in a later letter, was divided into twelve groups: six boys' groups and six girls' groups, with a teacher in charge of each. Grades 7, 8, 9, and 10 were mixed together in the groups, largely for extra-curricular activities. Our classroom teacher in Grade 7 was a Miss Miles. She heard me sing, probably the national anthem or something, and told me I should work on my voice. Consequently, I joined the school choir (and was the only boy) and under her coaching would learn various songs that I performed at home. The one I remember particularly was Handel's "Where e'er you walk," and it apparently impressed others that I had a good treble voice.

A few days after my last letter, on 8 September, Mother cabled us to say she was safe. Surviving the Blitz was no longer a matter for calm—being bombed was now far more likely than being hit by a thunderbolt—and we were all worrying. On an everyday level, however, life continued on in a happy, normal fashion for us boys, with "free time" taking priority over dull routine.

Sunday Sept. 8th

Dear Mother

I woke up on Sunday morning very early, but I had better tell about Saturday first. We have free days all Saturday so I did not hurry over breakfast. After breakfast, David showed me his magic lantern and put on a few pictures. Then we wrote some envelopes wrong way round and showed them on the lantern. Then after a bit David remembered that some signals for the farm were waiting to be painted white. David had done a few for me the night before. I painted the two of them then banged in nails like this [illustration] so that we could hang them almost any direction. Then we had to go out shopping. We got a few things and a fountain pen for each of us for school. I am writing with David's because mine is no good.

After lunch we went to the farm. We hoisted the signals and I had mine on a tree while David had his on the old barn about twenty or thirty years old. He had to climb inside and then climb up the side of the barn while I gave him the hoisting rope. We had great fun playing about with them. David is going to use the binoculars as I can see the barn quite well and plainly. We came home quite late and did not have lights out till ten to ten.

Sunday Sept. 8th

I woke up very early and got up at eight. Unluckily David did not feel well so I could only read all morning and finished half a book. We had lunch at the usual time and oww [now?] I'm writing my letter. I have just got your cable and I am so glad your alright we were so worried.

Monday Sept. 9th

I woke up to remember it was David's birthday on Monday and was very excited. David was quite calm about it. I thought it was such a shame that it was his birthday on a school day and so did he. Still, it was going to be fun on Saturday as we were going to the farm to celebrate his birthday.

We did hardly anything else on Monday, as there was hardly anything to do. We went to bed at the usual time.

Tuesday Sept. 10th

I got up same as usual, got my schoolbag ready (I had been given one on Sunday), and after breakfast and making my bed set off to school with David. We did hardly anything in the way of work except French in the morning and then it was all easy. We came back at twelve and had lunch at 12:30 and were back at school at 1:30. We did not do much in the afternoon and had free time from 3:30 p.m. onwards. We went to bed at 8 o'clock.

Wednesday Sept. 11th

I got up everything happened the same all day till 3:30 p.m. then we had to go to the dentist and doctor. We were met by Aunt Mavis and taken to the medical arts building. We got into a lift there and went to the seventh floor. We went to a door that said, Dr. Brown and Dr. Cowan. [Dr. Brown was one of Canada's foremost pediatricians, and Dr. Cowan would save me from having terrible buck teeth a year later.] I sat down in the dentist chair directly I got there. I had an x-ray photograph taken of my teeth and found that I had to have a baby tooth filled. Dr. Cowan (who was a lady) said she would not use the drill as they were so small. David had his teeth cleaned as he liked it then we left. We went downstairs to Dr. Brown on the third floor then. He asked about my health and said I must be a very healthy boy. He looked at me through an x-ray thing and

teased me about my brain. He said I had sat on it. I had tea in
a Honey Dew with Uncle Harold as well as David and Aunt
Mavis.

Thursday Sept.12th

I woke up on Thursday to find everything the same as usual,
had breakfast and went off to school. I did not do much in free
time because I had nothing to do. I have nothing else to say
about Thursday except that it's bedtime so—goodnight.

Friday Sept. 13th

We did all the same things on Friday too. School, lunch, school,
free till bed and bath so that's all I can say about Friday.

Saturday Sept. 14th

I woke up to remember it was free time for the day so I got up
quickly and got over breakfast. I'm afraid I was very inactive.
I sat down here all morning, but David had to stay in bed all
morning, Doctor's orders. He had to on Sunday too. He hates
having breakfast in bed, but that's the only time he eats a lot. I
read a book all morning I'm afraid. After lunch we were going to
the farm so I thought that we would make up for it. We started
out in the car and were just going by the jail farm when a car
in front of us stopped twenty or thirty yards ahead of us and
we put down the brakes hard but had a little accident. Nobody
was hurt except Aunt Mavis, and some soldiers gave us a lift
to where Uncle Harold was waiting for the car in his Ford and
he took us to Dr. Routley's, who fixed it up for Aunt Mavis and
we went home in the Ford, went to bed early and woke up on
Sunday morning same as usual.

With lots and lots of love from
Alec

73

Aunt Mavis added a note:

Phyllis Darling

I have broken my right arm so cannot write! Alec is flourishing and doing very well at school—They have been moved up already so they seem to be pretty well on a par. We were glad of your cable, as there have been no letters for ages. I wish I knew where Mummy and Davina were. Oh Dear, do take care of your precious selves.

Heaps and heaps of love
Mavis

···

[Undated, but probably 29 September 1940]

Dear or Darling Mother

You wanted to know exactly what happened in Auntie Mavis's accident so I will tell you. We were going to the farm and were going to take a friend with us. We had to go down a very busy street—actually it was the main street—to their place and passed the jail farm. We were jogging along quite merrily when a man stopped dead in front of us. Auntie Mavis put down the brake as hard as she dared but it was not hard enough and we bumped. It was quite a jolt as we were going thirty-five miles an hour, and David bumped his tooth on the dashboard so that it broke. Like this [crude illustration]*! ... I broke—at least, helped—a chair[2] I bumped it so hard. I fell in front of Susan and stopped Susan flying through the windshield, and Nurse held Jeremy tight and bumped her nose on his head, and* [Jeremy] *bumped his head on the chair while he threw Auntie Mavis on the steering wheel so that she broke her arm. The people in the back seat got off best except Nurse whose nose was*

---

2   i.e., the front seat of the car

*aching for weeks afterwards. Soon there was a crowd around
and some soldiers came and helped us out. They brought their
car up to ours and then they took us to the nearest garage—
gas station in Canadian—and told them about the accident,
where it was, what it was, what colour it was—in fact, a general
explanation. Then they took us to where Uncle Harold was
waiting in the Ford. Then he took us to Dr. Routley who dressed
Auntie Mavis's arm and put it back into position. We stayed
there until she was ready then.*

*I am very sorry about the Jews, I won't say anything about them,
what did I say in my letter?[3] I had better start my letter though
as I have wasted a lot of time ...*

Monday

*We had manual training [woodworking] on Monday morning
and we were doing a cigar box violin which I am getting on well
in. I have got the cigar box and I have done all the planing and
it is in the right shape which is rather hard to do, and I have
done most of the filing and there is a place for the cigar box.
Funnily enough I am better at that than anything else I do in
woodwork. I seem to take much longer than anything else. In the
afternoon we had gym and we played soccer and I nearly scored
the winning goal but the goal keeper caught it just in time and
another boy scored it for me. Nurse, Susan, and Jeremy were
going for a walk and Susan saw me so she cried at the top of her
voice "There is Alec," and everybody looked at me so I felt very
bashful as you might think. But no more was thought of it. I
had my music lesson afterwards so I went into the Junior school
gym, did my homework till it was time to start. We had it* [the
music lessons] *in classes and it was the easiest work you could
do. Auntie Mavis is paying for* [them]. *They are five dollars for
twenty occasions and we have them twice a week. We had half*

---

3   *Whatever I had written has not survived among the letters my mother kept, but both Mother
and my grandmother had very close and dear Jewish friends.*

an hour and I forgot to tell you I have learnt four poems, they are these: "Indian Summer" [by William Wilfred Campbell. Canadian poetry was being taught in Ontario schools: I wrote out the words of this poem] … "The Ranchman's Ride," "Robinson Crusoe's Story" and "Rain and Wind." I will not write these down as they will take up too much room.

Tuesday

On Tuesday morning we had a study period and I studied for my history and geography exam. Is Aunt Chrissie having any raids or anything, she never tells me and I don't even hear about her house, how Kitty is or even how Maidenhead is.[4,5]

I forgot to tell you about David's machine-gun bullet that has not been fired and is for a Vickers machine gun of the last war. This is the exact shape of it. [crude illustration] *David is always bragging about it. But I have rather gone off my subject. The rest of the day was just dull.*

Wednesday

Wednesday was dull except that I got 15 cents for pocket money and we practiced for our programme we were going to have on Thursday week [possibly choir practice].

Thursday

Thursday was a French period and otherwise dull.

Friday

Friday was just school.

Saturday

Saturday was a super day. For one it was free, another we went to

---

4   *Aunt Chrissie is Christine Douglas, my father's older sister. She had introduced my mother to my father. Kitty is Aunt Chrissie's cat, and Maidenhead is her residence.*

5   *Presumably Mother answered these questions, but her letters to me have not survived.*

the chiropodist downtown—David has got a bad corn you see—
and we were going to an airoplane display at Simpson's. It was
super with all the ice thing that takes the ice off the sings [wings]
of the planes.[6] And it gave all the planes from the first one.

Goodbye then
Lots and lots of
Love from Alec

P.S. I had lunch at Simpson's with the family.

This is a song made up by a boy at school.

Mother, brave and strong,
We will send our aid to thee
Naught can go wrong.
To the tune of Ah poor bird.

[On the back of this letter, I wrote in block letters:]
"KEEP YOUR SPIRITS UP WE ARE AT HAND"

[Undated, but probably 13 October 1940]

Dear Mother

On Monday morning we had manual training for three periods.
I played with a little girl called June [June Glasgow] *who*
was actually very boyish. She could play rugby very well and
kick better than me. David had a cap put on his tooth in the
afternoon. He was taken by a lady called Mrs. Crevaille. He
had white gold put in but only temporarily.

On Tuesday the morning was very dull. We played soccer
instead of the opportunity period.[7]

At 3:45 p.m. all the "war guests" in the school were given a
reception by the students' council. A Daily Star *camera man*

---

6 Presumably a mechanical deicing machine for aircraft.

7 *As I recall, opportunity period was a class in the timetable without instruction in which we were*
   encouraged to read books or magazines.

even came. He took a picture of all the people possible. They
gave us a lovely glass of chocolate milk and a cup of tea each.
We had piles of cookies too. I could not eat my supper at
home either.

Friday

Friday was a Red Cross tag day[8] so we all had to buy tags in
the classroom because of the advertising of the masters. We
had the auditorium first period and an English woman painter
came and lectured to us about England, its fine people, its great
buildings, and all its customs. She gave us lantern slides, which
were all her own paintings. We had French and spelling exams,
then Films. The students' council president gave them. They
were about a trip up the British Columbia coast and happy
hunting grounds, which was nature. After lunch we had a Red
Cross meeting.

Saturday

It rained on Saturday morning so we couldn't go to the farm.
David and me gave or made a lantern show to pass the time. It
was about the U.S. Coast Guards …

Sunday

I am writing my letter now. After I had got up to date in my
letter I went to church. It was a new one for Forest Hill Village.
When we were back from church we were surprised to hear that
a cousin of Aunt Mavis, whose name was Ronald Smith, had
joined the air force and had come out to Toronto from the west.
He came to lunch with us and we showed him round the city
right to the Island. Then they came back and had tea with us.
("They" means his [Ronald's] pal as well.) They both signed their

---

8   In the early twentieth century, Tag Days were fundraising campaigns regularly held in cities
    and towns across Canada when charitable organizations collected funds. Donors would be
    given tags acknowledging their support.

names in electric pencil on David's autograph book. Then we took them back to their depot, which was the colloseum at the exhibition grounds.

Lots and Lots of Love from
Alec

P.S. I was on the back page of the Globe and Mail *on Saturday morning. I'm quite public.*[9]

9 As I recall, newspapers including the Globe and Mail and the Daily Star published pictures of war guests from various schools. The published photos could not be located and perhaps the photos that were taken were never sent to press.

CHAPTER 4
OCTOBER TO DECEMBER 1940: CANADIAN THANKSGIVING AND HALLOWEEN

[Undated but probably 20 October 1940]
Monday

Dear Mother

Monday was a whole holiday as it was Thanksgiving Day. We were going to the farm all day. Well—we started out at 11 o'clock and got there at 12 o'clock. The first thing I did was climb up a tree and see if I could see a nice long way. I climbed down again and found some wood for a fire. We gathered a lot of stones and made a base for the fire, then we got some dead wood from a pile we had made before for a fire. We put them on the fire and sat down and started lunch. First we had a dish of tomato soup (actually only Susan and Jeremy had dishes, we all had cups). Then we had sandwiches and Jeremy and Susan had rice pudding. The sandwiches were bun sandwiches of turkey and ham and ordinary ones of turkey, ham, peanut butter and jam. After lunch I found a whole tree lying on the ground and lugged it to the stream and left it there to see if it was still alive next time I went to the farm. Then climbed up a tree for fun and it started raining. I rushed down and found shelter in the trees and David joined me. He had been making a wigwam but he took it to a clearing in the wood when it started raining, and made it there as it was sheltered and a very good place. Then we went to the car and left. So that ended a lovely day.

Tuesday

Tuesday was School. *We had an opportunity period and in the afternoon we played around with another war guest on the other side of the road. He wanted to have a war so we did it to please him—and us. It was rather exciting as I was good at crawling on my belly most of the time and shooting from [that position]. The other boy (his name was Holland[1]) was climbing up trees all the time. We never won because we never had an armistice. Towards the end of the game we decided to not be allowed to shoot more than ten feet away. Then we had to go.*

Wednesday

On Wednesday we had recess and we had a very good game of soccer in it. I was playing and so was David. He scored a goal too. The score was 2-0. Y.A. [unknown] *was playing B.B.* [unknown] *and won. I played pretty well. I missed two periods because I had to go to the dentist. They were both Art. For the first time I had to go on a bus as Auntie Mavis couldn't drive me with her broken arm and Uncle Harold was at the office. I went there by bus and it stopped right in front of the building. I got out with Nurse and went up to the seventh floor and walked into the dentist's office. She looked at my teeth and said she would do four fillings that day. She started off and finished about 4 o'clock and we walked out. Then we got the bus home and had to walk half a mile to a long-wanted supper. (By the way we stopped a bit at a Honey Dew.) I went to bed tired and happy that night.*

---

1 *John Holland. He later became a Justice of the Peace in Toronto, and was a neighbour of my parents in Toronto in the 1960s.*

Thursday

Thursday was a whole holiday and we were playing about with John Holland (the other war guest I told you about) and Stronie Bongard. At first we had a war then we collected leaves for a collection. We had lunch at 12:30 and half an hour's rest then we played about with John and Stronie. Stronie had a rugby ball and we played touch rugby till supper time. Then we went out and had another game after supper. We went to bed at 7:30, ready for another long whole holiday. Friday. It's not worth writing on this line so turn over.

Friday

On Friday morning we went to Eglinton—a shopping district north of us. We had to buy some provisions from the A&P store and Loblaws. Then David went to bed in the afternoon as he did not feel well at lunch. I played about with Stronie and John and another boy who everybody called Eddie. The two other boys came along. We had fun with all the dead leaves we could find. First Stronie and me made a pile and practiced diving on it, then we buried him. Then John was buried with him then I joined him. Then we all got out and buried the boy who buried us. Eddie and a boy called Nichol had been away pumping up their tires and a rugby ball. I went to bed very tired again that night.

Saturday

On Saturday morning I stayed indoors writing my letter. I got down to Thursday on my fifth page, which shows I am improving in my letters as much as you. David was in bed. Then I had lunch and wrote my letter for a bit till David and me were told we were to be taken to the library to take back our books my book was at school so I just walked up to Aunt Edith's and went with her on the Davisville bus then on a street car (that is a tram) to the library. Then we had something to eat at a Honey Dew then we went back. We had something to eat at Aunt Ethel's [Harold Fry's sister] *then went home.*

Sunday

Now comes a surprise. Auntie Mildred was up in Canada at Montreal for a concert and Auntie Mildred was coming to Toronto to see us. *We were all very excited and prepared to receive her. We only had her for Sunday and Auntie Mavis said that she would be much too tired to have her all day with her broken arm, so Uncle Harold, David, Auntie Mildred went to the Granite Club which David, Uncle Harold and me (I only half) belonged to. Paul and Lilian had a duplex house of their own now (duplex is one floor to you and another floor to someone else.) They lived quite a way from us so we took the car and took them along with us. We had a super lunch. Turkey and pineapple juice and water, ice and ginger ale. It was as David says a super supper or an acey ace meal. Then we were shown round the club. There was a swimming pool, skating rink, badminton courts, lounges, parcel office, [and] a dining room about 200 yards long and 50 yards wide. There is any amount of waiters and waitresses and the[re] is even a place where they sell candy and cigarettes. There are lots of members as well. After dinner we showed Auntie Mildred about Toronto. We arrived home to find Auntie Mavis waiting for us and Jeremy, Susan and Nurse just going for a walk. We were comforted by the cozy fire and Auntie Mildred sat herself down nearest to the fire and put her feet on a footstool as she had a bit of a cold. We talked on and on. Auntie Mildred telling us about Montreal and that she had earned something like sixty dollars and had put it in the Canadian bank and left it there. She told me that the Canadian weather must agree with me as I weighed 91 pounds and was 5 feet, 1 inch tall. I never had as much in one day. I went to bed at 7 o'clock as I had done so much and so;*

Goodbye, or as the Marx brothers say, Hail and Farewell[2]
From Alec

P.S. My overcoat is too small already.

David Fry wrote to my mother on 3 November. Mother was delighted and sent it back for his mother to read. "Isn't this the nicest letter," she wrote. "I know you'll love to read it."

Dear Auntie Phyllis

I am sorry I haven't written sooner but I am a very bad writer. I wouldn't make a very good war guest.

Alec and me are having a wonderful time together, it's nice to have someone to play with. I have a Besuca,[3] a sort of wart or corn I am not sure which, on my foot and it's just being burst out and is rather sore but it is very useful. I do not have to do nearly as much work, on Friday I missed school, and I do not have to have a bath.

Alec must have a hard head as he bust the seat of the car in the accident but there must be an awful lot of bad accidents in the blackout.

What is it like to sleep in an air raid shelter? Is it easy? I would not like to try it. How many narrow escapes have you had yet? It seems everyone is having them nowadays. I do wish you were here, it would be much safer! Last Thursday was Halloween and Alec and I went shelling out ... we got a whole basket of candy each. People are very bad at Halloween. In Forest Hill alone there were two fires, lots of broken windows, and For Sale signs

---

2 This is a reference to the 1938 film *Room Service*, directed by William A. Seiter, based on the 1937 play of the same name by Allen Boretz and John Murray, and starring the Marx Brothers.

3 This may refer to Bezuca, a type of gel used on warts.

in front of people's doors. The candy was good though.

With Much Love From
David
....

,

A week later, on 12 November, I sent Mother my own account:

Dear Mother

Last week I did not tell you about Halloween on Thursday. It was super. We dressed up and went around shouting "shell out" and all the grown-ups had to give us candy or something. We got almost two baskets of it and one person gave us money. We stayed up late till 9 o'clock and David had a red tail coat and white trousers with a hideous mask. We had super fun and Aunt [Auntie Mavis crossed out] *gave us each a caramel sucker about a foot in length, huge really. I am writing this amidst a tin can band and an underage Soloist—Jeremy—and David is the tin can band. Susan is out of it. I think it is worse than any old air raid. Now David has got his old gramophone on or else it is Susan. I will start Monday on the next page. We need not to save paper so much out here.*

Monday

Monday morning was manual training and we were doing our [cigar box] *violins still. We did not have anything else unusual* [or] *interesting, so there is nothing else to say.*

Tuesday

Tuesday was all the same. We had art opportunity and that is all interesting on Tuesday.

Wednesday

On Wednesday it was pocket money and I got twenty cents.

Thursday

Thursday we had an auditorium period and we sang.

Friday

On Friday it was just school.

Saturday

On Saturday we went to the farm and we took another boy from England. His name was John Holland and Uncle Harold had seen me David and him playing about together so he invited him. We had super fun climbing trees and climbing up hay ricks and picking apples. ["He really started being," crossed out] *He went and made us pretend we were looking for gold but we offered him an apple and he forgot about it. We just climbed another tree and that started him into birds nesting and he tried to climb a huge oak for one but he soon forgot that when the branches began to fall off.*

Sunday

On Sunday there were parades because Monday was Remembrance Day. We saw them and were they super. They had lots of different parades of different regiments.

Well Goodbye and Good luck
Alec

....

[undated, probably 17 November 1940]

Dear Mother

Sunday

*On Sunday there were parades. Me and David and the whole
family went to see them. They were super fun. I only saw one
but it was super all the same. Auntie Mavis, Uncle Harold
and the babies sat in the car while David and me ran to where
the General was inspecting the troops. It was a super view.
There were all different kinds of regiments there. The Governor
General's Horse Guards[4] and the motorcyclists and the Eton's
[Eaton's] memorial machine gunnist,[5] veterans of the last war
and the militia and I don't know how many others watching.
But that was really all to it. But it was fun watching it.*

Monday

*Monday was Armistice Day and I was listening to the ceremony
at 11 o'clock. Did you have one in England, or did an air raid
stop it? I have not anything else for Monday so I'll go on with
Friday, at least Saturday, because I did not do anything really
eventful in the week.*

---

4 A Toronto unit of the militia originally raised in 1889. The unit sent many men for overseas
   service in the First World War. During the Second World War the Horse Guards were
   equipped with motorcycles in 1940, which probably accounts for the motorcyclists mentioned
   here. In 1941 the unit was converted into an armoured regiment (tanks and armoured
   cars) that served overseas in Italy and North-West Europe in 1944–45. National Defence
   Headquarters, Directorate of History and Heritage, "The Governor General's Horse Guards,"
   https://www.canada.ca/en/department-national-defence/services/military-history/history
   -heritage/official-military-history-lineages/lineages/armour-regiments/governor-generals
   -horse-guards.html (accessed 25 January 2023).

5 Probably refers to the veterans of the Eaton Motor Machine Gun Battery, a unit of some 300
   soldiers and equipped with armoured cars, raised at the expense of Sir John Eaton, president
   of the T. Eaton Company, the famous department store, in the fall of 1914. The unit served in
   the Canadian Corps on the Western Front in 1916-18. Library and Archives Canada, *Guide to
   Sources Relating to Units of the Canadian Expeditionary Force: Machine Gun Units*, 62, https://
   www.bac-lac.gc.ca/eng/discover/military-heritage/first-world-war/Documents/machine%20
   gun%20units.pdf (accessed 25 January 2023).

Saturday

On Saturday was Santa Claus's Parade, and I have here what it was like in the paper. I have marked where we were watching on the advertisement. [Evidently the paper was sent but not preserved!]

By the way I want to tell you about the rodeo I saw in the afternoon. … First two cowgirls sang some songs that were called "Songs of the Ranch." They sang to a guitar and were from the Wild West. Then came a grand entry of cowboys and cowgirls. A Red Indian band played and they danced and did everything. Then we had some bronk [bronco] riding. The rider who kept on longest won. The rider who won was on for 72.3 seconds. The next item was steer riding. This was really exciting. The first steer (I am sorry they were Burmha [Brahma] bulls) burst out of the pen, almost knocking it down. He was really wild. … [there were seven contestants, and the second won with a time of 39.6 seconds; the letter describes several other events, leading up to] *Gene Autry, the most famous cowboy in America with his two wonder horses, "Champion," and "Champion Junior." He made a ring shaped like this* [illustration of hexagonal ring in which were two round shapes] *where the horses danced …. Then he DANCED THROUGH A RING OF FLAME ….*

Then we had a mounted basketball game between Canada and America …. It was a really tough game. Then we had a wild cow milking contest …What you had to do was catch a cow and milk it …. We had a few other things … then we drove home in a snowstorm.

Sunday was same as usual except that we did not go to church and Virgil Markham came to lunch. He said he remembered you from a party.

Lots and lots of Love from,
Alec

The next letter is adorned with a sprig of holly and in large capital letters: CHRISTMAS GREETINGS.

[undated, probably 21 November 1940]

Dear Mummy

Monday

On Monday morning we stayed with Mr. Grass all the time and in the afternoon we did too. It was rather a shame because we missed manual training but had fun drawing boxes for Maths as we are in volumes. This is how we did it. First we put in three equal lines like so (Fig. 1) [rough drawings] *then we added some more like so (Fig. 2) of course they were all equal. Then we had to make it as though it was transparent like so (Fig. 3) … or if we liked as a wooden box without a top by rubbing out the lines that I darkened in Fig. 3. We had a bit of geography too and then we had to draw a map of Saskatchewan* [Illustration showing Churchill and Saskatchewan rivers and principal cities].

Tuesday

On Tuesday morning we went to study period. I was learning a poem in it called "Santa Filomena."

[Here I included five verses of the poem by Longfellow, a lament for the army of the dead—"honour to those who by their deeds have helped us in our daily needs, and by their overflow have raised us from what is low…"]

That is all I know but you see what it is like. We had opportunity too so I went on with my stencil I am doing for the lantern show David and me are raising.

In the morning David and I saw an accident with two cars but it was only minor and I forgot to tell you, too, about the sheet of paper I signed that is put in a book with all the other classes of Ontario's signatures. Tho it was to be sent to the KING AND QUEEN, Mr. Grass said, he did not know about the other provinces of Canada.

Wednesday

Wednesday morning was cloudy and it looked like snowing I am afraid. David was sick and had to go to bed. I was at school in good time and was ready nice and early in the morning, 20 English, 205 English, 211 Literature 207 Maths 203 Music.[6] In English we were doing singular and plural, and in Literature we had to correct a test we had done on Tuesday. These were the questions in it. What book did John Oxenham's story come in, and who wrote it? Answer: Westward Ho[!] *by Charles Kingsley. I put John Oxenham's story by George Henty as I knew nothing about it in the slightest. Why would the maiden likely marry Edmund? (Two reasons). It was from the "Outlaw's Song" by Walter Scott. I got both my reasons right. I shall not tell you more about it as there is not room. In Maths I did not do too much except volumes and things. In Music we had Christmas carols.*

In the afternoon we had 211 Literature and 211 Health, then sat in the basement. In Literature we had memory work but I did not recite, and in Health I received a new health book, and in Art I did an all-over pattern. There were four to choose from which were stripes ... squares ... and drops ... and diamonds ... I chose diamond pattern.

Thursday

On Thursday morning we had Audortorium, 207 Spelling, 203 Music, 207 French opportunity. In the afternoon we had Study, 205 English, 207 Spelling or Maths, 211 Literature.

In Audortorium the junior band played and three boys lectured

---

6   Class numbers allocated by the school.

about airoplanes. We learnt a few carols in music and played a few games in French like Simon Says *or* I Spy with My Little Eye. *In opportunity I did a Christmas card like this* [two illustrations showing front and back of the card] ... *I learnt another verse of "Santa Filomena" in study. I found I got 72 out of 90 in my test for Literature or 74 1/10%.*

Friday

On Friday morning we had nothing but French and Maths. In the afternoon we had Films, Social Studies, and then we just read books.

Saturday

Saturday was miserable as it was raining on the snow.

Sunday

Now I am writing my letter and it has started to snow again so goodbye.

Lots of love from
Alec

P.S.

Darling Phyllis

I can't really write much yet—just a line to say Merry Xmas & that Alec is flourishing. He's grown FEET, has a wonderful colour and looks grand He had a session at dentist—three out & eight fillings in October—&— now wears a man's 7 ½ in shoes, & 14-year-old clothes! Wonder Boy! David about two sizes smaller in everything—Boo & Coo! Mildred insisted on donating twenty-five dollars towards his clothes but Harold wouldn't let me use it (men!) so it's into Bank as an emergency fund for him. He's doing splendidly at school— the boys are very equal in work, & Alec is shining in Music. I haven't heard much, mostly slow dirges,

91

but the teacher is pleased! I love your letters, Alec is so proud of you—so are we all! Wrist agony, no more now—

Thine, Mavis

Sent you some tea, hope you get it & it is of use. You may get a photo of the children soon if they come out!

The approach of Christmas was very much in mind. On 28 November, I sent Mother a copy of my half term report:

"I am sorry I could not send you this report but I will be able to at the end of the year ..." The overall comment had a familiar tone: "Alec is rather too absent minded and is rather late." The music teacher, Miss Miles, had evidently taken a shine to me— "Splendid response," she wrote, giving me a mark of 80%. I seem to have done well in Spelling, English and Maths, but had not done my project assignments in natural science. The rest of this letter seems to offer distraction from my academic progress.

[28 November 1940]

In my last letter I did not tell you about the bucking Ford in the rodeo. It was really super. It looked like this [illustration]. *It kept on going on its back wheels and bucking like a horse and spurting water and firecrackers went off—it was marvelous.*

Monday

On Monday morning we had manual training in which we were marked for our reports. In the afternoon we had gym and played a game called dodgeball in it, you play it like this [diagram]. *The people behind the black line on side of gym throw the ball at you and you have got to run to the other side area without being hit. If you are hit you are out.*

Tuesday

We had study period on Tuesday but nothing else.

Wednesday

On Wednesday we had Health period. We had to do diagrams and things in that. Then we had Art. In Art we had distance effects. We had to show a distance effect in paint.

Thursday

On Thursday we had opportunity class and I am taking Art. We had to do a poster for the milk foundation. I am making a milk bottle lighthouse and saying as a slogan MILK! THE GUIDANCE TO GOOD HEALTH.

Friday

On Friday we had Gym and we had to go for a walk. It was supposed to be a march. We had to do it to see if we could enter for five years Rugby Training.

Saturday

On Saturday we went downtown and bought some winter clothes. Me and David looked like parachute troopers when we came out of the store. It was Armenian and there was a sign which said "No admittance" and they spelled response "respons."

Lots and lots of love from
Alec

P.S. Did you ever get the pollyphoto of me and David together? If you did you never mentioned it. Well—Merry Christmas to everybody and a happy one.

This next letter (undated) seems, from the references to school pre-Christmas activities, to have reported in the period from 9 December to 14 December (a Monday to a Saturday), and was written on odd sheets of writing paper.

[9 December 1940]

Dear Mother

Monday

On Monday morning we had manual training. David and me were doing a swing for Christmas and we were going to give it to Susan. This is what it is going to look like [rough illustrations of top and side views of swing]. *David and me were told not to be* [dissapoiinted, crossed out] *disappointed if she did not like it at first sight, (sorry about spelling) as she did not like things like that till she saw their use. In the afternoon we had Gym and did a game called dodge ball (I told you all about it in my letter before last). Our group won and I was hit toward the end. We had a hard battle though because they stayed 10 minutes and we stayed twelve minutes. We had exersizes after that and they were rather dull.*

Tuesday

*Tuesday morning was absolutely horrible. Rain had spoiled the snow and made it very hard as well as melting it. We had a study period while the girls had gym. I was making up a ditty for my ditty bag on it.[7] In the afternoon we had Literature and we did a play in it (*Pied Piper).

Wednesday

On Wednesday we had Health and Art. And we were busy in

---

7 *David and I were filling "ditty bags" for sailors on HMCS* Forest Hill *containing such things as socks and preserved food. Whether they were received or appreciated, we were never told.*

Designs and hardly anything in Health. We had Literature as well and in this we did a play called The Three Witches. *A French play.*[8]

Thursday

On Thursday we had Audertorium and in it we had a play called The Birth of Christ. *It was very good, done all by girls. The angels looked awfully good too, like this* [crude and child-like illustration].

Friday

Friday was just rather dull. All morning we stayed with Mr. Grass, and in the afternoon we had a Red Cross programme.

Saturday

On Saturday we went to the farm. Out there it was lovely and I just had super fun with David. You could almost skate on the pond and the roads were better looked after than the city. David fell through the ice but we did not worry about that.

I have just received your letter, it is lovely.

Lots of love from
Alec

P.S. Please excuse paper. Ran out of writing paper.

---

8   *As I recall, this was a French version of an excerpt from Shakespeare's* Macbeth, *featuring scenes involving the three witches.*

Dear Mother,

Monday Dec. 16th

On Monday morning we had manual training and me and David were working like wildfire to finish Susan's swing as it was the last manual training period before Christmas. First we got the plane and planed it down to this shape: [drawing]. *Then David marked the places to drill the holes while I got the drill ready. Then David brought the swing over to the electric drill. I turned it on while he pulled the drill down slowly and drilled right through. It spit a bit but we could not help that as it was a special drill and the only one of the right size for the rope. When we had finished that we rushed it over to the bench and sandpapered it hard. When we had finished that we got some* [boiled? word unclear] *oil and a rag and thoroughly rubbed it till it had a nice dark shade. Just as we had finished, Mr. White, the manual training master, called out, "Tidy up" and "Duties are Alec Douglas, row 1 and 2; Noel Enright 3 and 4; George Fine 5 and 6; Ralph Fox and Alan Gordon, tool room."*

We took it home safe and sound, all nicely oiled and looking nice. It was the quickest I ever did something like that in my life. In the afternoon we had Gym but we didn't do much in it.

Tuesday Dec. 17th

On Tuesday morning we had study period and David was having fun writing letters like this.

Dear David Sime.

Please meet me at the dance hall tonight as I want to tell you something. From your tiny sweetheart, ... (who is the fattest girl in class).

P.S. If you don't I will cry.

[Marginal comment by Mavis: *David's sense of humour! Sounds awful but is very harmless really!*]

We had opportunity on Tuesday morning as well and I was making Christmas cards. (They did not turn out very well though.[)]

Wednesday Dec. 18th

On Wednesday we had memory work, Art, Health and Literature and Music. I did not recite anything in it as my name was not called. In Music we had carols as it was so near Christmas. Only one week. It seemed impossible, but I suppose you always feel like that at Christmas and your birthday. In literature we read a poem about the pipes at Lucknow.[9] In Health we [studied?] the teeth: we had to draw one like this [drawing of cut-away of a tooth] and do an article about your teeth and how many roots they had (one, two and three). The underlined word is how many I have. In Art we were given portfolios to put our art in and anything unfinished had to be done in spare time. They looked like this. [drawing] They were quite simple but served their purpose. We did Christmas cards but I'm afraid I did not do much in that period as I made a mess of my coloured paper and just couldn't think of what to do.

Thursday Dec. 19th

On Thursday morning we had opportunity period and I did not do much in it. In the afternoon we had study and did a bit of studying in memory work. We bought a Christmas tree (at least Mr. Grass did) at noon and it didn't look bad. I was about 5½ ft. high and held a lot of ornaments. Out here trees are so plenteous that a tree about 40 ft. high only cost[s] about £1.5s

---

9   "The Pipes at Lucknow" by John Greenleaf Whittier (https://www.poetry.com/poem/23166/the-pipes-at-lucknow#google_vignette).

whereas in England they would cost about £10.5s. This one only cost about 3s. [Comment by Mavis: *(I must say I haven't seen a 40 ft. one!) M.*]

Friday Dec. 20th

Friday was a big day. Everything we wanted to have seemed to come to us. First It was very dull. Just Arithmetic and Spelling. Then, in the afternoon, it livened up a bit. First came carol singing in the audortorium. Then we had our party! *First we had some films. The first one was about skiing at Lake Louise[10] in Banff [National] Park. You saw these skiers climbing up mountains and going through caves formed by ice and up to the very top and skiing down a bit and so on till comes the end of their journey and the top of [the] Banff mountains to the station. Then was one part where they had to go between two trees a foot apart. The next one was about trout fishing in the Nipigon River. Then we presented Mr. Grass [with] a present of an auto compass. Everybody gave about 4d and we could just pay. Then we had presents given out to everybody and I got a scribbler and a Scripto pencil from a girl who had to give it to me when we had to draw names out of a hat and whoever you drew out you gave a present to. I had to give one to a boy called George Caldough. Then we had something to eat. After supper we went to a nativity at St. Timothy. They are exactly the same as at St Martin-in-the-Fields. It was lovely. The lighting affect was awfully good at first, rather dim and gradually growing. It stayed on till 10 o'clock or after.*

Saturday Dec. 21st

On Saturday morning I was indoors and in the afternoon I was buying Christmas presents. Then all evening I was wrapping them. I had better not say what they were because Uncle Harold and Auntie Mavis will be reading the letter.

---

10 Corrected from "Lake St. Louis" by Mavis.

Sunday

*On Sunday we delivered a present to a friend and visited
Grandma Fry.*

*Lots and lots of love from
Alec*

[Note added by Mavis:] *Your darling is in the throes of Xmas
excitement! He and David both saved up $1.50 and I added the
same so they did their own shopping together (with me hovering
in the distance) they were terribly funny—I do wish you'd been
here to see them!* SO *important! The boys get on so well together
& have a grand time. There hasn't been a letter from you for
weeks, I expect some have been lost. More news from me soon.
Alec is* awfully *well—*HUGE *& much fatter! Very good looking
in fact.*

MFF.
....

CHAPTER 5
DECEMBER 1940 TO MARCH 1941: FIRST CANADIAN CHRISTMAS AND WINTER

The letters home at this season provide a fairly vivid portrait of the world we were living in at that time. On 29 December 1940, I wrote:

Dear Mummy

Christmas Day

On Christmas morning we woke up to find our stockings and found this on top [rough sketch of a maple leaf, presumably in maple sugar, with "Alec" and "Canada" written on it]. We put on our dressing gowns and walked to Auntie Mavis and Uncle Harold's room. Then we started to open them [the stockings]. There were lots of lovely things in them. I had a tie-rack and a box of crayons and a humming top and at the very bottom 10¢, about 5d. Then we had breakfast. After breakfast we all listened to the "Empire broadcast." Did you listen, it was from the "BBC"?[1] When that was finished Grandma, Aunt Edith and Uncle Art came with most of our presents. We had to wait a bit before we could go down as they were getting the presents ready. When we could go down it was about 10:15 a.m. Uncle

---

1   *Of course, she did. The family in England always listened to the Christmas programme, and my grandmother, Nellie Fernie, always insisted that everyone stand to attention as "God Save the King" was played.*

Art gave out the presents. The first one was to Jeremy. It was the present me and David gave him, a cute little (or you might say big) ball that was made into a dog's face. It was called Rover the Pup. Then came Susan's. It was a little cut-out book. Then came mine. It was the gloves, name-tapes and book of explorers. Were they Christmas presents, I'm sure we had them in England, anyway, thanks awfully.[2] The gloves are just what I want and the nametapes are what Nurse wants, and David and me share the book. Then came David's present. It came from England too. It was a Charles Letts schoolboy diary. He got it from Aunt Davina. She had sent him the same since 1939. Then Susan got a cut-out book and David and me got a postal telegraph set that you send Morse code with. Susan and Jeremy gave it to us. Uncle Harold got David and my present to him. A lovely box for shaving things like soap and after-shaving cream. Then I got David's present. Four destroyers for our navy. David's present from me was a battleship for our navy. [At this point my writing changes into a slanting style for one sentence.] I'm afraid were taught to write like this at school but it is not my ordinary writing so I am rather bad.[3] I got lots of other lovely presents including ICE SKATES, ICE HOCKEY STICK, ICE HOCKEY PUC. The puc is the same as a ball but it is very hard rubber and looks like this. [sketch] Jeremy, Susan, David and me all got between us an electric hair dryer. [sketch] I got a Boy's Own Paper from Auntie Mavis and Uncle Harold. I cannot tell how many lovely things I got but I will be able to bring most of the things over after the war. After a lovely lunch (dinner) Susan's school teacher, Miss Boyle, came as Susan was one of her favourites. Actually she came for lunch and helped Susan with her cut-out books. Mrs. Kinnear,[4] you know Mrs. Hartley well,

---

2   *I blush to read this! But there were times when I used to wonder if Mother had been a little careless about these things.*

3   *Penmanship, an attempt to teach us copper-plate writing, was one of our least favourite and most pointless classes.*

4   *Aunt Louise Kinnear.*

it was her daughter came to see us and Mrs. Cavell. Mr. Cavell
gave us a penlight. One of those torches you put in your pocket.

There followed several days spent quietly, recovering from Christmas. I noted that "On Saturday I saw a marvelous film called *The Thief of Bagdad*.[5] It begins with a ship sailing to Bazra and a blind man telling his story and everything in Technicolor. You must see it when it comes to England...."

New Year's Day in 1941 was equally memorable, as recalled in my letter, probably written about 3 January: a letter that although thoroughly disjointed contains a lot of information!

Dear Mother

I told you about Christmas so now I'll write to you about New Year's. Since you said you liked the letter that was not written in diary form best so I will write this ordinarily. In the morning we stayed indoors then had a marvelous lunch of roast DUCK and CHICKEN. Then we had a super pudding. Out here we call it dessert. Then we all wished for the new year's happiness and drank a toast of Madeira wine. I wished for good luck on the farm and David wished for a house on the farm and Auntie Mavis for peace in 1941 and Nurse for good health in 1941 and Uncle Harold for happiness in 1941 and Susan and Jeremy had a sip. David said he did not like the taste of the wine but I loved it. After lunch we had a rest and then went to the country. All was well until we got to the road where we should have gone on to get to the house. Then we found it too rough and got stuck but after about 1½ hours we got out. We phoned up to Miss James[6]—the lady who had invited us over to the house—and she was very relieved, she had worried about us all the time and

---

5   British film from 1940, directed by Ludwig Berger, Michael Powell, and Tim Whelan, and starring Sabu, June Duprez, John Justin, and Conrad Veidt.

6   *Freda James, a successful interior decorator in Toronto and a close friend of Mavis and Harold Fry.*

was just going out to look for us. She said she would meet us.

We went by another road and got there to find she had left and gone the other way. Uncle Harold found her though and we went tobogganing on a super hill. Then we came in at sunset and dried as well as washing in cold water. Then we read magazines and Miss James's nephew, Ronald Ray, who had come skiing while we were tobogganing, read a book. Then we had a super supper. There was chicken and baked potatoes, and spiced grapes and salad and spiced pears. We had some pudding and that finished supper. We had cranberry sauce with our chicken. I forgot to tell you about Miss Veach. She is the lady who stays with Miss James. She entertained Auntie Mavis while Uncle Harold was looking for Miss James. After supper Ronald Ray got an oil lamp and took it into his room where we played with his soldiers.... Talking about Christmas presents, thank you very much for sending over that postal order. Auntie Mavis is trying her hardest to change it but it is rather hard as most banks won't take any English money, and I wouldn't be surprised if all of them won't, but Uncle Harold is in the banking business and he might be able to sell, I mean change it. When I was writing about Christmas I forgot to tell you about the wonderful present David got. It is called KOPY-IT and it transfers things from paper like the example I have here [presumably attached]. *You have a piece of waxed paper and rub it with something like a pen or pencil but not with the nib or lead. Instead you do it with the other end.... You can do it once on anything except newspaper....*

I'll go back a bit in my letter to where we got stuck and tell you exactly what happened. We had gone up this road and got stuck on the way down. There was not room to turn in because it was so narrow. We were almost at the bottom when we went back first into a snowdrift. We got out and tried pushing the car out ... Uncle Harold got out and Auntie Mavis drove. All three of

*us pushed and found out it was no use. Then David and me
found a service station and found there was only one man there
looking after the petrol and the other was at Nobleton (a town
nearby) fixing his truck. We tried pushing it out again but failed
and then David and I were just going to get assistance from a
farmhouse when we saw the truck go by that belonged to the
service station. We waved to it but it went by us but came back
soon, having been told about us probably at the service station.
Then they helped us out in about half an hour.*

*By the way Nurse thanks you very much for the bedjacket you
sent Nurse. It fits her* ["lovelyly," scratched out] *very well and
she is very pleased.... When we went to the farm yesterday we
had super fun tobogganing and, coming home, we got stuck. We
drove three extra miles and when we got home we had lovely
waffles to eat. I did not write very exactly about that as I want
to get my letter off by tomorrow morning post and will not be
able to write in the morning.*

*Lots of love from
Alec*

A letter from Aunt Mavis to my mother at about this time gives
a charming picture of family life in Toronto, and reveals certain
character flaws that members of my family today may recognize!

Darling Phyllis

*You were a naughty darling to send so many presents— & thank
you from us all! Harold is deep in "Taffrail's"[7] Navy book—&
the boys are dieing to get it away from him. The little doll from
Lafayette's came without a card in it, but I guess it was from*

---

7 Pseudonym of Captain Henry Taprell Dorling (1883–1968), a Royal Navy officer who was
decorated for distinguished service in the First World War and returned to serve in the
Second World War. He published more than fifty books of naval history and historical fiction,
including works for young readers. "Captain H.T. Dorling," *Times* (London), 4 July 1968, 10.

you, & Susan loves her! David is writing himself to tell you how keen he is on the weekend book—it is good. I am awfully glad to have the Eliot poems. I wish you were here to read them with me! Jeremy's gloves are adorable! Also thanks for the charming bedjacket. I did a dreadful thing, & hope you won't mind. But our nurse—a perfect darling, a very superior person—has been wonderful to Alec & does all the extra mending & washing & chivvying when I'm not around—so I pretended you had sent it to her. She gave Alec very nice presents, & I thought you'd like to make her feel good! I'd have told you more if I'd been able to write! So if you get a thank-you letter don't faint! Writing is still difficult & painful—hence this awful scrawl. Then yesterday came the money orders to Alec & me—Darling you shouldn't— with everything so expensive & uncertain in England—please don't run yourself short to send him money. We don't know yet if we can save the rest for emergencies. I'll let you know what happens!

Alec is a lamb—and looking very big & well, almost fat! He's still very slow getting on with things—such as dressing, getting to bed, etc. & loses his possessions all over the place—but we keep on prodding and exhorting as we do to David over his peculiarities! & I daresay someday he'll "snap out of it" as the Canadians say! Harold thinks he's a splendid little fellow, & so level-headed & good-tempered. We think we're awfully lucky to have such a darling! With boys of Alec and David's age there seem to be so many things to correct & nag about sometimes Nurse and I feel we're being perfect pigs—but they seem sublimely indifferent—I don't think they notice our attempts to make then Wonder Boys—and we have grand times together especially at the Farm (as we laughingly call our 100 acres of rough woodland & stream & pasturage). I hope you'll feel your boy is being properly brought up, when he's handed back to you! I don't profess to be an expert in raising boys—but I do my best!

*In one thing I feel Canada will do him good. Aunt Chrissie,
I find, had managed to instill some of her typically snobbish
ideas in his dear old head, you & I know the sort of thing, from
long & close experience—if you don't, ask Davina!!!— & they
are getting nipped in the bud! David is quite a democratic
young Canadian & firmly squelches any Christina Douglas-
isms that issue from Alec's lips—& I notice he is getting over
them! Alec on the other hand is awfully good for David, &
we notice a big improvement in David since Alec came. They
get on wonderfully—never seem fed up with each other &
play & work together splendidly They got a lot of war toys at
Christmas & play war by land, sea and air—very realistic and
exciting—during which they address each other as Air Marshal
& Admiral as seriously as judges. They both believe in top of the
ladder in one easy step!*

*Alec certainly loves you, my dear, & happily and easily includes
you in his conversations. Usually as a super cook (!!!!)—or
things you've done together. I was so interested in your last
letter (end of Nov. was date) to read of your new collection being
photographed. I wish I could buy my undies from you—I adore
the nightie you sent by Alec. After the war I certainly shall,
darling. I hope the pictures arrive.*

*I am sending you the picture I had taken on our staircase of the
four children. I hope you'll like it! Harold & I are [extra?] fond of
the four of them!! I do hope the letters & tea & cards for Xmas
arrived—so many mails have been lost. I also hope the picture
arrives safely!*

*I can no more, my wrist aches! More soon—bless you my
dear—I hear on every hand how brave you are being—take care
of yourself.*

*Ever thine
Mavis*

Jan. 19th 1941

Dear Mother

On Sunday we went to the farm and I think I told you about it in my last letter but not very thoroughly. Anyway, I'll tell you about it now. We took the toboggan in the back of the car, although it stuck out a bit. We had to tie it on a bit so it would not fall out. We wore the hats Aunt Edith gave us for Christmas to keep our cheeks warm as it was cold out there. They look like this .... [crude sketch of a balaclava, with my caption *"Not a very good example"*]. *We had super fun out here at a super hill that looks like this ...* [another crude sketch] *We had a super run at the bottom too. When we came home we got stuck. We were being pulled along behind the car and had stopped on a hill, and he could not get up at it.... so we went all the way back to the farm and charged both the hills from the farm to where we were at the moment and farther. We had to run about a mile to catch the car up again. We got home at last and had waffles for tea. On Monday we had manual training and after school I had my music lesson and I finished my letter after supper. On Tuesday we had a study period. I learnt a poem called "The I Cart ["Ice Cart"].[8] It goes like this:*

Perched on a city office stool
I watched with envy while a cool
Lucky carter handled ice
And I was wondering in a trice
Far from the gray and grimy heat
Of that intolerable street
Oer sapphire berg and enamelled floe
Beneath the cold, still ruby glow.
It goes on and on but that is all I have learnt. It ends rather like

---

8 There are further lines quoted from the same poem in the second of the two letters dated 16 February 1941 below, which gives the full title. The poem, by British poet Wilfrid Wilson Gibson, was published in 1915.

this:
Drifting ... into ... sleep ... sle-ep
Drifting ... into ... sleep, BANG!!

This letter went on to report further school assignments, a "home-made museum with our English friend"—probably one of the boys staying across the street—and visiting some friends "who were experimenting with chemicals."

Feb. 2nd 1941

Dear Mummy

On Monday David was in bed and otherwise nothing eventful happened except in school. In the morning we had three periods of 207 [spelling], Mr. Grass [maths], and three of manual training. In the afternoon we had reading and English and Gym. In Gym we just did exercises and races. [A routine and dull report of daily classes until Thursday follows]. *In Auditorium Miss McCullough's class performed. They did not do much and the band played. They had one good thing though, called "Little Lady Icicle," where a girl was balley [ballet] dancing.... On Saturday morning I went to see the parade that was on to advertise buying War Savings certificates and stamps. It was super. I'm afraid I could not see all of it as we saw it start from the middle of the whole thing. The first things (for us) were motorcycles and army lorries. Then came gun and ammunition carriers. Then came the air force. It was huge, I would say it was at least a mile and a half long. Then came some Boy Scouts with posters saying LEND TO WIN and PLEDGE FOR VICTORY. Then came some Canadian Mounted Police. Then came veterans with flags that looked super. Then came the women. We all get the giggles with them. One was about as tall as David, very fat, hunch-backed and could not walk properly.... She had*

her feet on the side. Do [you] remember when Auntie Moo Moo
[Mildred Dilling] corrected us about walking on the promenade
in Etretat.⁹ Then came ambulances and after that Salvation
Army trucks and after that a huge air force truck, like the ones
at Winchester¹⁰ with a picture of a ship being torpedoed. Then
came a huge fire engine with the words: 2000 FIREFIGHTERS
HAVE BEEN KILLED IN LONDON ALREADY. DON'T LET
IT HAPPEN HERE. I forgot to tell you that on Friday I got my
Maths test. The marks were 30 out of 35 or 6 sums right out of
7. On Sunday we went for a ride in the car to the lake shore.

This letter concludes with routine accounts of daily events, report-
ing progress in skating, piano lesson—"There'll Always be an
England" was the latest achievement—and Jeremy's birthday. The
subsequent two letters are both dated 16 February, and only parts
of some letters in this period seem to have survived. Evidently
around this time, a bomb had fallen on Gloucester Place¹¹ during
an air raid. As Mavis Fry had written on the back of the 19 January
1941 letter:

Dearest Phyllis

Alec is very well & busy—he does not feel the cold as much as
this [an illustration in my letter headed WINTER IN CANADA
showing a figure beset by wind, shivering, and saying "brr"
with the comment "even the wind is cold"] would lead you to
suppose!!! His work at school is progressing quite well—I saw his
master yesterday & he says he [Alec] is still a little dreamy, but
improving a lot—& really his tests in Maths and spelling were
excellent. He is doing well skating & loves his music. School has

9 A reference to a pre-war trip to Étretat, a small coastal town in the Normandy region of France famous for its white cliffs.

10 *My mother had probably taken me to Winchester, a city in Hampshire County, England, before the war, although I do not remember it.*

11 The bomb had landed opposite 49 Gloucester Place, permanently damaging the structure of the building. After the war, it had to be reinforced with massive timbers.

started too & there is great competition! All very happy and blooming, and thinks of you a lot!

Lovingly
Mavis

We were all sad to hear about your bomb, but hope everything is cleared up now! You are a brave girl, bless you!!

Two letters dated 16 February[12] include the school report that Mavis Fry summarized on the back of an earlier letter. An A in General Deportment is printed in capital letters (the original report had to go back to the teacher so that Mother only received my handwritten copy). Courtesy, work habits and homework received As, effort and attention span Bs, and marks for French, Spelling, and Composition and Grammar were in the 80s, well above class average.

Dear Mummy

I shall tell you about Saturday the fifteenth first as it is the most exciting day of the week. In the morning we (David and I) went to have our haircut as we could not comb it well. I was a naughty boy and started reading the comics and I had reached a horrid story about a certain man called the Mummy who raises corpses from the dead by murdering people and giving the murdered people's blood and putting it in the corpses.

---

12 Although the two letters have the same date, and each reports on the preceding week, the events described for each day are different. This suggests that the letters cover different weeks. The difficulty is that the internal evidence suggests they both refer to the same week. The first letter specifically mentions that the week covered includes Saturday, 15 February 1941. The only potential date indicator in the second letter is that the family attended the "original ballet Russe" on the Friday of the week. Coverage of the Ballet Russe appearances in Toronto in the *Globe and Mail*, however, show that the performances were in the week starting Monday, 10 February 1941, which places the second letter's coverage in the same week, 10–16 February 1941, as the first letter. (*Globe and Mail* [Toronto], 11 February 1941, 18; 15 February 1941, 19; the latter was the date of the last advertisement for a performance to appear, which suggests the run was not extended beyond the original week planned.)

We did a bit of shopping then delivered my sweater to Aunt Edith's house as she wanted to make an alteration on it over the weekend. Uncle Harold stayed home from the office in the morning and then went to the farm in the afternoon. We took our skis and a toboggan for me as I had no skis and I could not ski. When we were almost there we saw a man driving horses and a sleigh. He offered David and I a drive and we had a super ride. He drove us as far as our farm then we got out. Then after a bit of tramping about in the snow we walked towards Miss James's farm. Miss James was the one we stayed with on New Year's. We sighted Aunt Mavis and Uncle Harold coming back. We signalled him to stop and he gave us a lift back to the farm. We got everything off but found that Uncle Harold's boots would not fit into Aunt Davina's skis. I had some super rides on the toboggan and went down hills like this; [rough sketch]. *I started by the road and the log cabin,* [and] *we had a super time. David was going down a hill like this* [another rough sketch] *and went like this:* [another rough sketch!]. *We never thought he would get down safely even. David can ski quite well now and he has never really been taught. Then we came home and had some sandwiches. On Monday we had manual training ... Reading and gym, etc. I had a music lesson too. I'm getting on pretty well in music ...* [similar descriptions of the school program with special attention to a famous hockey player—Bill Taylor—who visited one afternoon]. *On Friday it was just normal and ... today we're going to Christian Science church.*[13]

Lots of love from
Alec

....

The next letter, also dated 16 February, continues to report school activities and lessons: "In Health we were learning about

---

13 Aunt Mavis had probably wanted to let me see a Christian Science Church since my grandmother Nellie Fernie was a Christian Scientist.

sinosuses and antrums and the way it blocks up something or other in the skull ..." There follows "a super poem in memory work. 'The Ice Cart.'" I didn't bother to break it up into stanzas:

Feb. 16 1941

It goes like this: Perched on my city office stool, I watched with envy while a cool and grimy heat Of that intolerable street, O'er sapphire berg and emerald floe, Beneath a cold, still, ruby glare Of everlasting Polar night, Bewildered by the queer half-light I stumbled unawares Upon a creek where big white bears plunged headlong down with flourished heels, And floundering after shining seals, Through shivering seas of blinding blue. And as I watched them ere I knew, I was stripped and swimming too, Among the seal pack young and hale Thrusting on with threshing tale, With twist and twirl and sudden leap through crashing ice and salty deep. That is as far as I know but don't you think it's pretty good.

Thursday

... we had Auditorium and it was a super play ... It was supposed to be introduced by Piller Cough Drops and Old Man's Pills for Pale People. Then the characters were announced. "Oswald Axle Grease," the most astonishing, astounding, marvelous Hero and our beautiful, sweet, slim Heroine of the naughty nineties and a fat old thing skipped across the stage, "the worst, most horrible villain on earth," the Ivan McKee Mactavish. Then—just as the curtains opened— "you forgot me, brother" and an old lady hobbled across the stage. Then the play started. The old lady was hobbling to and fro across the stage frowning. Then the slim "Heroine" entered. "What ails you, mother? We are about to lose the old homestead." Then ... enter the villain, and asks about marrying her. Then, at the last moment, in rushed Oswald Axle Grease

112

and saved them. I saw a marionette show after school but I haven't time to tell you. On Friday we saw the original Ballet Russe. I am sending a programme to show you what it was like. I think the graduation ball was super.

Ronald and Leslie[14] came in the night. On Saturday we had a lovely day out with Ronald and Leslie, and I visited the museum. Now I'm writing my letter.

Lots of love from
Alec

....

Mar. 2nd 1941

Dear Mummy

How's goings on and your "Gloucester Pl. fire-brigade?"[15] I just got your letter dated Jan. 29th on Feb. 28th. It's quite amusing, you being called "glamour girls." Remember when I used to say you should go on the stage. Probably the sand bags are to prevent such "treasure," as an incendiary bomb, being hurt by its comrades. Don't you wear gas masks to put out fires or are gas masks part of the dungarees? Do you have to put out fires as far away as Oxford Street or Regent Street when you are Fire Watching? Are you having as many parades in London as in Toronto? Last time we had a parade we had SIX TANKS in it. I should have thought they would be bad for the roads.

I'd better be telling you our news now. Jeremy is as wild as any three-year-old could be and Susan hasn't been quite "up to it" for a few days. Yesterday we were having super fun in the garden with Jeremy. David and Jeremy got on the toboggan and I pulled them around a bit then I got on and David pulled ... [rough

---

14 *Ronald Smith was a distant cousin of Mavis Fry, who was stationed in the Toronto region with the British Commonwealth Air Training Plan. I do not remember who Leslie Walker is.*

15 *Mom was a firewatcher, a civilian position to watch out for fires caused by incendiary bombs. As I remember this was a volunteer position because she was not serving in regular wartime units. At the same time she also worked on an assembly line in a factory in evenings.*

sketch] ... *I made them skid and turn sharp corners and once I made them think they were going right in the hedge I'm sure. I'm learning another poem now. I'm sure you know it, "Jabberwocky."* [The letter goes on with the words of the Lewis Carroll poem, omitted here] ... *Have you received the photo of David, Susan, Jeremy and me on the stairway. I hope you have. On Thursday we had a rehearsal of the demonstration of the intermediate school. It is very good but I will tell you about it in my next letter as I am going to it. It is Chinese, Irish and Scandinavian and Canadian. They were not very good in the rehearsal, but we were promised they would be better. I forgotten Miss Burnie's Christian name. I am thinking of sending Mr. Willink a letter today. I haven't written for ages, so, goodbye.*

Lots of love from
Alec

P.S. [Added by Aunt Mavis] *He must have been in a somewhat crazy mood when this was written! I hope you enjoy these long poems word for word!—I feel they are rather space fillers—but hate to be too critical. I'm enclosing the letter to the ex-master so you can send it if you want to!* [The letter to Mr. Willink did not survive, nor does he appear to have answered.] *All well and flourishing here—your letters much enjoyed, what with canteens and fire-watching do you ever sleep? I love Alec wondering if you put out all the incendiaries on Oxford and Regent streets! Busy girl!*

Love
Mavis

Two more letters in March no doubt kept my mother well informed and, perhaps, amused. A more serious note from Mavis at the end of the month reported some problems with my teeth that had to be addressed sooner rather than later. Attached to one letter were my measurements: "—these are exact measurements so allow for growth" wrote Aunt Mavis. "Waist—28", Cuff—29½" Chest—28," Sleeve—16½" Length of coat—25", Shorts—12½" inside, Breeches—19" (average English 11½, Canadian 16)."

Mar. 23rd 1941

Dear Mother

This letter is going to be pretty exciting, and we have just started Spring so you will know what Spring is like out here (vaguely)!!!

I was listening to the radio rather a lot yesterday and everybody were doing nothing but making up silly poems about Spring. The weather is lovely out here, the sun shining bright and temperature only about 50° F ... Last week Ronald Smith and Leslie Walker came for the weekend. Ronald was in hospital with artheritus. I don't know how he got it because he is only twenty-one, but he came on Sunday. Then we found he had sick leave because he had to gain weight or something of the sort. We had quite a time with him. Yesterday he gave David and me ten cents to buy something in the Village. Guess what, I have saved out here $1.00 or one dollar. I have got a penny in my money box still [presumably an English penny]. *Do you remember in England you never let me see a skating carnival, well I went to one the Wednesday before last. It was really super. When I have finished my news I will tell you about it. Last Sunday, I wrote to Aunt Chrissie. Last Saturday (not yesterday) I went to the dentist and in the afternoon had my haircut. The Friday before last I saw a show, with* [short films] Ferdinand the Bull, The Practical Pig, Donald's Lucky Day *and* The Ugly Duckling *as well as Artie Shaw's band and Blue Barons. There were four others I cannot remember. On Monday I had my music lesson. I can play "There'll Always be an England" without the music and ... "God Save the King."*

Now for the Carnival.

115

It was held in the Maple Leaf Gardens. The first thing was called "Capt Kidd in the Southern Seas." This was all about pirates and things. Then we had a thing called "Neptunes Kingdom" where Captain Kidd went down to the bottom of the ocean in a diver's helmet and saw mermaids and "Neptune" "Himself." After that it had Cinderella at the ball. Aren't you dog tired every day after coming home from work? How is "Aunt" Lucille. [Presumably I had been told to address this very old friend properly!]

Love from
Alec

P.S. Did you hear about the Italian plane surrendering in midair the other day? [Crude illustration of two British fighters zooming towards an Italian fighter]

Mar. 30th 1941

Dear Mother

I wrote a letter to Aunt Chrissie today and am writing a short one to you. Auntie Mavis suggested putting in a ballad or something, so here goes:

Coronach

She sent him over to Canada
And said to the poor little fellow
"Now you must be very good over there
And don't start getting all yellow"

She saw him off at the station,
He had a bodyguard with him,
It wasn't a big celebration,
'Cause his mother got all out of Rhythm.
"Now your Aunt'll take care of you,

Don't be frightened," she said
Then his face grew rather blue
And hers began to grow red.
Wild Scotch lamentation
"Are you sure you wont come with me
It will be kind of nice,"
"I've got to stick to my job" she said
"Go forth and learn to skate on the ice"

He went forth kind of sadly,
But now he's over there,
He can skate very well,
And is sorry for his mama dear.

But when the war is over,
Over the sea she'll fly,
She'll leave old Adolf sober,
While Musso long shall sigh.

I hope the end is true anyway.

I am going to make Shakespear jealous when I've finished.
By the way it was snowing and it is supposed to be Spring on
Friday. Paul and Lilian have gone to live in Brockville now as
Paul is working in the mental hospital now.

Lots of love from
Alec

Mavis Fry followed this letter up with her own, explaining some
of the references in the last few letters:

Mar. 31st 1941

Darling Phyllis

The Tooth Problem of your son is now at a stage where I feel I'd like your re-actions before proceeding further! As you know Alec's jaw is unusually small and his palate unusually high and narrow, and the result is that there isn't enough room for his new teeth to come down. Our dentist has gone into it thoroughly and made a plaster model and taken x-rays—and they show that the new teeth not yet erupted (if you get me!) are absolutely locked out by the teeth already in. It's quite a tricky situation. At our dentist's request I then hoicked him up to a specialist in jaw problems who was very nice and talked to me for ages— and the net result of his deliberations is that Alec must have four teeth (good ones, I'm afraid) taken out (see illustration) to allow the teeth not yet through to come down. Then for a year his mouth must be left to see how they spread around, and then perhaps some bands might be indicated. By that time it will probably be your problem!!! However, my dear, I think we'd better get the four extra teeth out as soon as I hear from you, as it may lead to serious trouble if the ones in the gum grow much more and can't get down. I'll have them taken out by the best man and I suppose he'd (Alec) better have gas, don't you think. Four teeth would be rather an ordeal for the little fellow with just a local. It's too bad he has this problem, but really it's his only health complication—otherwise he is so well and rosey, enormous appetite, enormous growth, and looking marvellous. Just send me off an airmail when you get this, as I'd like to get it over with. [illustrations in pencil showing which teeth had to come out and how the new teeth were already imprisoned by those already in]

I suppose you have heard that Lilian is having a baby in September. They are very thrilled, but Lilian isn't feeling very

*grand yet. What with her miscarriage, then a quite severe
operation and now a baby, she is certainly having a strenuous
time. However, I think that when it is all over, the baby will be a
grand idea and make her feel much more at home. We are just
getting ready to really know each other, and now Paul has been
moved to Brockville, a small town 240 miles away—too bad
because doctors and things are rather far away—and I hope he is
able to buck her up a bit during the waiting time. However they
may be back in the autumn. I hope so. Of course things are pretty
difficult for her financially still, and I'm so glad to have been
able to lend her cots and various things. We went shopping for
maternity dresses before she went and found some nice ones—it's
extraordinary how things improve—even in the few years since
I had Jeremy there has been a vast improvement in maternity
dresses and underwear. Marvellous slips with a back-wrap—
and all the dresses wrap in mysterious unobtrusive ways that are
such improvements on mine! Do write to Lilian to spur her on
her way—I hope her family will be able to send her some clothes
for the baby and things—I know it would help—and perhaps
some nighties for herself. I imagine she'll need some new ones.*

*Has Davina picked up her present from Walpole's yet? I'm
longing to hear what she gets. It was a great idea of yours. Oh,
I wish I could be over with them all. I was so sorry to hear
(in Alec's letter) you had a touch of flu'—but really you are
marvellous, my dear, what with your real work and all this
night work for the fire watchers and canteens and things. No
wonder you feel a bit exhausted! When all this is over you'll
have to come over here and have a real rest. Your young man
is very happy and busy but I know he is dieing to see his very
wonderful mother again. Sometimes I envy you being the
wonder woman on the horizon, while I'm the old grouch on the
spot! I wonder if David would have such glowing memories of
me if we were parted????*

You mustn't take Alec's choice of poetry for learning too seriously—he's at the stage where comedy is all important—and I seem to remember his little mama has always had a yen that way too. [the remainder of the letter is in pencil] *... Anyway he has good literary sense and loves poetry. I hope you like the ballad he has produced for you this week. He and David are hot mad about old Scotch ballads at the moment and reel them off by the yard!*

I must get this off so I can get an answer. My love to everyone & take care of yourselves.

Ever yours lovingly,
Mavis

CHAPTER 6
APRIL TO AUGUST 1941: SPRING CELEBRATIONS AND SUMMER HOLIDAYS

There is a gap in correspondence until Easter, when, on 17 April, my letter was accompanied by a long one from Mavis. Finding ways of addressing a parent evidently gave me pause—"Dear Mother (Darling Mummy)" was followed by description of Easter presents. The list includes towels with cross-stitch for Mavis, chocolate eggs for Uncle Harold, and a chocolate boat for me from David. However, he wrote, "I got exactly one egg." The roller skates were the real excitement:

> ...they are super ball-bearing ones. We were so excited about it that I'm afraid I forgot to write so I am writing now. Poor old Jeremy had his tonsils out as well as a front tooth so he is laid down for a week. We are having fun amusing him.

I mention a letter from Aunt Chrissie and an "absolutely hilarious" George Formby movie, as well as shopping at Eaton's for summer and spring clothes. There follows a report on the Spring Festival, probably at Maple Leaf Gardens, the first half of which was "Sacred" and the second half "Patriotic." I noted that the choirs and orchestra "were from nearly 100 schools of Ontario."

Mavis Fry's letter of the same date puts the above letter into context.

Darling Phyllis

Just a note to add to Alec's. I hope you've been getting his letters. He hasn't had one from you for ages—nor have I from the family. So I suppose a lot has gone down. I'm afraid, poor darling, you've had some terrible raids lately—how we think of you all! I do hope you are very sensible & careful & not too brave!! Sit in shelters when things are very bad—& not just go on dancing!

Alec has grown out of all his clothes—he now wears a Canadian size 16 (I wear 14!!) Though, of course, he's not quite as tall as I am yet. We went down on Monday & I got him a very nice new (enormous) navy-blue trench coat—his old one is a joke—sleeves up to his elbow. Neither of the flannel suits he came with will go near him—anyway they're pretty worn out—so I've ordered him one new one, also some shorts for school & a new light-weight green sweater with a V-neck. The boys don't wear suits for school over here, mostly shorts, slacks & sweaters, & it's really rather sensible as they are so hard on clothes. You said something about sending him a suit so I am enclosing his measurements. A rather heavy grey flannel or a grey tweed would be very useful. Don't send a navy blue as the one he had new this winter will be alright again. Boys' suits here are very expensive & not nearly as well cut as England. The one you ordered him is an awfully light flannel—all I could get—and will do for the hot weather, so if you could send one for the autumn & cooler days it would be lovely. The one I've ordered (he's too big for stock sizes with shorts here, at his size they all burst into longs, but he's much too young, don't you think?). Costs about $15, which seems a lot for such a lightweight flannel, so I imagine you could do better at Harrods!

I hope to hear soon about his teeth—I'd feel happier to have it over and know his mouth was alright.

About his birthday present—I don't think the fishing would be good enough for real fishing rods—or the boys patient enough yet! We gave him roller skates for Easter & he loves them—you should see the knees!

Love to you, my pet,

Write often.

Lovingly,
Mavis

PS A few white shirts would be a help, too, if you see any in his size! Don't worry if they're too expensive.

May 11th 1941

Dear Mother

I received your letter this week, dated April 17th alongside with Aunt Chrissie's, dated April 19th. Auntie Mavis says she is going to put me into longs next year as I would be too tall for shorts. [Mavis comments: *I don't recollect that rash statement. It must be the wish is father to the thought!!*] *On Friday we got our reports, which were real surprises. Believe it or not I got 96% in Maths and 95 in English. Sue Norrington, a girl in our class, got 100% in Maths. I got 84 in French and 69 in History, but I cannot tell you all I got as I can't remember all I got. My lowest mark was 64 and 60 was a pass. On Friday night we saw the film* The Great Dictator.[1] *All about the Fooey of Tomania. Charlie Chaplin wrote it and directed it. He acted as the Jewish barber and Heinkel, the Fooey of Tomania. The film started in 1918, where the Jewish barber is manning the Big Berthas. The first shell hit a hut just outside Paris, then the next one made a wheezy sound and dropped out of the end of the barrel and*

---

1 British film from 1940 directed by Charlie Chaplin and starring Chaplin and Paulette Goddard; it was a political satire aimed at Adolf Hitler.

stayed there. They just stood still there, then the leading officer said, "check the fuse" to the man behind him who passed it back to Charlie. Charlie turned around to do the same but there was nobody behind him so he did it himself. Now I come to think of it you saw it in England, didn't you. Anyway, I'll run through it sketchily. He couldn't check it and it exploded. Then they found the British had broken through the lines and every man had to get to the front. Then he got lost in the smoke barrage and came out with British Tommies. Eventually he got in the cockpit of a plane, which crashed. He was put into hospital and it showed different headlines and then it showed him in his barber shop and he fought back against the storm troopers and eventually invaded Austria and gave a speech of democracy, etc.

Yesterday we went to the farm and had super fun. We were helping to clear the orchard of dead wood and got super bumpy rides in the wood cart. Auntie Mavis was telling us about the letter you wrote to her on the Blitz. She told me about when you started to go out in the Blitz without your tin helmet when you remembered what I had told her, and went back for it.

There is no signature to this letter, just an illustration of the front door at 49 Gloucester Place and a figure (presumably my mother) approaching the front steps.

May 18th 1941

Darling Mummy

Did Aunt Davina's wedding to Archie Whitehead go well, or did you go to it? I do hope it did, what with bombs, etc. How did you like my report? I'm not trying top swank of anything, but I was rather proud of it.

This year I am trying to get into UTS, that is, University of

Toronto Schools. UTS is the brightest school in Toronto, and boys have to keep up to the average, as well as pass a very hard exam with only grammar, composition and maths. All the hard subjects, although I am good in grammar and composition. I do hope I get in, because it'll mean a lot in my education.

Yesterday I went to the dentist and found that the doctor who was to take my teeth out had just gone for a two-week holiday, so now I won't have them out till June.

Next Friday we are going to have two periods in the auditorium celebrating Empire Day. We are going to have one period and the other classes the other. We are having broadcasts for different countries of the Empire. These are the countries in their right order: India, Australia, South Africa, Scotland, Ireland, England and Canada, I have to do England and I divided it into four parts: London, Liverpool, Birmingham and Newcastle. There are four war guests in our room, so I gave them each a part. Sue Norrington, Liverpool, Pamela Christie, Birmingham, Noel Enright, Newcastle and me London. I am doing London because I made up the broadcast. This is my part: "Hello Canada, and the British Empire. This is England, Motherland of the free. I am speaking from London. Many interesting things are to be found in England, so I will turn you now to Liverpool. Here ships are coming in Daily." Then I wait until the rest have finished speaking and say:

"This is the BBC in London." "You have just been listening to an interesting program (I hope) from all parts of England. We hope that you have enjoyed it and now say goodbye. Au revoir till another time."

"This is the BBC signing off." "Carry on, Canada."

We are going to sing patriotic songs, too. These are them. First "God Save the King" in three parts. Second "Carry On." Third "Thumbs Up," and last, a song that I do not remember. We

*made the words something like this: "Children of the Empire,"
"Rally Round the Flag" … etc. I hope it comes off well, because
it's the first auditorium period I've ever played a major part in.*

*Just now, the weather is lovely and spring flowers are just out, as
well as the trees, in fact everything is lovely, as well as the farm.
There is a wild duck nesting there, and we are going [to] prohibit
hunting. All the trout are getting bigger and we expect to be
living there this summer.*

*Yesterday we were squirting maple sap at each other. I was
splitting the maple seed when out came some sap, and we had a
regular battle.*

*Lots and lots of love from
Alec*

....

June 8th 1941

Darling Mother

*I had a lovely birthday on Wednesday. My first present was
from Nurse, a book called* Biggles Hits the Trail, *by Capt. W.E.
Johns, the next was from Susan and Jeremy, a dinky toy. It was
a model of the "Mayo Composite," you know, the big mail plane
with a smaller plane on top.[2] Auntie Mavis and Uncle Harold
gave me Arthur Ransome's newest book—*The Big Six. *Then
Grandma, Aunt Edith and Uncle Art gave me the 1941* Modern
Boy's Annual. The Big Six *is super. This is the introduction.*

---

2 *The Short Mayo Composite was a piggy-back, long-range seaplane/flying boat combination
produced by Short Brothers to provide a reliable long-range air transport service to North
America and, potentially to other distant places in the British Empire and the Commonwealth.
Co-designed by Mayo and Shorts chief designer Arthur George, it comprised the Short S.21
Maia, which was a variant of the Short C-Class Empire flying boat fitted with a trestle or pylon
on the top fuselage to support the Short S.20 Mercury. The aircraft was destroyed by enemy
bombing on 11 May 1941, but how were Susan and Jeremy to know that, let alone me!* "Aircraft
model of Short S.21 Mayo Composite," Powerhouse Collection, Museum of Applied Arts and
Sciences, Australia, https://collection.maas.museum/object/241324; https://m.newsreview
.uk/2021/11/dinky-aircraft-forgotten-greats/

"But who are the Big Six," said Pete.

"It's the Big Five, really," said Dot, "they are the greatest Detectives in the world. They solve one mystery after another."

"Why 'Six'?"

"There are six of us," said Dot.

Dot and Dick, who had taken to photography, had come to stay with the "Death and Glories" and found that they were being blamed for crimes they were perfectly innocent of. Tom, Joe, Dick and Pete were in a dreadful fix when Dot came with Dick to stop thinking that the "Coots" (Tom & co.) had been stealing shackles and casting off boats. They formed a Detective club and use[d] the Coots's shed for Scotland Yard. After many clues they got evidence with a photograph that George Owdon and his chums, who didn't like the Coots Club, had been the culprits and had blamed the Coots all along.

I haven't finished Biggles yet but I'll tell you about it in my next letter.

I like Gaffer Gilling's[3] poem:

A wonderful bird is the pelican
His beak holds more than his belican.

I don't mind about the birthday present being late at all, so don't worry about that. I will put the number of my passport at the end of the letter, as Auntie Mavis has it at present and she isn't up yet. Do you remember me waking you up to get to work on time when you were at Peter Jones [in Sloanes Square, London]. *By the way, has Peter Jones been a target for the raiders yet? They have a hard time blacking it out, don't they. I am glad the canteen is fit for service again. I called my poem*

---

3   *The first reference in the letters to Captain (later Lieutenant Colonel) Walter J. Gilling, a chaplain in the Canadian Army and, the future Dean of Toronto. Known as "Gaffer" to his friends and family, he became my stepfather in 1943.*

"Coronach" because once I saw a Scotch poem by Sir Walter Scott with the same name. Yesterday we went to the farm with a guest. We had quite a time and once we were going along the other side of the farm we saw a snake. Our guest (Allison Little) wanted it for school so we hunted it out of its lair and killed it. Then we took it home in the back of the car. Auntie Mavis didn't know about it and we were hiding it from her all the way until she got home, because she didn't like dead animals.

Well—goodbye.

Lots of love from
Alec

P.S. My passport number is: C9752

I got another fountain pen for my birthday too.

P.S. I think your boy had a happy day, bless him—mostly books, it seems. At his age that's what I liked best! He's very well & big—growing rapidly still. Shoes men's 8!! I'll write soon, but Nurse is on holiday & I'm busy from dawn to dusk!

Lovingly,
Mavis

....

June 29th 1941

Dear Mother

School broke up last Wednesday and since then we have done a lot. In the afternoon we were helping in school to tidy up and helping Mr. Perry to garden. Then on Thursday morning David went to school as Mr. Grass wanted to help him and I went roller skating. On Thursday afternoon we went to Dr. Brown to be examined. I weigh 94 lbs and David 76 lbs. David is 51" high and I am 61". In other words David is 4'8" high and weighs 5 st 6 lbs and I am 5'1" and weigh 6 st 10 lbs. After that we went to Dr.

*Brown's office. He asked us if we shaved yet and felt us. He told
David his posture was abominable and said pointing to me, "now
look here this is the way you should stand." David was then given
a lot of exercises for round shoulders. Then we went to the library
to get some books. I got* Three Men in a Boat, The Call of the
Mountain *and* Oxus in Summer. Three Men in a Boat *is about
… well … I guess you know what that's about. I haven't read the*
Call of the Mountain *but* Oxus in Summer *is quite good.[4] It is
by two girls who are following Arthur Ransome's footsteps. After
that we went and had an ice cream soda then went home. On
Friday morning Nurse came back and in the morning Aunt
Edith took us up to Maple to see Grandma and the Routleys off
to Muskoka. Yesterday we got the new plans of the house …* [a
rough drawing of the house] *… I am not sure about the placing
of the windows and doors and the veranda may be screened in.
The roof slopes slightly and juts out about three feet which will
protect us from the sun and rain. We went to the barber shop
on Friday and on the way David bought a new addition to our
army—a despatch rider. I forgot about telling you that Nurse
brought us an oil truck and transport.*

Well, lots of love from
Alec

....

July 12th 1941

Darling Mother

*It has just started on a raining spell here after weeks of dry
weather without one drop of rain. It is rather a nuisance now, first
because we are going to Muskoka tomorrow, and, second, because*

---

4 *Three Men in a Boat* (Jerome K. Jerome, 1899); *The Call of the Mountain* (Cornelia Meigs,
1940). *Oxus in Summer*, written by Katherine Hull (1921–77) and Pamela Whitlock (1920–82),
follows the adventures of a family of children in Exmoor, with much horseback riding and
a vivid landscape soaked in imagination; Arthur Ransome wrote the introduction to the
series. https://en.wikipedia.org/wiki/The_Far-Distant_Oxus; "Whitlock, Pamela," in *Oxford
Encyclopedia of Children's Literature,* Jack Zipes (ed.), online edition (Oxford: Oxford
University Press, 2006).

all the farmers are just getting in their wheat they planted last September. It is doing some good though. All the farmers who own pasture land need rain to keep their grass green, and it will help stop the forest fires that are doing such damage.

Yesterday we went to the farm where our architect's assistant, Mr. Fowler, and the contractor, were staking out the places where the house was going to be. It looks tiny at the moment but it won't look so bad when it is actually built.... [Another attempt at drawing a picture, and the comment *"Please don't study that picture because I am a rotten artist."*]

By some miracle I was able to swim in the stream yesterday quite well. It is rather cold, but what do I care. Jeremy loves the water so I think he will be a good swimmer. Ronald Smith was discharged from the air force because of his eyes. He stayed with us a week and went to the farm with us last Saturday. He was very useful there as he cut down a huge branch from a dead willow that we had been fretting about for ages. That reminds me that yesterday we pulled a lot of dead wood off a tree with a rope. We had super fun doing it. We pulled and David pushed, then when it fell we had to run. Last Friday we went to Riverdale[5] and Jeremy was staring open-mouthed at everything. Ronald took us to see The Great Dictator *again and I'm sure I liked it as much as when I first saw it. Do tell me how* [Aunt] *Lucille is getting on now. By the way if she has any stamps she can spare, I would love some.*

*Lots of love from
Alec*

P.S. Auntie Mavis received an album full of snapshots of Auntie Davina's wedding this week.

---

5 Riverdale Park, which spans the Don River in Toronto, bounded by Cabbagetown on the west and Broadview Avenue on the east.

July 21st 1941

Darling Mother

This week we went to Muskoka and had a lovely time. I hope you got my postcard. It wasn't very good but all the other ones were pictures of about 50 miles away. It was a super cottage ... [two drawings showing the view from the lake and from the back of the cottage. David and I had the front attic bedroom evidently, and Aunt Edith the back attic bedroom.]

It was a lovely week, and we were doing something different every day. On Sunday we were swimming with an American boy from Washington whose name was Robby Gindsmore [it may have been Dinsmore, which seems to be a more common name], and saw Uncle Art off going back to Toronto. On Monday we were fishing for quite a time and swimming too. Nellie [presumably a friend of the Frys'] caught two fish, a 13½" bass and an 11" pickerel. On Tuesday it was unbearably hot. We tried trolling but had no luck—except bad luck. We were trolling merrily along when I felt a hard bite so I pulled. We had quite a hard job for a while then the pulling stopped. I pulled the line in to find the hook and bait gone with some blood on the line (what was left from it). On Wednesday we went on a fishing trip and fished quite a while. David caught six undersized sunfish in succession, I caught one small bass, Nellie caught two sunfish and Aunt Edith one bass too. We went back for our picnic as it was so rough and ran out of gasoline halfway there so had to row half way. After lunch we went fishing again and Nellie brought up a stick. On Thursday it was rough as ever and we hung around and went rowing once. On Friday we played with Robby. On Saturday it was raining all day. Sunday was a lovely day and in the morning we went for a long walk while the others were at church. We went home on Sunday night arriving at 11:15 p.m. in Toronto.

Well, lots of love from
Alec

Chapter 6

Darling Mother

*I received your letter with all the photographs in it this week.
I think they are super. [Because photographs would not be
allowed on board ship in July of 1943, when I went home, these
photographs remained in Canada. By war's end, I had forgotten
them!] I put the one of Capt. Gilling and of you (Capt. Gilling
had his uniform on) on the dressing table. Auntie Mavis says
she had tweeds exactly the same as yours once. I think you had
better be slimming pretty soon. [The cheek of a twelve-year-old.]
I feel quite jealous of Auntie Lulu [Louise Wheatley] living in
Cornwall. The house is super now—it looks like this* [some very
rough sketches: "from road, from fence, from orchard, from
old cabin"]. *They have just got to put in the insulation, put on
the roof and glass in the windows and they'll have finished the
exterior part of it, then they'll get workmen to do the interior.
The farm is getting on really well and so is the vegetable garden.
Yesterday we brought home more than a basketful of beets. We
are growing corn too (on the cob!). It is getting on well. The cob
is gradually forming; so we're hoping to have a corn roast this
year. The Clarks, who live next door, moved to their cottage
last Thursday. They have a cottage in Muskoka and go for their
meals in a hotel. I wouldn't like to be them much, since they
have to go for their meals to a hotel. I'd rather have home-cooked
meals. I guess they are giving their cook a rest. Talking about the
Clarks, they rescued a cat the other day and brought it home.
They fed it while they were here and now Mr. Clark feeds it with
a pint of milk every day. Jeremy can't be pulled away from it so
we have to feed it once in a while. Once, the dog next door had a
fight with it and it scratched him (the cat scratched the dog) and
the dog ran away. Auntie Mavis is going to phone the Humane
Society about* [the incident]. *Its name is Lily.*

I hope things are getting on alright at Walpole's. I never see anything about it or here either.

Well, love to everybody;

Your loving son
Alec

P.S. I hope you like the photo. [not identified]

We spent a great deal of time at the Farm, where besides a successful vegetable garden, we had plenty of work to do clearing deadwood while the cottage was under construction. There was a large apple orchard behind the cottage, where we gorged on freshly picked apples (on at least one occasion with disastrous results) and came to appreciate bird watching.

Later that summer, we learned that the Canadian Broadcasting Corporation and the BBC were planning a broadcast on 24 August between war guests in Canada and their parents in England. We were to be allowed a minute and a half each.

Aug. 3rd 1941

Dear Mother (or Darling!!!!)

Isn't it thrilling for August 24th. Aunt Mavis says I should be more excited but can't be, much more than I am right now. I think it was very [nice?] *of Mr. Connor to arrange it. I can't think of anything to say unless I know what you're going to say but I suppose it will be something like this.*

Alec. *Hello Mother, I've been longing for today for ages.*

You. *I don't wonder—it's the same with me. Tell me, how is the house at the farm getting on?*

Alec. *It's nearly finished, we've just got to varnish the floor and we're finished. (I'm not sure about that.)*

You. *Oh I am glad, do send me a picture of it!*

Alec. *Oh sure.*

You. *I wish I could see the farm.*

Alec. *I know, it's super. The vegetable garden is getting on well, and the apples are almost ready. The corn is ever so high and we [can] almost eat the cobs. The shrubs are getting on well and the petunias are lovely.*

You. *I guess I'll have to go to Canada.*

Alec. *You bet, but I'm beginning to miss England.*

And soon the Announcer says "The minute and a half is up."

This letter went on to talk about the farm.

Yesterday we went to the farm and had a super time. The glass was in the windows and all the roof was finished. Most of the floor was finished. I think it's going to be very cozy. The stream was lovely and cooling and we were in it nearly all afternoon. There was an old log in the stream that we lay on. It would float if we lay on it but if we sat on it, it sank. We did a lot of work yesterday like cleaning trees of dead wood. There was a lot there. We were burning caterpillars off trees too. We got a lot of fun out of it.

How is everything at home? All my love to them.

Love from Alec

Aunt Mavis wrote the same day:

Darling Phyllis

I don't know how this happened, but I find I've neglected to post two of Alec's letters—do forgive me, but my excuse must be—

- *Maid on holidays— & endless cooking for large family.*
- *Trying to make curtains and paint furniture for farm in order to get family in for a few weeks before school.*
- *Red Cross work.*
- *a particularly vicious heatwave*
- *a bad cold!*

So you must forgive me if I forget something occasionally! I wish I could get away from it all for a week or so, but no hope—too many taxes!

Much love—longing to hear your voice on [the] 24th—wish I could talk to my family too!

Thine etc,
Mavis

CHAPTER 7
SEPTEMBER TO DECEMBER 1941: SCHOOL, THANKSGIVING, REMEMBRANCE DAY, CHRISTMAS

School had begun the first week in September. We had been to the Canadian National Exhibition again before that, but "All we could see really was the crowds..." Aunt Mavis took us to lunch at the women's building. We had a window table and saw the Labour Day parade, "things like Down with Fascism, release C.S. Jackson[1] and other anti-fascists[,] Up With Unionism..."—all very obscure to a hungry boy. As usual, Mother was given a detailed description of what we ate—apple sauce, creamed chicken and ice cream with chocolate sauce, "dee-licious!" Once more I complained about the penmanship we were forced to do—"Auntie Mavis doesn't like that writing either..."—and told Mother of the science, maths and social studies we were taking. Later in the month, just before Aunt Mavis wrote her long letter of 25 September, we celebrated the completion of the new house at the farm.

Sept. 23th 1941

Darling Mother

I am sorry about being late writing my letter, but I wasn't able to on Sunday, being at the farm. That reminds me, the farm is

---

1 C.S. Jackson, international vice-president of the United Electrical, Radio and Machine Workers of America, and a thorn in the side of management, had been interned on 23 June 1941 under the Defence of Canada Regulations (just as Germany invaded the U.S.S.R.!) because of his supposed links with the Communist Party, and was released in December 1941 after his case had been reviewed. Doug Smith, "Remembering C.S. Jackson," *This Magazine*, 27 no. 5 (December 1993), 18–20.

finished! Next time I'm out there I'll have to take a picture of it.
[A rough plan of the house, showing living room, kitchen with cellarette, four bedrooms for Susan, Jeremy, David and me, and Uncle Harold and Aunt Mavis, a bathroom with shower.] ...

We had a lovely house-warming party. David made a cocktail of Coca-Cola and we drank to the well-being of the farm. Then we presented the presents to Aunt Mavis and Uncle Harold. David gave Aunt Mavis a syrup jar, and I gave her an oven glass that she could put things in or keep in the oven without cracking. Susan gave her a lovely handkerchief with "M" woven on. Then Jeremy gave her some soap, three cakes. Then Nurse gave two towels to Auntie Mavis and a box of candies to Uncle Harold. This week we are voting for the president of the students' council of the junior high school. David and I are for Arnold Irwin. David [made] some posters like this [one with musical note and one with naval flags spelling AHOY VOTE FOR AN ABLE PRESIDENT]. *David is super at those kind of things. Next Friday we are supposed to have a wiener roast, but I don't know whether we can go or not as the thing is at 4:00 p.m. and we might be going to the farm then. It'll be a shame if we can't go, but I'd rather go to the farm. There is going to be a paper chase, and games too. We will get (if we go) two or three hot dogs apiece, and a bottle of chocolate milk or ginger ale or something.*

We've got nearly all the curtains up at the farm, each room has its own colour. The kitchen red and white, Susan's room pink, the spare room purple, Auntie Mavis and Uncle Harold's room yellow and green, Jeremy and Nurse's are red and blue. The living room's colour is red and white but its curtains are sackcloth, and the kitchen's are blue and white. I hope this weekend is as good as last.

All my love to everybody.

Love from
Alec

[Two figures are drawn at the end of this letter, Goebbels from the rear, and Hitler from the side, with the note "THESE ARE MEANT TO BE CHARACATURES."]

Mavis wrote a long letter on 25 September that reveals most affectingly the generosity and love that had gone into the invitation that brought Alec over to Canada.

Sept. 25th 1941

Darling Phyllis

I'm sure I'm the worst "foster mother" in Canada—I keep meaning to write you long interesting letters all about your boy, & weeks and weeks pass in rapid succession & it never gets done. To be honest I've had a hectic summer—building the cottage on the farm (constant supervision necessary!) besides making all the curtains, painting furniture, having Nurse and Cook away on holidays—& the usual housekeeping, etc. Phewew!

Alec has had a good summer—lots of fresh country air & two weeks at Muskoka, & is looking very rosey & well. They are both back at school again—in junior high school now (very proud) & to home in a little less haste! Our cottage is finished & we are starting to take our weekends in the country which is heavenly! In the winter we'll be able to go out for skiing—so I'll get Alec skis for Xmas!

Wasn't the broadcast thrilling? We were so proud of you both— as the Connors cabled "much the best!" I practiced pretend broadcasts with Alec beforehand, and fortunately for him the conversation went pretty much as expected. He was so calm about it all but—inwardly thrilled! And <u>what</u> a lunch he put away when it was all over!

*You dear thing to send the suits—also the $9 (nine dollars),
which arrived last week from Mrs. Ritchie (who is she?).[2] The
tweed suit is exactly like David's best tweed so they're both
delighted—& the flannel I'm putting away for the Spring, as it
seems a shame to start it at the end of the season. I thought I'd
spend the $9 on knee breeches for the tweed (for cold weather) &
new school breeches. He has [a] good navy overcoat for best, &
the new leather jacket Harold gave him last year for school, & I
think they have plenty of shirts between them plus Alec's three
new ones you sent. He has nearly grown out of his pyjamas, and
will need new school socks & best socks, & shoes & overshoes—so
you can guess how glad I am his new suits arrived! Did you
get them before rationing? Even now you can't get suits of that
caliber over here for twice the money—the tweed suit over here
would be about $27!!*

*I often wish you were here to talk things over about Alec. He &
David both have their little peculiarities—& Alec's besetting sin
is still slowness & dreaminess. I think he is waking up a lot—
but one has to remind & remind him about every little thing!
Also he isn't very fond of work!! School's not too bad—but nose
in a book is the rule when there is anything about the house
or farm to do. However, I think work is good for boys, don't
you? I mean little helpful jobs—especially in a big family—so I
keep him up to it! I think he sometimes thinks I'm a nuisance,
but he never says so! Bless him! I have a little trouble over the
bycycle business—they both want one, but in the town I feel
it is unnecessary, & at the moment could not afford one for
both, anyway. But there have been so many accidents with
children on bycycles, that I have forbidden them to ride on
other peoples except on this road. However I know Alec rides to
school whenever he gets the chance & I follow them all the time*

---

2 *Mavis is asking about Eva Prager, a dear friend of Mother's who, with her husband, Ritchie, had
escaped from Nazi persecution in 1937. She joined the staff at Walpole's as the window dresser
when Mother became the fashion buyer there in 1938. I eventually did meet Eva when I returned
to England in 1943.*

to check up. I feel he's likely to go into a dream & forget what he's doing, but I can't do more than ask him to co-operate. Next summer when we're in the country I'll try and get them both bikes of some description, but I don't *like it in town! I don't know how you feel about it, but I thought I'd let you know.*[3]

Otherwise I think everything is splendid—we're a very happy family & have lots of fun & games & jollifications!!! I hope your child will be all you hope when he returns to you—all I can do is treat him as my own—& I assure you I do that. In fact I feel he is—almost! We talk about you & England & future plans a lot—& he never feels I'm taking your place, darling, I'm just the "man in the job" so to speak.

Love to all.

Ever thine
Mavis

Oct. 5th 1941

Dear Mummy

This week has been "just ordinary" except for the elections of "Junior Student's Council" for president. These were the people running, Bosworth Corbett, Geoffrey Johnston, Pat Yeomans, Pat Long, Dianne Abbott, M. Jane Gilmore, a boy called Irwin (I don't know his Christian name), and a boy called McConnell, and two more girls, Ann Neill and Anne Haley. [The "Irwin" here is the Arnold Irwin mentioned in the previous letter as my, as well as David's, candidate; there evidently had been new developments since 23 September.] *I nominated Geoffrey Johnston and wrote out the whole thing on a typewriter.*

---

3   *After returning to England in 1943, Mother bought me a second-hand bike for a song and let me ride it in London. I had no brakes and I knew very little about rules of the road but managed to survive with the help of some severe talkings-to by the odd policeman.*

Sept. 25th 1941

Group #20, hereby announces the nomination of Geoffrey Johnston for the presidency of the "Junior Students' Council" of Forest Hill Village School.

Moved by Alec Douglas.
Seconded by George Caldough.
Signed L.A. Rickard, Group Councillor.

David didn't agree with me as he is in another group and is all for his president who is Irwin. We had the election speeches last Wednesday. Irwin was first, and Geoff last. Poor old Geoff couldn't say much because everybody else had brought in what he was going to say. The elections were last Friday and Pat Yeomans won. He is an American with a terrible Southern accent. All the girls except three in one group voted for him.

We went to the farm on Saturday and did a good lot of work, but we were back very late. The week before last we had our Wiener Roast and had a super time there. [Exactly where this took place is not explained.] *First we explored the woods around then we had games. In rugby our side lost 16–0, but I don't know about soccer. After that we had our meal. We had wieners first, then we had something to drink. Then apples. After that we had a paper chase, and the one who caught a hare first got a bottle of Orange. Then we had stories and jokes, and the best got prizes. We got home about 9 o'clock.*

I didn't tell you much about the farm, so I'll tell you more. First we found a cat that had been there last weekend. It was a cute little thing, and I think it lives there. We were picking apples on a tree that was hollow, and went into a hole that went to the bottom of the tree. Luckily I was there to catch it. It is about six months old. We picked two baskets of apples, two baskets of tomatoes, and one potato. Send my love to everybody, and

141

tell me how Uncle David[4] is. Is he going overseas yet or has he finished training. I hope Elizabeth Anne is alright, she is my first cousin you know.

Lots of love from
Alec

[The rest of the page is taken up with a drawing of the student elections entitled

"ELECTION DAY WIMSY

VOTE JOHNSTON; YEOMANS, SHE'S A LEADER AND WE NEED HER; CORBETT IS OUR BET; VOTE IRWIN; VOTE "BUNNY" ABBOTT; WE WANT HALEY, SHE IS MEANT FOR PRESIDENT; GILMORE; McCANNEL FOR PRES...."]

Oct. 19th 1941

Darling Mummy

We have been having a lovely weekend at the farm, having a bit of Friday, Saturday, Sunday, and, because it is Thanksgiving, Monday. We arrived late on Friday. Directly we got there, we unloaded the car, and filled the coal oil lamps. Then we had supper after an hour, then to end the night listened to the radio and read a book, then we went to bed. Saturday morning was lovely, and I got up feeling ever so well. After a lovely breakfast I went out to saw some wood. I made some vain attempts to saw it but the wood kept slipping so gave it up and looked for some easier wood, but it was all wet. David finally came and we cut one piece, but then the wood was too short, so we played a bit in the wood pile. Then we found the cat and we played with it. Then we drove Mr. Barrie's pigs away. We did not do too much in the afternoon until we started helping Nurse cleaning up

---

4   David or Vivian (my mother preferred the latter name) Fernie was my mother's elder brother, who served as a sergeant in the Royal Marines. He was also a talented jazz drummer!

the rubbish round the house. Sunday was another lovely day, and as it was Thanksgiving Sunday, we took some old clothes to Mrs. Barrie for her children. The Barries are a very poor family (farmer's family), and we often give our old clothes to them for charity. David wasn't feeling very well in the morning, and he went to bed. We forgot it was Sunday, so we worked hard all day, clearing up the rubbish pile near the house. We carted the kindling to one place, medium-sized wood that could be used next to it, and the big wood next to that. [illustration] *We had a super turkey for lunch, and lovely apple pie! Dee-lich-us!!!*

Monday was about the same as the other days. Lovely and warm until late in the afternoon, when it started getting cold, then it rained. Uncle Art came for lunch, and left soon after. We finished clearing up the rubbish, then cleaned up the vegetable garden. David and I drove the pigs home, and Aunt Gert and Uncle Fred [Routley] came to supper. We left late Monday night and arrived home about 9 o'clock. School has been quite nice, as opportunity has started. I am taking Glee Club, and I think it is super.

Lots of love from
Alec

Oct. 28th 1941

Darling Mummy

I'm sorry I haven't written before, but I've been having such an exciting time I forgot. Last Saturday morning we went to the dentist, then we went shopping. I had one baby cavity at the dentist which was filled in no time. David, I'm afraid to say, had six cavities. He has to have camphorated chalk, and some stuff called "Enzodent" [tooth powder]. After the dentist we went to Eaton's. There, we bought socks, stockings and gloves. David got a new pair of shoes! I did not need any as I have got

Uncle Harold's old ones. They are size 8 and he says they are the most expensive he ever bought, so I'm going to take real good care of them. Then we went to Simpson's and I got some new rubber boots. They are size 9, and I've got a big pair of ski socks to wear with them. After that Auntie Mavis picked up Uncle Harold from the office and we drove home. By the way, I wore the tweed suit for the first time on Saturday. In the afternoon we went to the circus!! It was marvelous. First there was a parade. First in the parade was a queen on a camel, led by an attendant. Then came all, or most of the performers. There were clowns, and elephants, and lots of other things. Then we were all requested to sing "Carry On," but David was about the only singer. Then some clowns made a performance. There was a pile of tables like this [illustration]. A man got on the top of them then was passed another table which he pile[d] on top of the rest, then on the top he put a chair, then on the top he was swayed back and forth, and finally the whole thing fell. There were lions and tigers, a bang car, performing seals (the same ones as in the Olympic Circus). There were elephants and acrobatics, and at the very end a daredevil got to the top of the building—came down a ramp on a bycicle and jumped about 60 ft. into a pool of water 3 ft. deep… [picture] There was a firecracker at the end of the ramp. On Sunday we went to the farm with Noel and Bobby.[5] We had a lovely time there. On Monday, school was the same as usual.

Well, Lots of Love from
Alec

....

---

5   *Noel Enright was a war guest staying on Ava Crescent. I do not recall Bobby.*

Nov. 9th 1941

Darling Mummy,

In your letter you said that you hadn't received any letters for ages. I'm so sorry, but I've been writing regularly, except for two weeks, and once I was writing to Aunt Chrissie. I hope she likes her new house. In her last letter she said your birthday was Sept. 17th. I wasn't quite sure, so I didn't send you a present, or a cable, but don't worry about not getting a Christmas present. Since I wrote last, I've been having a lovely time. I think I told you about the circus and that weekend so I will tell you about last weekend. We were at the farm and had a lovely time, of course. We went out on Friday evening, and arrived at about 6 p.m. We had supper at about 6:30 p.m., then went to bed at 8:30 p.m. On Saturday morning we got up at about eight, to find it a miserable morning, drizzling rain half the time. All morning we were indoors, and absolutely in everybody's way. In the afternoon it was a bit better, and I went to saw wood. I wasted half the time, looking for a sawhorse, and by the time I had finished the others had gone to help Miss James decorate her house for the Halloween party—I had forgotten to tell you that Friday was Halloween—so I walked over, and arrived just in time for a bit of a party for the children that she had started. I was given a puzzle and my name ALEC to put on my coat. A farmer's boy made it with macaroni treated with shellac. We had a girl to supper, but David and I weren't very good hosts to her I'm afraid, Susan was much better, and showed her round the house. We could not go to the party as it was too late for us.

On Sunday it was much nicer, and we all felt better. We did not do too much in the morning except bring in a bit of wood for the fire. In the afternoon we had a long—at least, about a mile— walk. I'm not a very good walker anyhow—you ought to know that. Miss James and the girl who had come to supper the day before (her name was Kathleen Cherry) and Mrs. Cherry came with us, [and] we brought home some apples with us. We came home on Sunday night.

Yesterday we were in the city, and I think we are going to be here this afternoon too. I wear the tweed suit you sent me every Sunday in the city now.

Lots of love from Alec

P.S. Please don't send me too much for Christmas.

[The last half of the page is taken up with a large V for VICTORY and a picture of Hitler split up into a head, arms, legs and chest unattached to a body]

The next letter is adorned with a sprig of holly and in large capital letters: CHRISTMAS GREETINGS, and is in pencil. I wrote, "The reason I am writing in pencil is because I broke the nib off my last one and lost another I had. I'm terrible with pens, I think I'll have to tie the next one round my neck."

Nov. 24th 1941

Darling Mother

This letter is supposed to be for Christmas, although I don't know if you will get it in time, but if you are lucky you will … Since my last letter—if you got it—I have been doing a lot. On the afternoon of the 9th of November I was singing in the Remembrance service, and on Armistice Day we had a holiday in which we went to the farm. It was snowing softly all day, almost raining in fact. However we got some work done. Nurse was working hardest of all of us, like she always is. On Wednesday we had our auditorium period. Mr. Trott's troubadours played "You and I" and another piece. Mr. Myers, one of the trumpeters, got out of tune in the middle of it, and it sounded awfully funny. Mr. Trott is one of those conductors who throw their hair about, and his is that long, loose hair that flops about so easily. We had some other numbers too, like a solo on the trumpet and one on the piano. On Thursday we had Glee Club. On Saturday was the Santa Claus Parade.[6] We have one every year. It is a wonderful thing. Starting with Mother Goose and ending with Santa Claus, including five bands. There were lots of things like Cinderella and Gulliver's Travels. *After that David went to the dentist and shopping for the ditty bag.[7] I went with him. After supper we packed it. On Sunday morning I wrote two letters, one to Aunt Concey,[8] and one to Mumsmum.[9] In the afternoon we went to the art gallery with Bobby Reidelmeier,[10] and afterwards went to supper with him. We have been doing a lot this week …*

On Saturday afternoon we went to the farm, and woke up on Sunday to find snow for miles around. David wished to high heaven that he had brought his skis. In the morning we had a snowball fight, but it soon melted away. We got home at about 7:30 p.m. This morning we celebrated Aunt Mavis's birthday and tonight Uncle Harold is taking her out.

Well—lots of love from
Alec

---

6 *I had sent the newspaper clippings in my previous letter but possibly decided to describe the parade here in case the previous letter did not get through.*

7 See note on page 94, note 7.

8 *My father's older sister.*

9 *My term for my maternal grandmother, my mother's mother, thus 'mum's mum,' which I shortened.*

10 *Bobby Reidelmeier was a friend of the Fry family. He was in Toronto to train for the RCAF, but he was rejected for health reasons.*

Dec. 6th 1941

Darling Mummy

This week has been very exciting. On Tuesday the choir had to sing at commencement night. We had to be there at 7:30 p.m., and I was there on time. We had a practice in Mr. Gochiers [Gauthier?] *room, then at 8:30 we went up to the auditorium. First we sang "Now the Day Is Over," then we sang a song called "Wooden Shoes"* [this is followed by the words of the song with instructions for the singers]. *Then we sang another song called "The Humming Bird," then hummed "Now the Day is Over."*

Yesterday we went to the [school] *"Social." It lasted from 7:30 till 10:30, but we only stayed on till 10 o'clock. First we played in the games room, then we danced till 9:30, then we had refreshments, after which we went home. In the War Savings drive at school we have a large V like this:* [illustration follows of a large "V" with dollar amounts starting at 0 at the bottom of the "V," rising up to $1000 at the top of each arm of the "V" over the caption "TOTAL NOW $2056"] *which we fill in every week with red paint. Our group contributed $480 towards it. I think we are going to get a theatre party for contributing the most.*

Well, Lots of love from
Alec

Dec. 21st 1941

Darling Mummy

I wrote to Aunt Chrissie last week, so this week I'll write to you. I don't know whether I'll have room on this pad to write all of what I've done in such a little time. I told you about commencement night and the social evening. Well, the very next Friday I was invited to a party with Debby Smith. Debby is an

*American from the state of Maryland. She is a very nice girl
in our class. She is a very good hostess too. We arrived a little
after time and were just in time for the first game. The game was
to sit down in a circle on the floor. I was given a doll and a girl
was given another* [object]. *We had* [to] *pass the two round and
round, and see how long it took for the other object to catch the
doll. Then we put three pillows on the floor, and told a boy he
had to walk over the books blindfolded. He practiced as much
as he liked and when he was blindfolded we took the pillows
away. Then we put five books on the ground:* [there follows a
somewhat confusing explanation of a game that evidently did
not have great appeal to me]. *Then we danced! We danced until
it was time for refreshments, then we danced again. (Such are
American parties, dance, dance and dance all the time.) I'm not
saying I don't like them, I do, but you get quite sore feet with all
the dancing. We left before the rest, but it was half an hour after
we were supposed to leave.*

*The next Thursday we had our theatre party. It was a very
funny film called* Lady Be Good.[11] *On Friday morning we had
carol singing for the first hour. The Glee Club sang two of the
numbers. We left at half past two in the afternoon as it was
the last day of school On Friday night we saw the Nativity play
at the Holy Trinity church. It is the same one that was at St
Martin-in-the-Fields before the war. On Saturday morning I
went down to the post office to post some parcels, and walked
back with John Holland. When we got back we played Ping-
Pong together. We went to the farm yesterday, and brought
home a load of Christmas decorations.*

*Well—lots of love from
Alec*

V ... – For Victory

---

11 American musical film from 1941, directed by Norman Z. McLeod and starting Eleanor
Powell, Ann Sothern, and Robert Young.

149

Chapter 7

Never in my letters home were the events of the war mentioned. Thus Pearl Harbor passed unremarked, as did the German invasion of the U.S.S.R. in June of 1941. It simply did not seem necessary to say anything about these distant happenings, and Mother certainly did not want to hear about them from me. Of course, many of our letters did not get through. There was only one letter in January of 1942, no letters from 8 February to 11 April, and none in May, which suggests that even if my letter writing was not as frequent as it should have been ("I'm getting terrible nowadays, only writing on alternate weeks ..."), some of our mail must have been lost at sea during that terrible year in the Battle of the Atlantic.

CHAPTER 8
JANUARY TO SEPTEMBER 1942: THE FARM, SUMMER CAMP, AND NEW EXPERIENCES

Evidently many of our letters in the winter of 1941 never reached their destination, The only ones that seems to have survived up until April of 1942 were one in January describing the holiday season, and one in February to my grandmother.

Jan. 11th 1942

Darling Mummy

Thank you ever so much for the super frog planes.[1] They are perfect models. We had a marvelous Christmas. Everybody liked it and Jeremy wanted to know when Christmas would come again. [marginal note: 8:30 a.m.] *We got up about 8.30 a.m. and took our stockings into Auntie Mavis and Uncle Harold's room, singing "Merry Christmas to You" in the tune of "Happy Birthday." Then we opened our stockings. I got a pen and collar-pin, and an orange, three books, soldiers for our army, and nearly everything that I could want like thumbtacks (drawing pins) and a film for my camera. David got similar things and Jeremy got a cute little hobby horse. Susan got a boot-full of candies. When we got dressed and*

---

1 "Frog" (possibly for "Flies right off the ground") was a line of flyable model aircraft, powered by a rubber band attached to the propeller, produced by International Model Aircraft Limited of the United Kingdom. https://www.oldmodelkits.com/index.php?manu=Frog; https://www.frogmodelaircraft.co.uk/

Fig. 4: Alec Douglas, David Fry, Susan Fry, and Jeremy Fry at "Moocowsgarden" (also known as "the farm"), 1942.

*had breakfast, after which we listened to the king. Then we
waited for Grandma and Aunt Edith and Uncle Art to come.*
[marginal note: 10:30 a.m.] *Then we had a lovely time opening
presents. Yours was one of the first to be opened. I got presents
from everyone I knew.* [marginal note: 10:30–1:30] *Please thank
Captain Gilling for sending the presents to me. I got a shooting
game, bedside lamp, a conjuring trick (hocus pocus tiddley
ocus stuff) and a printing set, skates* [three exclamation marks

with commas instead of full stops] *(the exclamation mark with a comma is my own invention), a shooting game, a suitcase, a pencil from Susan and lots of other things. (Remember [in England] how we went down to breakfast to open the presents) we don't do that here, we open our stockings, have breakfast, and then open our presents. Our Christmas dinner was lovely. A huge 18 lb. turkey, cranberry jelly, stuffing, sausage meat, but if I go on like that you will get too hungry. Plum pudding, mince pies and raisons finished it off. (We had hard sauce with the plum pudding, but the holly did not burn very well.)* [marginal note: 2:30–6:30] *After that we played with our toys (or read our books) and went to bed early. I got all the presents that were sent from England for me,* Alice *and* Thomas *and* Jane *(a book from Auntie Florence),* So Few *[a book] from Aunt Chrissie, and you can tell her that Auntie Mavis did get her sewing bag and tea cosy. Aunt Davina and Uncle Archie did not send one, as the (postage) restrictions started before they sent it.*

The holidays as a whole were very nice, although there was very little skating and skiing, but after Christmas it was better. We saw the nativity play, but I told you about that ....

We went to the farm ... and got the plumbing going. We went again after Christmas to get ready for New Year's but we did not get out until after we had planned. The week end after Christmas we had a very good turkey dinner, with Miss James. That night we did not get home till 11 o'clock. We only got about an hour's skiing in the whole holidays, and that was the last day, when we had to get home early because it was Nurse's day out. ...

With the Christmas gifts, the armies David and I were building up for our military campaigns at 3 Ava Crescent assumed ever more impressive proportions: "In the artillery: one heavy coastal gun, one dragon [*motor truck*] pulling an 18-pounder field gun, three eighteen pounders and a searchlight truck pulling an anti-aircraft gun. There are eleven machine gunners. We have fourteen foot troops. Four soldiers, two bombardiers, two sailors, two airmen, an Indian and an Italian, and two [S]cots. We have seven transport trucks, four oil trucks, two scout cars, one pom-pom gun, one ambulance, one motor-cyclist, three fire trucks, four staff cars and six mascots."

Feb. 8th 1942

Darling Mums-mum

Mummy told me all about the present you got me for Christmas, thank you ever so much! It was a lovely idea. I had almost forgotten my old money box. The weather here has just turned marvelous. As Mummy probably told you, it was terrible. Rain and slush etc. It started turning about a week ago. We got up in the morning to see some snow on the ground and it was still snowing hard. By 10 o'clock a.m. there was enough snow to make forts and have snowball fights. We were sorry it wasn't skiing snow. but had to make the best of it. Then in the afternoon our spirits fell, [as] it started raining. It was terrible and slushy and everybody was downhearted. In the night it suddenly froze, though, you can imagine what the roads were like then!!! After that it got better and better, and now the snow is over a foot deep in drifts. Miss Dilling (Auntie Moo-Moo) [Mildred Dilling] is visiting us today to give a concert at Kitchener. (Kitchener is a town north [actually west] of Toronto.) The snow is so deep on the highway that all the buses have been cancelled, and she can stay till 6:20 p.m., when the train leaves for Kitchener. School is going very well. In our group meetings we are having debates etc. for entertainments. Next Wednesday we are going to have a debate, "Resolve[d] that the Air Force or Navy has harder entrance requirements and more preferable life." I am speaking for the navy. This week some Normal school [teacher's colleges as they

Fig. 5: The author's grandmother, Nellie Fernie, at her house, 49 Gloucester Place, London, c.1947.

*were called then] students came to teach us in various subjects.
A Mr. Thompson taught us writing. He came from* Yorkshire!!!!
*He had a perfect Yorkshire accent too. I think he must have been
a war guest out here. The inspector was there this week too. I'm
glad Elizabeth Anne is well, and I hope the rest of the family is
getting on well, Soon I will be a pretty good skater if the rink is
shovelled and I can get the practice. My ankles are still rather
weak, but once I get over that I'll be alright.*

*Well—lots of love from
Alec*

On 12 April, in the letter to my mother, after apologizing for not
having written for two weeks, I reported my latest exam results:

*Literature 89, Spelling 90, Maths 60, Science 61, Social
Studies, 78, Music 83, Composition and Grammar 70,
Courtesy A+ Work habits A+, Punctuality and Absence A+.*

*Maths was very hard, and I only got 60 because of my
previous marks. Science was quite easy and I got 71% on the
exam but I was brought down by a previous test in which I
only got 50%. All the other exams were easy ...*

*Last weekend we were at the farm and had lovely fun. We
arrived at 1 o'clock Friday, and after doing our chores and
having lunch, we played around in the lovely sunlight, or played
games, that is all except Nurse, who was busy gardening and
washing dishes. Aunt Mavis was working too. We had supper at
7:30 and went to bed nice and late. The next morning I got up at
8:30 and had a nice morning. David, Jeremy, Susan and I were
out for a walk for about an hour, then I came and helped Nurse
for a bit, after which I climbed trees and watched for David,
Aunt Mavis and Uncle Harold, who were getting some maple
syrup from the neighbouring farm.... We got up about 9 o'clock*

Sunday morning ... cleaning up the so-called front lawn....
Nurse raked, while we put all the sticks, rocks and dead grass
into the hole where the old house used to be.... We had quite a
party that night with easter cake and a lovely hot meal. I got
a book and a tie for my Easter presents, David got the same,
while Uncle Harold got an Easter egg and a tie. On Monday
we walked over to get more maple syrup and look at the maple
syrup being made. We left after lunch on Monday.

This week has been a nice week although the house has been
very topsy-turvy since Wednesday.... David was in bed with
a cold, Aunt Mavis was getting flu, Susan was going to have
her teeth out but it was postponed, I was at the theatre in the
afternoon, and Nurse went home for a few days because her
brother's house was being sold [in Pembroke, Ontario] *... at the*
beginning of the week. On Thursday Aunt Mavis had the flu,
David was just getting better, Jeremy was in bed, and David
and I were doing the housekeeping upstairs. On Friday I was in
bed with a cold, and it was snowing hard outside (the snow is
melting now), and David had to cook breakfast. Saturday was
better and today Nurse is home.

Yours lovingly
Alec

....

The spring of 1942 followed a similar pattern to 1941, except that
the family now spent every weekend possible at the new cottage on
the farm. Skis added a new dimension to farm visits, although the
opportunities were scarce, and my skating, despite weak ankles,
was improving. School work was not greatly challenging, music
lessons were proving fairly successful, and work on the farm had
become quite fascinating. There were chores which we found
taxing, especially the task of pumping up the water pressure by
hand every time we came back to the cottage. This was something
we really disliked, but no mention of it appears in my letters. We

were planting vegetable and flower gardens and meeting new people in the area. Mr. Butler of Nobleton provided Mr. Fry with an impressive quantity of trees that he planted in the spring and summer, and the owner of the farm next to the Fry property, Mr. McAllister, sold us seed potatoes that David and I cut up and planted. This was a learning experience. As I wrote late in June, "The potato crop failed in the vegetable garden, but we've quite a crop in the old hole. We thought those ones wouldn't grow, but I guess we made a slight mistake ..."

Apr. 24th 1942

Darling Mummy

I received your letter of May 7th [presumably the letter written April 4th] *this week, and it sounds very exciting. I must ask Miss Belt if she knows a Miss Lennie at the conservatory,*[2] *and in that way I might be able to get in touch with the Lennie family. I am certainly thrilled about Auntie Moo Moo paying for my lessons. I wrote her a letter last week. You're right about my doing lots of things* terribly, *for instance, mathematics. I am improving but I wasn't so good at Easter. Please don't take on an inferiority complex about being a good cook, as you can make pie and fix up meals as well as you make fruitcake and apple and blackberry jam, you're pretty good!!!! It oughtn't be hard to live up to either, as long as you have the right material.*

You seem to be in quite a royal position now, in every letter I get you are taking or have taken somebody to the Albert Hall, and every time in the Royal Box too! North America seems to be having a good time in England from what I hear. I'm long[ing] to hear about the wedding.[3]

Yesterday we (David and I) went to see a wonderful film called

2 Royal Conservatory of Music in Toronto.

3 The wedding of Davina and Archie Whitehouse.

Mr. V. *Maybe you saw it in England as* "Pimpernel" Smith.[4] *It is very funny and very serious with a bit of love attached and a bit of gruesome stuff. Mr. V is an absent-minded professor at Cambridge and very humorous in parts, for instance:*

"You're late for your lecture sir."
"But my lecture's not until Friday."
"Today is Friday, sir."
"What! Well, what happened to Thursday."
"We had it yesterday, sir."
"Unbelievable!"

Then he is very serious too. He takes ["archaeolo" is crossed out] *archaeological—what a word, I looked it up!—expedition in to Germany to cover up his work. There is an American who is very fresh, and a boy who is very serious, and doesn't know what all the secret is about, and who is very busy looking for relics when the others are planning. They get thousands of narrow escapes, and finally they rescue five men from [a] concentration camp and one of their daughters. Mr. V. is nearly caught but makes the official about to shoot him angry, and escapes from him. The official calls for him to come back, and Mr. V says, though you can't see him:*

"I'll be back, we'll be back, we'll all be back."

We had a lovely afternoon in the theatre and afterwards got a hot dog at a Honey Dew.

Next Monday we have a holiday for Empire Day. And on Tuesday I have my second shot for diptheria.

Yours lovingly
Alec

---

4 British anti-Nazi film from 1941, starring Leslie Howard.

> *P.S. I just got your letter delivered by a friend of a friend of*
> *yours. Susan loves her little book and thanks you very much*

On 11 June, a letter thanking Mother for her birthday wishes (sent by cable) gives a fairly complete idea of our activities in Canada.

> *Thank you ever so much for your cable, it is nice to know that*
> *you are thinking of me. Aunt Chrissie sent me a cable too. I have*
> *been doing lots of things lately, going to the farm, working on the*
> *school garden, etc. Last Friday we drove out to the farm with*
> *a long weekend in prospect. What a super one too. We stopped*
> *for a bit on the way and David and I walked till the car caught*
> *us up. On Saturday morning the men came to fix the telephone*
> *for us. We could speak on it by evening. In the morning Susan,*
> *Jeremy, Uncle Harold, David and I walked up to a blister in the*
> *side of a hill—a blister is a bare spot on pasture land, generally*
> *on the side of hills, where grass can't take root—and covered*
> *it over with brush and dead wood after planting clover seeds*
> *there. Uncle Harold had to go back once to see some men about*
> *sodding the ground around the house. After lunch we had a lot*
> *of fun, and fooled around most of the time. Sunday morning*
> *was rather dull and we split wood so that it would fit in the*
> *stove most of the time. It was—as David called it—"misting"*
> [a type of light rain] *and there wasn't much to do, so we had*
> *lunch quite early. After lunch it was nicer weather and we had*
> *more fun. I forgot to mention that we cut grass in the morning*
> *of Saturday, and on Sunday morning when it had cleared up*
> *a bit went for a nice walk along the road. Monday was lovely*
> *and bright and the men arrived at 8:30, before we had got up,*
> *and started getting the ground ready for sodding. They did it*
> *pretty soon, and drove off to the field to get some sod. We helped*
> *Uncle Harold to paint the screens, otherwise it was a very easy*
> *morning. In the afternoon David and I went off in the truck*
> *and loaded the sod. We got 112 in the first load, and 150 in the*

second. The men didn't have time to finish sodding on Monday, but I think it's finished now. Uncle Art arrived in the afternoon and drove us home. We stopped twice to help stuck cars and then at Maple to see Aunt Gert and Uncle Fred.

We are having great fun working in the school garden. We are decorating it with red petunias, white petunias and blue alyssum in the shape of a V with other beds all around. It is going to look very nice from the road. ...

P.S. I had a lovely day on my birthday, and I had Noel to tea with me. David gave me a model tank to make, and I got a lacrosse stick from Aunt Mavis, while Nurse gave me a new book. At tea, Uncle Harold brought me a beautiful jackknife for a present.

The garden at the farm was something in which we all took an interest, and considerable pride. I reported weeding sixteen rows—onions, cabbage, lettuce, cucumber, beets, radishes, carrots and peas, as well as the failed potato crop. I am pretty sure Nurse was the expert in this area, but Aunt Mavis and Uncle Harold—particularly Uncle Harold—found enormous pleasure in these pursuits. Not mentioned in my letters is the constant campaign he waged against groundhogs, who—if they were unfortunate enough to wander on to his property—soon came to a sticky end after he plugged up their holes at one end and inserted cyanide into the other.

By far the most exciting event of the summer was, as my letter of 22 June anticipated, going to camp.

Darling Mummy

Can you believe it, this time next week, I'm going on a CPR [Canadian Pacific Railway] train, on my way to Sherwood

Forest Camp, which is in the Haliburton district.[5] I'm thrilled about it and I'm sure you will be. Aunt Mildred is paying for me too. It is going to be ever so exciting. Remember the camp I was going to go to in France? We are in an awful hurry, because my trunk goes on and nothing is packed yet, rather like coming out here, with only thirty minutes to pack everything at school, and then only a day to get all the stuff resorted and packed properly. That was a real rush, and a gyp too, really, fancy wasting three days in port! But to come back to the subject, I think it was very kind of Auntie Mildred to pay for camp, and later for music lessons.

Talking about music lessons, I had my music exam last Thursday, and really it wasn't too bad at all. It was all over in fifteen minutes, and a milkshake afterwards really pulled me up from an[y] depression I had at all. I hope that's so. I was thinking afterwards, how kind Aunt Mavis had been to pay for my lessons so far. She has spent at least $80.00 on my lessons so far, and four dollars for my exam, which she had done without any complaint at all. She is very kind to me, and I wish I could show how I really appreciate what she has done for me.

This weekend at the farm we had a lovely time. On Saturday we were busy cutting the lawn and on Sunday we weeded the vegetable garden. We got six rows done, and now it looks much better. The onions were the worst to hoe, and we got only one row of them done. We have tomatoes, cabbage, lettuce, cucumber, beets, radishes, carrots and peas growing. The potato crop failed in the vegetable garden, but we've quite a crop in the old hole. We thought those ones wouldn't grow, but I guess we made a slight mistake. On Sunday afternoon we sewed watercress in the stream and clover on a bare sport on the side of the hill. The clover is growing there quite well now. Aunt Gert and Uncle

---

5   Better known as the Haliburton Highlands, located 200 kilometres north of Toronto, a two-and-a-half-hour drive.

Fred came over in the afternoon, and had supper with us.

I'm out of school now, as I'm recommended, and don't have to write entrance exams, so I'm in Grade 9 now, and also in high school.

Yours affectionately,
Alec

June 24th 1942

Dear Phyllis—A bit of paper conservation—I'll scribble a note on the back of Alec's letter. I tell him he must *write on both sides of the paper & save for Victory—but we forget!! You know! Well he's off for a grand treat on the 29th—Sherwood Forest Camp— and I'm sure it'll be a wonderful experience. Mildred, the dear, is paying his fees—$150—& we are paying for fares, laundry, extras etc: about another $40 (forty!) I imagine. It's a lot for one child's holiday, but I'm sure it'll be an experience he'll never forget. David thinks he's* very *lucky, but with the new income taxes, etc., we don't feel we can afford it for him—so perhaps he'll get his chance after the War. However David loves the farm so he'll have a happy time—and we'll all love to feel Alec is having a good time. Also one child less in out tiny cottage at the farm will make a little less congestion & give me one less to cook for!— Oh, and mend for, too—wait till you get Alec back & you'll find all your free time is spent mending his socks & putting on buttons & repairing tears—your little boy is a genius at wearing things out! I suppose it's because he's so big & coltish! His new trousers for camp were size 16 (bigger than I wear, as I'm a 14!) & yet he's only thirteen in sense and carefulness. Looking* very *well—and the tooth extraction & furcation last year has improved the shape of his mouth & jaw enormously—so he's really getting quite good looking! I'm sure you'll be proud of your large son when you see him.*

*I like the dress design you enclosed in Alec's letter. Clever girl!
I'm glad business isn't quite dead with rationing & taxes.
Have you seen my family lately? You never mention them, so I
suppose not!*

Do write some day.

Lovingly,
Mavis

*P.S. I love Alec's remarks, about my "uncomplaining" music
lessons—he is a scream! I expect he'll go on with the same
teacher—she is a Conservatory one, & very nice!*
M.F.

....

SHERWOOD FOREST Camp

July 12th 1942

Darling Mummy

I hope you received my last letter [from 22 June] *telling about
the journey up to camp, because there is such a lot to tell you.
The routine is very good, filling up every bit of time. We get up
at 8:30 a.m.—have a morning dip or wash, get dressed and have
breakfast at 9:00, except on Sunday, which is half an hour later.
After breakfast we have morning watch, in which a counsellor
talks about the more serious attitudes in life with us. After
morning watch we are given an hour to tidy up our tents. Then
we have call-up, after which we have instruction periods—
canoeing, swimming, life-saving and archery as examples. The
first period we are assigned to, the next is free choice. There is
a swimming period, then we have lunch! Phew! The afternoon
isn't quite the same. We have 1½ hours for rest right after
lunch, then we have different activities such as games, sailing,
canoeing, hikes and life-saving. After those activities we have
another swimming period, then have supper. After supper,*

*we generally have games on the playing fields, then go to bed
at 9:30. I have passed my swimming test to go canoeing—200
yds, and also my "P" proficiency test in canoeing. This week I
was on a canoe trip which I will tell you about later. We had a
regatta last week, and last night we had council ring, in which
we played Indian games, and were awarded tokens, etc. I got as
token for my canoeing.*

*We started our canoe trip last Thursday and we had a whale
of a time. We camped the first night on the veranda of an
abandoned cottage, and I had a terrible sleep. I woke up three
times to fix my bed—or it might have been the effect of the
coffee we had mixed with the stew (slightly flavoured with
tobacco (wisecrack), but it might be true.) We had a sumptuous
breakfast Friday morning, and paddled to Trout Lake. I've
never seen such a beautiful lake in all my life—not a bit of
habitation on it either. We paddled into Hawk Lake and stayed
there all day, then camped for the night on a special camping
ground. We had a swim and shower, then went to bed. I haven't
ever seen so many mosquitoes in my life. I put up a mosquito
bar* [mosquito netting], *but when I woke up, it was black with
mosquitoes, and I was a mass of bites, even though I had socks,
pyjamas and an extra sweater on. They still are itching. We
were back at camp by 3:00 after a wonderful trip. That's all to
date, and I'll write again soon.*

*Yours affectionately
Alec*
....

3 Ava Crescent
Toronto, Ont.

Aug. 4th 1942

Dear Mother

I haven't written for about two weeks so I had better keep up correspondence. I have quite a lot to tell you about so I will tell about the regatta first. The first event was a freestyle swim for the intermediates, and at first I didn't want to enter, but at some trouble I was persuaded to enter. To my surprise I came THIRD in swimming THE BREASTSTROKE! Next there were Keewi[6] races, and a junior tug-o-war in the water. There was a punt race and several other events. In the breaststroke race I came **First**! *The canoe races were postponed because of the canoe trips—there were two out and neither had arrived, so we only had two old canoes. I hope to be going on a canoe trip next week, so I hope to get letters before I go, as it is quite long.* [I seem to have forgotten I had already told her about the canoe trip.] *We had a camp game last Monday (yesterday), and our side won easily. It was Pioneers and Indians. The pioneers try to get supplies in the form of slips of paper with things like salt 10 points, or powder 50 points, or water 10 points, on it. You can hide it wherever you like and you try to get through the Indians to the fort, which is hidden, and the Indians search you to get the slip of paper.*

Yours affectionately
Alec

....

---

6 *Probably a name made up at the camp.*

My letters failed to mention a girls' camp across the lake from us, which was the source of much speculation. We knew some of our counselors paddled across the lake after we had turned in for the night, but what happened then was a matter of wild speculation. We were sure they were up to no good.

3 Ava Crescent
Toronto, Ont.

Sept. 21st 1942

Darling Mummy

Here I am back in the city again after a wonderful—and ever so long—summer holiday, [and] starting school tomorrow. We had three months holidays practically, from Jun 16 to Sept 22nd, which is three months. The extra time was because of boys working on the farms. Some can even stay till Oct. 9th! After leaving camp I was at the farm. We had ever such an exciting journey, up starting at three in the morning! We all had slept in the lodge and I slept on a converted couch with another boy— Graham Purdy, maybe I told you about him. We washed and all waited around for the truck. When it finally came everybody got aboard with their luggage. We had an uneventful ride until we got to Gelert—the station. It was rather chilly where I was, but it was fun. We got off at our station, and got our luggage. A few of us played cards till it was time for the train to come. The luggage was checked, then we went to the carriage, or coach, and waited for the engine to come, passing our time by playing with the chairs—[illustration]—or trying to balance on them— [illustration]. Nobody could do it with their eyes shut for 10 seconds. The engine finally came, and after a lot of shunting and pushing and banging—we got started- -very—very——slowly. After a bit we were Kinmount, where we changed engines and had our breakfast, which consisted of sandwiches, cake, biscuits and an apple with chocolate milk. We arrived in Lindsay at about 8:45 a.m.—that's around 70 miles sou'sou-west of Haliburton and Gelert, and 50 miles northeast of Toronto. Having left Gelert at around 6:45, you can imagine our speed. We arrived in Toronto at 9:15 and I was met by Aunt Mavis and we drove off with my trunk. We had lunch then I saw the movie Wings for the Eagle,[7] *all about making planes for America. It was quite good. I met Aunt Mavis at Simpson's parking place after that and had supper at Muirhead's Cafeteria after which we went home and got ready for the farm. We drove out around 8 o'clock and arrived at nine.*

The next day Dave and I went over to Mr. McAllister's farm and helped them get in oats. Dave had been doing this all summer. Dave drove the horses, and I helped pitch. We got in six big loads and the next we got in around twelve—we had two wagons. David drove the horse to pull the oats up into the mow and I helped in the mow. That evening I drove the cows in to be milked. There were ten—counting heifers—to drive. The next day I'm afraid I was sick from eating too many apples, so we never worked at Mr. McAllister's again, but he has offered us a job next spring—helping with the maple syrup.

I was over at Miss James's on Sunday for the afternoon, and we played deck tennis most of the time.

Last weekend—not yesterday and the day before, but the one before, David visited Ottawa with Uncle Harold and Aunt Mavis. He saw all the sights and is a travelogue about it. Aunt Mavis got me a lovely pen there and I've vowed not to lose it.

Tomorrow I start school, as I said, and I will be in the same group as David, Mr. Carter's group. The only catch is that I'm in 9A and David is in 9C, which is just as good, only there are

---

7   American film from 1942, directed by Lloyd Bacon and starring Ann Sheridan and Dennis Morgan.

too many pupils in 9. We were at the school this morning and found out all this. We had our hair cut this morning and this afternoon went to the public library for David to take back the books he had out for the summer. While we were there we saw the John Ross Robertson collection of paintings. Some of these were beautiful. Most of them were Canadian or about Canada.

I do hope you're better from your operation now.

I passed my junior lifesaving test for the YMCA with 252 out of 300 or 84%. Thanks ever so much for thinking of the suit for me.

Yours lovingly
Alec

CHAPTER 9
OCTOBER TO DECEMBER 1942: VICTORY IN MIND

Oct. 5th 1942

Darling Mummy

I've started school now properly, the last week we were at home most of the time, the furnace not being in proper functioning order. We used to have an oil furnace, so it had to be changed to coal, and they took an age to do it.[1] We had lovely fun, Dave even made an "Eskimo Club," and both Dave and I are honorary, honorary, honorary, honorary, honorary members, having been frozen out of school five times—every day. We've had lovely fun at the farm, and on Saturday we planted eight pine trees: two Scotch pines, four red pines, and two Austrian pines. Mr. Butler from Nobleton put them in, and he was in high spirits. His son had been missing at Dieppe and he'd had news that he was a prisoner in some German Camp.

On Saturday we had whole lot of carpenters in the house, and there were some men painting. There were six in all. Mr. Sibbit, the contractor, and his son with an assistant, were painting,

---

1   Likely a measure to conserve petroleum products as a result of the shortage caused by German U-boats sinking many tankers in the western Atlantic in the first part of 1942, including tankers that supplied refineries in eastern Canada with oil from Venezuela. See Robert C. Fisher, "'We'll Get Our Own': Canada and the Oil Shipping Crisis of 1942," *The Northern Mariner/Le Marin du nord* 3, no. 2 (April 1993), 33–39.

while two carpenters who had been working on the house in the city with another man were working inside. We had molding put around the top of all the bedrooms and the bathroom while the hall and Sue's bedroom had a new ceiling. Mr. Butler was there too, and he showed us how to divine water with a fork from a willow tree. Aunt Mavis is quite good, and so is Dave, but the rest of us aren't so good. Mr. Butler is wonderful. Aunt Mavis took us to lunch in Nobleton, where a lady served meals as she (Aunt Mavis) could not get into the house for lunch. She served us delicious pork (roasted) with mashed potatoes, and we had pie for dessert. She had a lovely garden outside her house, and she told us she had 250 gladiolus bulbs.

The weekend before last, when we were at the farm, we had a lovely time, and when we were there, the man who had sold us our fruit trees visited us and we bought a whole lot more, and beside that 150 strawberry plants, two *gooseberry bushes for Uncle Harold, a whole lot of asparagus, and I don't know how many grapevines! We're really going to have a farm next year! Today in school we haven't done much out of regular school work.*

I've found that we're taking British history from Queen Elizabeth to present times. This year we were behind a month in school, so we are rushing like anything.

We had our elections in group last Friday, and David is second vice-president. I didn't have a chance to be in the executive this year, as this is my first year in Mr. Carter's group.

Last week I was at the dentist, and, to my relief, I found I had no cavities.

Out here we are awfully excited and proud to be making Lancasters and Mosquitos.[2]

2 The Avro Lancaster was a heavy bomber that was designed and produced by the British company Avro; after early 1942, it was also produced by Victory Aircraft in Malton, Ontario. The de Havilland DH.98 Mosquito was a multirole combat aircraft designed by the British de Havilland; during the Second World War it was produced by de Havilland Canada in Toronto.

Uncle Harold was in the Victory loan again this year, and the insignia is a dagger [that is] supposed to be the Commando dagger, pointing at the heart of Berlin.

We have had to buy a whole lot of books for high school this year. I will tell you what I have now.

English	
Jim Davis—Masefield	50
Myths—A Heritage of Wonder Stories	50
Plays—Tempest, *Shakespeare!*	50
Poetry—Poems of Action	75
Living English	25
Dictionary	25

Britain's Story. General Maths. General Science. Basic French. The Essentials of Business Practice. Canada Sings: *Music Dictation book, five loose-leaf note books. It all amounts to approximately $8.05.*

At the first of the year I was in 9A, but 9A was changed to an all-art class, so I was transferred to 9B, which is for both. There is 9A, B and C this year and all are the same. 9A is all art and the other two are mixed. Dave is in 9C this year, so we are in separate classes but the same group—just the opposite of last year.

I got a letter from Aunt Chrissie the other day, and she told me about Peter[3] being in the convoy battle at Malta—it must have been, if he was on the Nelson,[4] *although I thought he was in the Pacific. I hope he got the letter from me.*

Well, my best love to you,
Alec

---

3 *Peter Douglas; he was my cousin and Aunt Chrissie's nephew.*

4 The HMS *Nelson* was torpedoed in September 1941 after escorting several convoys to Malta. After repairs, the *Nelson* continued to do so before supporting the British invasion of French Algeria in late 1942.

It was a busy fall. In mid-October, my yearmate John Holland had a spare ticket for the circus at Maple Leaf Gardens, which I was fortunate to share at the last minute, even though it was a school day. The letter I began on 24 October describes this event and various other activities:

Darling Mummy

I'm so glad your tonsils are better, we got your telegram last Saturday. I guess you had quite a good time convalescing.

We were out at the farm last weekend and had a lovely time. On Saturday we were over at the McAllisters, and chose a pumpkin that we never got for Halloween, and also we got a couple of bags of potatoes.

Uncle Harold wasn't able to come on Saturday ... He's very busy nowadays with the Victory Loan.

Last Thursday we (John Holland and I—Dave wasn't there) went to the circus. We were all invited—or I was—very suddenly. I was just about to leave for school, when I saw John at the door—he is a war guest across the road from us. He was going to the circus and had two tickets left. Dave was going to the dentist, so I went with John alone. Mrs. Merrick, John's host, or guardian, drove us to the Maple Leaf Gardens where it was to be held. We arrived in time and had a wonderful seat in the middle of the blue section—that's around 20 ft up or maybe 40—and we had a wonderful view—rather like Mumsmum at the coronation,[5] I thought.

The show was wonderful. We saw from the parade to the man coming from a two-foot-wide runway from the top of the stadium to a fall of around 80 ft into a tank of water three feet

---

5 The coronation of George VI and Queen Elizabeth at Westminster Abbey in London, on 12 May 1937.

deep, The first event was comedy acrobatics, then there were some trapeze acts. Then there were some lions, with a lady lion-tameress or whatever you call it. There were horse acts after that, then another trapeze act. There was a clown act after that—in a public wedding. There was a lovely bear act after that, with [marginal note *"3 Ava Crescent, Toronto, Ont., Oct 29th 42."*] *bears roller-skating and riding a bycicle. There was a super high wire (tight rope) act called the American Eagles—the leader is in the U.S.A. Flying Corps. The performers came from Sweden.*

There was a beautiful white stallion next, then a thing that made your heart go into your mouth, she [an acrobat] *went to the top of a huge Perch Pole—125 ft. high, and started to swing at the top, then she dropped, and her ankle caught on the pole which went over with her weight, while she screamed. All that happened was that the pole swung down, and hung in a vertical line down.*

There were more clown, trapeze and riding acts after that, then came the seals. They played "God Save the King" etc., all the tricks they usually do, then came six lovely elephants. After that there was a backward dive off the top of a ladder at the top of the stadium. Then there was a bycicle act—and that was all of the circus.

Sunday Nov. 1st
[Continuation of October 24th letter]

Last Tuesday we saw the Quints[6] in a Victory Rally at the Maple Leaf Gardens. The rally was wonderful—the stadium was full except for the seats around the scenery where you couldn't see a thing. We were in a box near the band [presumably Uncle Harold's position in the Victory Bond

---

6 The Dionne Quintuplets, the first quintuplets known to have survived infancy. Born in 1934 in Callander, ON, they became a major tourist attraction.

campaign entitled him to a box]. *The first item was the youth
of Canada. It was a marvelous show, showing sea cadets, air
cadets, Boy Scouts, Girl Guides, YMCA and even Jr. Red Cross
and schools. They all lined up in the middle of the stadium
and Harry "Red" Foster[7] told us a little about each. I forgot to
mention that the Boys' Brigade and K [Kiwanis] Club was there.
There was a Commando Raid with sailors and soldiers, and the
Germans were thoroughly beaten. The Quints were really sweet.
First Mr. Foster introduced us to them as they rode across the
stage on their trycicles. Then they came on to the microphone
and said hello and sang first a French song, then "There'll
Always Be an England." They did a splendid job considering
how hard it is to sing the high part of "There'll Always Be an
England" in broken English. Then they went off again and while
they were changing their tunics, John Collingwood Reade[8] gave
a wonderful address on the Victory Loan. The Quints then came
out all in Navy, Air Force, Women's Air Force and Women's
Army [uniforms]. They sang another song then they raised the
Union Jack and saluted it. Then the rally came [to an end].*

*Girls and ladies in peasant costume for all the Allied nations
came out, and after that came the navy, the army and air force.*

*This week we were at Dr. Brown's and I found that I weighed
<u>107</u> lbs and was 63¼ inches tall, 2¼ more than last year. I had
gained 3 lbs. It was really terrible and I'm trying to reduce.*

*Yesterday was Halloween. We went downtown in the morning
and I got a new pair of shoes, and also a pair of trousers. It
is unspeakable, but the truth, that one suit of mine [costs]
$24.50 around £<u>6</u>. That is really terrible, not counting, shirts,
underwear, socks or ties.*

---

7 Harry "Red" Foster (1905–85) was an accomplished Canadian sportsman, who played
   football and sailed, then became a notable sports broadcaster and advocate for children with
   intellectual disabilities. He was inducted into Canada's Sports Hall of Fame in 1984.

8 John Collingwood Reade (1904–63) was a British-born Canadian radio newscaster and war
   correspondent.

Luckily we have our winter overcoats or they would cost around $25.

After we got all the things we wanted, we had lunch in Simpson's Arcadian Court. We got home around 3:30, and I made a pumpkin into a face for supper. Uncle Harold got home for supper and we had a very nice little party.

We had movies of the farm and found to our dismay that half of them were ruined, because something had happened to the camera.

We had a movie of the coronation [of George VI in 1937] after that, then we found the farm movie again.

This year I am in high school, but it isn't separate ... as ours is a continuation school. Some boys have to go to another school for high school, when they have previously been to public school.

Yours very lovingly
Alec

....

Nov. 22nd 1942

Phyllis dear—

I have thought about you so much lately, & meant & meant to write, but I always think Alec is giving you all the news, & I'm always so hectically busy that letters are a very weak spot. But I know you understand, as you are busy yourself, & know what a weary creature one is at the end of the day. I haven't had a cook for nearly a year, & housework is not my easiest métier, but I'm managing, & not too badly, & improving as a cook!

I've been meaning to thank you for your cheques—which certainly do help. Four children & War taxation don't go well together financially—& it does help to have Alec's clothes taken care of! There seem to be so many little expenses with children,

*that added up consume a lot of money. Alec & David are now
wearing long trousers and look* awfully *smart. How I wish you
could have seen the pink, satisfied look on Alec's face when he
first donned grown-up socks & garters & long gray flannels &
a tweed jacket!! Then he had to have new school & best shirts,
new wool socks (men's type size 11½!) new shoes, underwear
(he only wears cotton winter & summer, as the houses are so
warm[)]. I bought a practically new navy-blue double-breasted,
long trousered suit from Mary Kilbourn, whose boy grows out
of things as quickly as Alec, & as it is pre-war it is beautiful
material & very well-cut. He looks awfully nice in it for best.
The suit you are sending will also be very useful, as the brown
tweed suit is getting very tight! Alec now weighs 107 lbs—& is
rather inclined to fat, so I'm trying to cut down a trifle of second
helpings & taken* [away? word unclear] *things—but he looks
very well & never has anything the matter with him. The boys
have both joined Scouts and are very keen. We're giving them
uniforms for a Xmas present, as they coast about $10 each—but
they want them very badly. Today they are off with the troop
on a hike; I made picnic lunches to take with them and they
have gone off very happy & gay. Life is very full & busy, with
music, games, Scouts, homework & the Xmas spirit!! I wish
you were here to see your young man! Alec is still inclined to
be slow, especially at jobs he doesn't like—sometimes I get a bit
exasperated over it—but I really think he is improving. It's really
his main tiresomeness, otherwise he's such a darling—I wish
he'd get over it, as the tendency may make life harder when he
has to stand up on his own feet. He has so many good qualities,
bless him—but, like David, his bad ones seem deep-rooted!
David drives us crazy sometimes, and yet he's such a lamb, too!
Funny little things!*

*I'm glad your tonsils are all better. It's a miserable business,
but a good thing to have over. Isn't it wonderful about Davina?*

I'd give anything and everything to be over with them—oh how horribly I miss them all. I'm dieing to hear all about Quentin. He sounds so precious. I wonder if you've seen him.

I hope you have such a happy Xmas—things are looking so much better, aren't they—perhaps this will be your last without your own little boy— oh won't you have a lovely time when you get together again? I know Alec will miss us, as we will miss him—but his Mother is very dear to him & no one will ever take her place—aren't you glad? That's one thing I'm sure, Alec will never be fickle!!

Much love, my dear—do write some time—

lovingly
Mavis

....

Nov. 29th 1942

Darling Mummy

A very merry Christmas! I hope this letter arrives around Dec. 25, do not open till the 25th so to speak (hopefully). As though this would arrive within a month!

I sent letters to the relations (Aunt Concey, Aunt Ethel and Uncle Gilbert, Peter, James, Mumsmum and Uncle Vivian[9]— the latter first).

We're all dreaming of a white Christmas out here, and somebody has even conjured up a song—something to the effect of dreaming of a white Christmas, like the ones I used to know.[10]

If it keeps on like today, we'll have a really white Christmas this year.

---

9   *My mother's elder brother, also known as David; see 25 Sept 1941 entry, page 142, note 4.*

10 "White Christmas," the popular song written by Irving Berlin was featured in movie *Holiday Inn*, starring Bing Crosby and Fred Astaire. Released in August of 1942, the song was at the top of the hit parade by October 1942.

In November, former U.S. presidential candidate Wendell Willkie visited Toronto, "and I heard a very good speech by the same." Mildred Dilling, a staunch Republican, had been horrified when Willkie failed to defeat Roosevelt, a Democrat, in the 1940 election. But, her political opinions notwithstanding and expressed as they were in no uncertain terms and at length in her visits to us, we were all Roosevelt fans. Then one day,

> I was just walking home from my music lesson, when I suddenly bump into the car coming out of the drive, and I get an invitation to see Willkie if I was ready in five minutes. I was ready in that time, believe it or not, and we arrived in good time for the programme. It was in aid of Russia so there were quite a few Russians there.
>
> Harry "Red" Foster was there and a good many important personages besides Willkie …
>
> There were a good many speeches including t[w]o Russian ambassadors.

Willkie, of course, was now a major supporter of the Allied war effort, not just a presidential candidate: Roosevelt's reputation did not suffer in the slightest in my mind, and probably benefitted, from this encounter. Sometime later we saw a newsreel of this rally for Wendell Willkie's Aid to Russia Fund, "and David and I saw ourselves as distinctly as we could have possibly seen, on the right and centre. That picture might be going to Russia."

Scouts had become a prime activity. We went on Scout hikes: "I passed my second-class test for firelighting, quite an accomplishment. We had quite a hard time, as the wood was wet and had been frozen. Next Sunday we are having a church parade so I have to get my uniform, although the belt is big, hat small and socks wrong colour, I look not too bad in it. The socks, hat and belt are being changed ..."

In December we had commencement night, "and did we have fun." This may have been written with tongue in cheek, if the rest of my letter is any indication:

> At first we sat on the platform behind a closed curtain for around ten minutes. I was wearing my new dark blue suit (long pants) the shirt you sent from England and a blue tie.

> After singing the "King" we had a few speeches, then the girls got their Entrance certificates. There was another speech, then the boys got their certificates. This must have taken around an hour, at least that's what it felt like. When everybody had finished with getting their certificates, we filed off, and in came the students with their junior matriculations. We had a lot more speeches and lectures, then they got their certificates. When all this was done, we went to the south prep. gym, had refreshments, and then for half an hour, we danced!

Both David and I had good enough results for us to take the University of Toronto Schools (UTS) entrance exam: "only fifty accepted out of 350 entries so I don't expect they'll get in but it will be good practice," wrote Aunt Mavis. In fact, David was accepted and I was not, but events proved that this would be of little account.

Two letters in December reported on the end of school festivities and preparations for Christmas. Aunt Mavis again added a note: "don't worry about the sleepiness Alec mentions—I never see any sign of it in ordinary life & imagine he may be dreamy when questioned.... I'm going to see his master and will report!" On Christmas Eve my letter had more news than usual:

Darling Mummy

Today is Christmas Eve and I'm ever so excited and impatient about tomorrow. We have a beautiful turkey, and today we saw Nurse taking out its insides—(ugh!).

Tomorrow night we are going to Aunt Gert's and Uncle Fred's and going to have a lovely time from what I hear.

On Saturday I will be going to Preston[11] to see Lilian and Paul for a week, which is going to be wonderful.

On Tuesday we had our group party and had lovely fun. The first thing we did was have the food, ice cream and biscuits for all. Afterwards there were three ice-cream cups left, one had been given for Mr. Totten so we only had three instead of four. We had contests to see who could imitate famous people or animals best, and who could solve what a jumble of letters on the board said. Dave and I sang "There's an 'ole in my bucket, dear Liza" etc., but didn't win anything.

Last Thursday we had a Scout party and had lots of fun except one game where the heaviest man in each patrol had to crawl on his hands and knees with somebody on his back seven times to the wall and back, a different man every time on his back. I happened to be the heaviest man.

We also had a game on our knees, where we hit a balloon with our hands, and tried to score a goal on the other side. The other team won 5-4. It was a really rip-snorting game.

At the end, after a bottle of pop and two doughnuts, we had skits. Each patrol had to make a skit of [a] 1942 version of Scrooge. We had some quite amusing performances.

---

11 *Paul had a new job at this point, so he and Lilian moved to Preston from Brockville. Located around 100 km southwest of Toronto, the Town of Preston later amalgamated with Hespeler and Galt to form the new city of Cambridge.*

Yesterday David and I went delivering Christmas presents around the village.

On Monday we decorated the Christmas tree and it looks beautiful now.

Well, I suppose that's all for now, I'll write again after Christmas.

....

Dec. 27 [continuation of letter started 24 December 1942]

I had a lovely Christmas, lots of presents and eats, and Santa Claus even remembered I had a stocking, and I got some wonderful presents in it.

I'll tell you what we did from about 7.30 or 8 a.m. to 12 o'clock p.m.*!!! First we got up and, in our dressing gowns, took our stockings into Aunt Mavis's and Uncle Harold's room. We opened our stockings, and found countless surprises in them, especially my first month's pocket money for next year and a cash book to keep track of all our money. We are going to get $2 a month now!!! We have to keep track of every cent of it too, which will be both educational and nice. It's about the most money I've ever handled, $24 a year! I have to pay for everything, of course.* [note from Harold Fry: "not quite!! H.F.F."]

When we had opened our stockings we went back to our rooms, got dressed and tidied them up, then listened to the Empire broadcast and the king's speech. Grandma, Aunt Edith and Uncle Art had come in the meantime, and when the speech was over we were called downstairs.

Some of the presents we had! David gave me a lovely gaudy tie, Aunt Louise (Kinnear) gave Dave and I handkerchiefs, we were given a game called Variety Bingo *from Aunt Margory, a game called* Blitz *from Mrs. Leeming* [and] *(the last were to both Dave and I) we were given Scout knapsacks, purses to carry*

Scout dues in, and at the end were given a tent!

When Aunt Edith and Grandma had left with Uncle Art, we had a light snack to keep us going till the turkey dinner.

We had dinner at 5:30 p.m. and had our first taste of Aunt Mavis's and Nurse's turkey cooking. Did it taste good. We pulled crackers in between times and wore hats for the plum pudding, which Aunt Mavis brought in on fire.

After dinner we changed into our blue suits and got tidied up as we were going to Aunt Gert's and Uncle Fred's for some more gaiety. We arrived when Uncle Art and Aunt Gert were playing a duet.

We gossiped until refreshments, which we all helped in serving and eating, and had a wonderful time. After that we had games and nerve tests which were very amusing. We arrived home at midnight.

Yrs. very lovingly
Alec

(only 365 days till Christmas)

CHAPTER 10
JANUARY TO JULY 1943: LAST MONTHS IN CANADA

1942 came to an end with a succession of parties, at school and at home, and at Christmas we did not get to bed until midnight, an unheard-of hour for thirteen-year-olds in those days and in that company. But the rules seemed to be changing in 1943. The first letter written in the new year reflected a rather disorganized period following the Christmas celebrations.

Jan. 17th 1943

I'm afraid I never got around to posting the letters I wrote from Preston, so I'm continuing it now.[1] You will probably be overjoyed to hear that our presents all arrived shipshape. The suits fit me perfectly, I'm wearing the brown one now. I don't know how to thank you. The games are wonderful. Uncle Gilbert's[2] daughter, Mary Jackson, said that she had forgotten what wonderful things you could buy in England.

We played "Plantit"[3] with her, as the other games took four players.

---

1   *After visiting Paul and Lilian Kingston in Preston, where Paul had a medical practice, I remember that I showed off my elementary skating skills at the local rink, but these letters do not seem to have survived.*

2   *Gilbert was the uncle of my stepfather, who had served with great distinction in the Merchant Marine.*

3   A gardening-themed board game, published by Geographia Ltd. London.

I didn't tell you all the Christmas [presents] I got, so as I have forgotten which ones I told you, I will start again from the beginning.

A Scout outfit, consisting of hat, neckerchief, shirt, belt, trousers, socks and garter tabs, from Aunt Mavis. Ski socks from Aunt Mavis and Uncle Harold. Gloves from Grandma. A lovely tent to use at the farm from Aunt Edith and Uncle Art. A game called Variety Bingo *from Aunt Margory, a game called* Blitz *from Aunt Agnes (Mrs. Leeming).*

Nurse gave me a lovely wallet and a book called Dave Dawson with the Commandos.[4] *Dave gave me a lovely flashy tie. Aunt Mavis also gave me a book called* Near East Adventure *and a lovely English (Reeves) paint box. I got two lovely handkerchiefs from Aunt Louise (Mrs. Kinnear). In my stocking I got stationery—rubbers, pencils, mending tape, thumb tacks and things like that. I also got a cash book from Uncle Harold with my first month's pocket money,*

Yrs lovingly
Alec

....

After visiting Paul and Lilian Kingston in January I came down with the mumps, and there is a gap in correspondence from mid-January until the third week of February. It is also possible that any letter written in the last two weeks of January failed to arrive in England, but I would not have written while I had the mumps. Whatever the reason, my letters began again in late February.

Feb. 21st 1943

Darling Mother

---

4   A novel by R. Sidney Bowen, New York: Crown, 1942. This was book nine in the fifteen-volume
    Dave Dawson series of adventure novels by Bowen.

I've been up two weeks now and having a whale of a time. I crowned my fun yesterday by seeing The Scarlet Pimpernel.[5] *It was a wonderful film, as well as gruesome—in the case of the guillotine. Leslie Howard was wonderful as Sir Percy Blakely. I liked especially his poem—"The Scarlet Pimpernel," by Sir Percival William Blakely ... You have probably seen this film so most likely this is all boring to you.*

This week I have been having a good time at school listening to announcements about reports and exams coming at the end of the month. I will really have to study, as well as learn about 100 lines of memory work in a hurry; as we have to be finished with all that stuff before Easter. This week we are having French and maybe German tests, and certainly Maths, so I'll be doing quite a lot of homework this week. I also have to copy out notes and improve notes and make diagrams to get my books complete. I have started off with Health. We had a music exam last Friday without much warning. I don't know how I did as yet. Talking about music, my music lessons are on Fridays at 6:30 p.m. now.

In National Defense we are taking knots and lashings now. Quite interesting, but the only trouble is that so far I know all the knots [required, but] there are lots I don't know as well, of course.

I think we will be having a parent's night in Scouts pretty soon, but everything is rather vague about it as yet. I hope to pass my first aid next Thursday.

We are reading The Tempest *in Literature now and I really love it. We really have to read it thoroughly. Mr. Trott (our English teacher) reads it slowly, clearly and thoroughly at first. Then afterwards we read it in play form. We have been reading it for two weeks, with about 4 periods a week, and haven't yet finished*

---

5   British film from 1934 directed by Harold Young and starring Leslie Howard and Merle Oberon.

Act I, Scene II.

Maths is getting to be interesting too now. We are studying stuff about Polynomials and Bynomials, and Monomials and Trinomials. Really complicated—what!

Yours very lovingly
Alec

....

Mar. 1st 1943

Darling Mother

This weekend I had a wonderful time at Miss James's farm. I started at 5 o'clock Friday evening and ended at about 7:30 p.m. Sunday evening. Miss James and Kathleen Cherry and myself were there. I did so much, I'll have to tell you about it in a sort of diary form.

Friday

We arrived at about 6 or 6:30 p.m. and directly we got there I went and got a dozen eggs from the Connells' farm (Miss James's neighbours) and a pint of milk and cream, but I won't dwell on that subject any more. We had finished supper and washed up the dishes by 9:30, and we then played hockey—the kind on a board with a ball and that you operate by a ring which works the men by a mechanism under the board. We played this till 10 p.m. Then went to bed.

Saturday

We got up around 8 o'clock a.m. and had a bite of breakfast, after which we started getting ready for a cross-country run on skis. I went ahead to ask the Connells for supplies such as eggs and milk to be spared for when we got back from the trek.

The other two soon caught up with us and I loaded my

187

knapsack (which Miss James—Freda as she likes us to call her—and Kathleen, had filled with supplies) and started off with them. We travelled along the roadside and turned in at a gateway and came to the most beautiful hill. It was long and <u>fast,</u> and at the bottom it went up and down another hillock. After a couple of runs down it we left and went along the road again till we came to a rail fence; this we crossed and came to two lovely fast and steep hills. They were terrible to climb up though.

We came back after about three hours and had some lunch; it was then about 3:30 p.m.; and afterwards stayed indoors, tending to the fire and furnace, and then having a quiet time playing hockey while Freda rested. I afterwards got some water, and we started cooking supper. After supper we again played hockey and darts, then I looked at the furnace, after which we went to bed.

Sunday

Sunday was very windy, and the skiing did not look so good. However, we had a wonderful time building a snow house. We left by skis and pulling a toboggan at around 5 p.m., and met the car at the highway.

Last Thursday I passed my Scout race test, in which I had to run and walk one mile in twelve minutes.

*Yours lovingly
Alec*

Mar. 14th 1943

Dear Mother,

The Saturday before last we were at the Youth Rally, for the Red Cross, at the Maple Leaf Gardens. It was a wonderful show. Everything from clowns to a military pageant. We had a wonderful box seat in the "reds." There are four sections: "Reds," "Blues," "Greys" and "Greens." The greens are at the top of the gardens, then greys, then blues, then reds. The box seats are just above the rail seats, so you can imagine how close we were.

The Rally started out with clowns, and a man who jumped over barrels on skates (the Gardens were flooded, as there were to be some figure skaters on the programme).

Officially the show started at 2:15 p.m., and the seats were open to the public then, (we had free tickets), so boys and girls were constantly pouring into the Gardens....

In the way of skating we saw the jumper, and a clown who copied him, then there were two figure-skating couples (one girl who goes to our school) and a man who skated on stilts. There was also a marvelous professional, who was a world champion or something, who came from some European country (Czechoslovakia or Switzerland I think).

Also there was an exciting game of ice hockey between Navy and Air Force. We cheered for Navy, and Navy won.

After the hockey game there was a game of broomball between the police and fire department. We cheered for the police and police won, as usual.

At first only the Royal Regiment of Canada's band played, but afterwards the Navy, Army, Air Force and Royal Regiment bands all played. It was the first indoor appearance of the Navy band. A girl in the CWAC [Canadian Women's Army Corps] *came and sang, and did a perfect imitation of Gracie Fields herself. She sang the song where she puts on a bandana. I'm afraid I've forgotten the words now.*

The pageant was wonderful. First the Navy marched in; with the "Wrens" (WRNS) in hot pursuit. After that came the Army with "CWACs"; the Air Force with the RCAF Women's Division, and all the branches of the Red Cross. The last to come in were the emergency nurses with their white uniforms, carrying huge Union Jacks. I forgot to mention that a girl with the Stars and Stripes came in on a big platform, with a big Red Cross on all four sides.

One lucky boy won the prize of a model of a Hampden bomber, and a picture of [George] "Buzz" Beurling, Canadian ace of the RAF, autographed by him and Capt. Roy Brown, Canadian ace of the last war.

Coming home was a terrible job, the street cars were like sardine tins, only worse. As somebody once said; "A crowded streetcar is like a sardine tin only worse, because sardines don't jostle you, or step on your feet, or knock you over."

We had to walk down a few steps before getting on, then we were last in the car. We were leaning against the doors most of the time, but finally a lot of people got off, and we were able to sit down.

On Saturday morning, I was at the dentist and found that I had no cavities.

Last Thursday at Scouts, Dave passed his first aid for Second Class. I couldn't [illegible] very well, as he was tying the slings and bandages on me. Also on Saturday, our junior basketball team won the championship. By the way, our group has a yell now, it goes like this:

In all the sports and on the field,
We're the boys who never yield,
We got the pips, we got the spunk,
We're the guys who never flunk.
Running, hockey, jumping high,

We of Carter's never die,
Sis boom ba, Sis boom ba,
Carter's, Carter's, Rah, rah, rah.

Last Tuesday I found that I had 79% in Manual Training, also, about 73% for German.

Wednesday was Ash Wednesday, so we had a service in the auditorium. Dr. Montcrief was the preacher. He comes from Florida.

On Friday Mr. Tamblyn came into group and we had a panel discussion of the laws of compensation.

We also had Health on Friday.

Yesterday I went roller skating for the first time this year.

Yours very lovingly
Alec

[Added by Aunt Mavis] P.S. Thanks for Alec's remittance—I think it's dedicated to dressing gown this month. His is in rags!
—Mavis

....

Apr. 4th 1943

Darling Mummy

Yesterday I had the time of my life canvassing for the Chinese War Relief Fund. I started at 9:30 a.m., and with John Dixon, went all along Vesta Drive, which is almost half a block from Ava Crescent. Our route wasn't very complicated .... David had a route right near ours with another boy .... [diagram showing how David's route was "full of apartment houses"]

It's quite educating to do that, you open a door, or a door is opened to you, and you see in the front hall a pair of slippers lying around, and in the distance you hear the tumbling of

191

breakfast plates. Dave told me that he once opened the door, at least the door was opened to him and he was just asking the maid if she would like to contribute ... and from the back of the house came a woman's voice shouting "NO"! and a couple of 50¢ pieces dropped down the stairs.

I had Auntie Marjorie's house to sell a tag to. David had the reeve and Aunt Agnes.

In the last two weeks I have received two lovely letters from you.

I like your description of shrapnel coming down on the pavement—devil's dance with dust-bin lids.

You never told me, or else I've forgotten, what you made in the factory[6] you tell me you are going back to.

I bet you liked the hockey game you saw in Brighton. I haven't yet been to a professional game yet, but I've seen a couple of amateur games and lots of it at school. It's awfully exciting.

Uncle David must be having a wonderful time in Africa, as long as it's not too hot or sandy. I suppose he'll soon be fighting.

Yours very lovingly
Alec

....

Apr. 11th 1943

Darling Mummy

This week has been ever so exciting, and rather unsettled, on the weather side. Last Sunday Uncle Art was here for lunch, and in the afternoon we walked part way home with him. It was a lovely day, with the sun shining, and a nip in the air that made you want to run. We, or I, restrained myself however, and we walked behind Uncle Art and Uncle Harold, holding Jeremy's

---

6 *This was my mother's wartime volunteer work; I do not remember what it was she made.*

*hand. We walked home another way, and found it quite cold
on Spadina Road. We met Nurse going on her day out on the
way back, and also heard bands playing in the distance. This
week was army week, and a recruiting campaign was on for the
Reserve Army. For that reason all the churches had soldiers,
and afterwards there were parades.*

Monday, to our surprise, was snowy, and not at all like Sunday.

*On Wednesday in Auditorium, Mr. Totten took the programme
over, and we had a lovely, dull, forty-minute period. Wednesday
was also Sue's birthday, and was she ever thrilled. She had
some lovely presents too, Uncle Harold gave her a gold wristlet,
that was to have her name engraved on it, and Aunt Mavis was
saying the other day, that it hardly seemed three years when
David was ten years old. She is twice as old as Jeremy now,
Jeremy being five.*

*Thursday was a very exciting day. We went to the Armouries[7]
to practice for cadet inspection in the afternoon, leaving school
at 3 o'clock, and arriving at the Armouries at 4 o'clock.*

*We got home at half past six, at least I did, Dave got home
about six. I had just time to get ready for Scouts and be there on
time. At Scouts I passed my signalling, which means that I only
have to pass my cooking now. That I hope to do this afternoon,
as we are having a hike. Our assistant scoutmaster is leaving
for the air force soon, so I want to get my Second Class before he
leaves. I have to pass my First Class at headquarters, so I don't
have to worry about scoutmasters or anything for that, although
First Class is by no means easy. Whereas you can pass your
Second Class at separate times, you have to pass everything in
First Class, except for cooking, swimming and journey at the
same time. Journey is where you have to camp overnight, make*

---

7   This is possibly the Toronto Armories, which was built in 1894 and was the largest armoury in
Canada. Located on University Avenue near Osgoode Hall, it was demolished in 1963.

a full report of what you did, and also make a map.

On Friday morning we had a group play. It was a great success, and Mr. Totten was there instead of Mr. Carter, to watch over the group. Mr. Totten is our principal. The play was a German radio broadcast, written by Dave. Dave was also presiding over the meeting, as the President and the Hon. Vice President were absent (Dave is the second vice president).

Yesterday we saw a wonderful pirate film called The Black Swan.[8] *It was all about pirates in the Caribbean, around Jamaica, and how all but one turn over a new leaf, and support the King, Charles I think. It ought to have been in 1674 anyhow, if I remember my history rightly.*

This pirate—the pirate's name was Henry Morgan—had been caught by the British, and he made terms with the king that, if he was set free, and made governor of Jamaica, he would stop the others being pirates. He stops them all but one, Captain Leech, who is finally killed at Tortuga. It is very exciting, perfect for boys. Of course there is a bit of love in it too.

After the movie we had supper and saw a lot of army equipment around the city hall. It was wonderful, although a couple of guns were slightly old (1918 and 1920).

We got home at precisely 6 o'clock, just when we wanted to get home.

Sue had been having a party and had been sharing some films (Uncle Harold was operating them) and so we saw some while we were about it.

Yours very lovingly
Alec

---

8 American swashbuckler film from 1942 directed by Henry King, based on a novel by Rafael Sabatini, and starring Tyrone Power and Maureen O'Hara.

There is another three-week gap in correspondence, no doubt the result of the latest medical event, marked by a letter written in pencil:

Apr. 26th 1943

Darling Mummy

Please forgive this awful writing, but I've been in bed with measles for ten days and I am slightly out of practice.

I'm really getting things over with this year, first mumps, then measles. Dr. Brown decided that I didn't have measles badly enough to stop reading, so that I have been catching up a bit for supplementary reading, and I might even learn some poetry for memory work.

Since the Friday before last Nurse, Sue and Jeremy have been at the farm, having some perfect weather; just lately it's been just like summer out. I peeked my head out of the window a couple of times, and the lawns are beautifully green, flowers are blooming, and the sun has been shining most of the time without a cloud in the sky. Early yesterday morning it was raining, but it soon cleared up enough for Aunt Mavis and Uncle Harold to go to the farm.

I've been reading a couple of books lately, novels by Percival Wren, awfully exciting, Foreign Legion and all that sort of stuff you know. They are both very exciting, with bits of humour inserted. Generally small talk. I like the way he writes, he's so lifelike.

Then I was reading a very exciting spy story called Faked Passports[9] *by Dennis Wheatley. It was quite astounding to see*

---

9   This was the third in a series about a proto-James Bond spy named Gregory Sallust. First published in 1941.

*Dennis Wheatley written in big letters at the top of the cover, I
couldn't quite see the Dennis Wheatley I know writing novels,
and practically worldwide at that.[10] It showed a map at the
back of the book, and all the countries that did not have Dennis
Wheatley's books translated into their own tongue were blacked
out. I think that China, Japan, Tibet, Mongolia and a good
lot of uninhabited South Sea Islands were about all that were
blacked out.*

*I tried out a couple of dull non-fictions at the school library
lately, but it was no-go. However I like biographies, and
autobiographies, very much. Truth is stranger than fiction. I'm
in the middle of the life of Napoleon, and a history of England
from 1840–1940 called* English Saga, *and have some more
biographies in mind.*

*I hope this letter isn't awfully dull. I'm just putting down what
comes into my head, filling space so to speak, with terrible
writing too.*

*I have a wonderful room while I'm in quarantine. It used to be
Nurse's room, then Bessie's (the maid)[11] and now it's the room I
have my diseases in, it was used for mumps as well. It is ever so
bright, and when I wake up in the morning, I can see everything
perfectly well. I can even read with the curtains drawn too.*

*I passed my cooking on the hike I told you about, so I now have
my Second Class, unofficially, as I got measles before, in fact,
on the same day we had Scouts, and I was to have received my
Second Class badge. As far as I know, our assistant scoutmaster
is in the air force now, but I'm not very sure.*

---

10 *The writer shared a name with someone I knew. In 1939 my mother and I had stayed in
Cornwall with Louise Wheatley, an old family friend, and her son Dennis and I were good
friends ourselves. We resumed that friendship after my return to England in 1943, but after the
war we lost touch. I learned later that Dennis eventually settled in Southern Rhodesia, probably
as a farmer.*

11 *Hired help was an off-and-on thing in these years. I recall two maids or cooks between 1940 and
1942, who were apparently unsatisfactory.*

Yesterday was Easter Sunday, and Nurse gave me a present of my favourite Dave Dawson *series book. I must have three now, at least, four now I come to think of it,* Dave Dawson at Dunkirk, Dave Dawson with the R.A.F., D[ave] Dawson at Singapore, *and my last,* Dave Dawson in [with] the Air Corps (U.S.A.). *Aunt Mavis didn't have time to get me anything, but she gave Dave his present a few weeks in advance, some showcard paints that he wanted badly, and quickly.*

Well, I think I've just about killed space as much as I can, and as I've run out of ideas, I will take leave of you till my next letter.

Your loving son
Alec

P.S. Aunt Mavis couldn't get me my present because she had very bad flu. She did, however, get me all candies and ornaments that she found time to produce.

It was not until April of 1943 that I became aware of the arrangements being made for my return to England. From rough drafts of cables Mother appears to have sent, she had "received Mildred's letter and understand your difficulties." Although I was never told about this, it appears that Mildred Dilling may have suggested that I go down to New York to stay with her, while Mother had already been discussing my return to England. Mother had written to Mildred, "Have cabled Mavis to arrange passage & temporary home. Dread passage and inevitable danger. Please advance necessary expenses—will refund." The cable to the Frys went on: "Please arrange permit and passage your end. Ask Canadian Pacific (CPR) Cable their London office for fare. Have contacted Children's Overseas (CORB) Reception Board for temporary home until Alec's passage available. Please send headmaster's survey Alec's work for public school entry. Fondest love grateful thanks for all you have done ..."

Aunt Mavis replied: "Cable received Alec thrilled and recovering measles enquiring regarding passage temporary home unnecessary pending completion school year writing regarding possibilities for Summer, love Mavis Fry."

It was at about this time that Aunt Mavis, evidently having been asked to do so, asked me if I would like Mother to marry again. Mother had mentioned "Gaffer Gilling" in her letters, and I knew that she was very fond of him, so it did not take much thought to realize that he was the person she had in mind. Although there is nothing written down about this, I never had any qualms about her marrying; the idea in fact really appealed to me, and of course I had every faith in her judgement.

May 16th 1943

Darling Mummy

I'm sorry for the absence of letters just lately, but I've been to the farm last week and the weekend before. Everything at school and everybody is in a dither. Exams come, next Thursday, and after that (the day after) the field day. What with everybody practicing for track and field, and baseball, and lacrosse games going on, Forest Hill Village School's playground is a hive of activity.

The Victory Loan went over the top yesterday, $1,100,000.00 was the objective!

You know that Dave and I have slept in bunks for quite a time now, well, yesterday we took the bunks down and made two separate beds, one for Jeremy and one for Dave. I have moved to the room where I had mumps and measles. I still use the old room in the daytime, but I sleep in the other.

A week ago last Tuesday I went to the Maple Leaf Gardens for the Victory Loan Show. It was very good. Jean Dickinson[12] and Lieutenant Oscar Natzke, RCNVR,[13] being the two singers.

They had demonstrations of machine gun drill and the Navy had a gun demonstration. The air force had a precision drill squad. It did everything without one order, and they did it in perfect time and precision.

The Canadian Provost Corps exhibited their skill in judo, a form of ju-jitsu. I wouldn't like to be caught by an MP [military policeman] of Canada after seeing that.

There was a flight lieutenant of the Fleet Air Arm who had been in the Navy FOURTEEN years and was only twenty-six years old being interviewed. He had been at Matapan, Crete and Malta.

I have had various hints of going back to England for quite a while now; isn't it wonderful to think of going back again. It'll be nice to see the downs, and all the places I remember from England.

Yesterday a Mrs. Maxwell phoned up, and is apparently a friend of Miss Marjory Fields. She is trying to get back to England, and she said that if she went, she would be glad to take me with her. I don't remember Miss Fields, but I think she is a friend of yours.

Last Thursday in Scouts I took out a badge card, that is, I took a card for a badge, to pass at school, and get at badge headquarters. It is my interpreter's, and I have to send and translate, write a simple letter, on a subject given by the

---

12 Jean Dickenson, American soprano (1914–??), was a popular singer on radio at the time. https://archive.macleans.ca/article/1942/7/15/the-lady-said-no.

13 This probably refers to Oscar Natzka, a New Zealand opera singer who was made a temporary lieutenant, Special Branch, in the Royal Canadian Naval Volunteer Reserve at the end of May 1942.

*examiner, and carry on a conversation in at least two modern
languages.*

*Talking about languages, Aunt Mavis remarked the other day
that I'm way behind where she was in French at thirteen, so I
suppose I'll be behind in French (and Latin too, for that matter)
if I go back to England.*

*Well, yours very lovingly
Alec*

....

May 18th 1943

Dear Uncle David

*I haven't written you since Christmas now but I hear you are in
Africa, or have you been transferred again?*

*I suppose you were pretty elated at the Tunisian victory.[14] If it's
not asking too much, were you in Tunisia or around there, or
did you stay in wherever you were before. Mummy tells me you
were in Durban [South Africa] at one time or other. It's pretty
hard keeping in touch with a fellow now.*

*In case you don't know, I'm in Boy Scouts, and have my Second
Class. I am going down to get my first badge on Wednesday.*

*We have a "group" system at school, and I am in the same
group as Dave. You'll probably remember him, he came to visit
England every other year, at Laleham[-on-Thames], with Uncle
Leonard and Aunt Florence (Mr. and Mrs. Thompson).[15]*

*The group system is quite ingenious. The school is divided into
twelve groups, six boys' groups and six girls', with a teacher
in charge of each. Grades 7, 8, 9 and 10 are mixed together in*

---

14 After the nearly six-month-long Tunisian Campaign, Axis forces surrendered to the Allies in
Tunisia on 13 May 1943.

15 Florence and Leonard Thompson were the mother and stepfather of Davina Whitehouse and
Mavis Fry.

*the groups. (I am in Grade 9.) We (our group) won two sports
championships this year, Jr. Basketball and Jr. Hockey. Our seniors
are not very good this year, but we might do better in the Baseball.
I have practically forgotten how to play cricket and rugger.*

Well, good luck till we meet again,
Alec

....

May 23rd 1943

Dear Mother

*This week we have been having exams, and will be having them
till next Thursday. This week at school has been quite fun. The
exams weren't too bad and school work was just reviewing. On
Tuesday it was announced that we were not going to have a
holiday on May 24th. All the other municipalities around were,
so we were really mad. Everybody went around writing on the
walls DOWN WITH VILLAGE COUNCIL or MAY 24th? and
things like that. There were pictures of Hitler, like this* [a circle
with a moustache and black hair coming down over the left
eye] *and an arrow pointing, like this ...* [illustration] *and the
words OUR DEMOCRATIC REEVE. Well, we were duly scolded
by the principal, who said—"This morning I had no feeling on
the matter, but now ..." When he got round to 9C, he started a
long speech about co-operating with the Dominion Government,
when one boy stood up and said,*

*"The Dominion Government said that municipalities could
decide for themselves whether it is a holiday or not."*

*Said Mr. Totton, "No they did not, they said definitely that it
was not a holiday." He was answered by the boy (Alec Freeman),
producing a paper with the announcement in it. Mr. Totton was
flabbergasted, to say the least. It must have had effects for next
morning, the village council announced that it was a holiday
after all: "They had just discovered that all the municipalities in*

201

*the neighbourhood had decided to have a holiday on May 24th."
So much for that.*

*On Friday we had an Empire Day Service at school, put on by
the senior high school. It was very good, with an excellent play
called* We Must Be Free or Die.

*Quote—I am working quite hard for exams, as I made such a
rotten showing in my last report. With ideas of going back to
England, I had better make an impression (good)—unquote.*

*We could not get to the farm this Friday, as it was teeming rain,
and, although the weather is now wonderful, Aunt Mavis and
Uncle Harold are in Hamilton. We are going out on Monday if
the weather is alright.*

*The garden is getting on alright in the city, and I expect the farm
is glorious now, but as I haven't been out of late, it is kind of
hard to know.*

Well, Love and kisses,

*Yours affectionately
Alec*

Aunt Mavis added a note:

*I'm enclosing this article in last night's paper—apparently the
Portuguese Line is the best & safest bet—You might enquire
at Cook's in London—it has to be arranged from your end I
understand. I know people coming that way in July who could
bring Alec.*

*(Later—I hear vaguely that it is terribly expensive—so probably
no good. Enquire anyway—perhaps we could do it between us)*

Love, Mavis

May 26th 1943

Darling Mummy

I am so glad to hear that I can go back to Housie [Christ's Hospital]. *I would certainly like to go back there.*

I certainly am prepared to work, and I realize what a necessity it is to work hard, I am sure that I won't let you down. I will certainly try not to.

I am rather vague about what I want to do when I get older, but I am interested in an engineering course or modern languages.

I am very keen on languages, and I am taking both French and German, although I am not very far advanced.

I would like to specialize in languages, but as I said before, engineering interests me.

I haven't been thinking of any other school, and I do like Christ's Hospital very much, and I would rather go there, I think, than anywhere else. I have been very dull, and so far this letter is very school-bookish, but I was trying to be concise about the answers for your questions, so I hope you will forgive me.

Auntie Mavis tells me that she has been trying very hard to get me passage over, but so far she has had no luck. I am enclosing a clipping from yesterday's paper, about going via Portugal, and apparently you will have to enquire about it at home. Aunt Mavis says that Cook's is the place to go, and she thinks that will be the best bet.

Aunt Mavis just told me that I ought to send the clipping in another envelope. With it I am sending as many exam papers as I can find, that we have had just recently. It will give the schoolmaster, or yourself, just what kind of work I am doing. At the end of the year, or term, I will get my report. Aunt Mavis thinks I have been working much harder lately, and I hope it is true.

By the way, Aunt Mavis knows some people who are going via Portugal to England in July.

Sincerely and hopefully yours
Alec

The following letter, on Mavis Fry's notepaper, is written in pencil.

3 Ava Crescent
Forest Hill Village

June 6th 1943

Darling Mummy

Please excuse the pencil writing, but I'm out at the farm, taking advantage of rain to write this letter. Yesterday the weather was lovely, not too hot, a nice breeze and the sun shone brightly. Dave and I got in the potatoes after about an hour of mathematical problems on where to put them, with the help of Uncle Harold. We put a hundred potato eyes in, and about ten of Uncle Harold's special ones. Today we put in some "Penguin Gourds."[16] They are creeping plants, and can be painted to look like penguins. Dave was planning on selling some. We are awfully late this year because of the wet spring.

On Friday I was given some lovely presents. Dave gave me a lovely model sailing ship to build, Aunt Mavis gave me a lovely summer tie, really smart, and Uncle Harold gave me a very nice book called A Picture Gallery of Canadian History.[17]

---

16 Also known as "calabash," these gourds are 5" in diameter, 12" long, and shaped like a penguin. Light green skin cures to a tan color. Ideal for craft projects. https://www.superseeds.com/products/penguin-gourd

17 *A Picture Gallery of Canadian History, vol. 1: Discovery to 1763,* by C.W. Jeffreys, published in 1943. Jeffreys was a Canadian painter and illustrator, best known for his historical illustrations. There were two more volumes to come in the series.

*It is a book, mostly of pictures, and quite a bit of writing about
Canadian history. I seem to have a bad habit of writing capitals
inside a sentence today. I don't know why. Nurse also gave me
a* Dave Dawson *book. Did I tell you that we had Field Day
[on] May 28th? Our group placed third. We had places in all
the classes—junior, intermediate and senior. I wasn't in much,
only the intermediate 75-yard dash, which I did not place in.
I must have been studying too hard to be in practice for track
running!!! We've had a few of our marks for our tests in school
lately—Science 73%, French 79%, Music 67% and over 60% in
Math (we have not been told our mark yet.)*

*Last Wednesday we were at [the] Scout Badge Center. Dave
passed his Healthy Man Badge, and I got my Debator Badge.
I am going to get two badges this week, Healthy Man and
Entertainer. I can only get six until I get my First Class.
Everybody in our troop is trying to get badges this year, as we
are trying to make a record year for badges.*

On Friday we had an excellent group period.

*Aunt Mavis wants to tell you that she will tell you as much as
possible in her next letter, about how I might be able to come
over to England. It is a sort of military secret, quite hush hush,
so she won't be able to tell you much. I will be very lucky if I can
come over this way.*[18]

*Mumsmum asked me in my telegram if I had received her letter
and photograph. I certainly did at Christmas, and I sent her a
thank-you letter immediately after Christmas. If she didn't get
it please tell me.*

*All my love
Alec*

---

18 This was the first indication of a passage to England through the Royal Navy, and I believe the
first of such passages for the return of "war guests."

June 16th 1943

Dear Mother

Here is my report (a copy [not included]*) certified and signed by Mr. Totton himself, principal of the Forest Hill Village School's Junior High School.*

Everything is present except some of the teachers' signatures (those who were absent). Mr. Carter's comments are perfectly genuine, copied from the original report.

School is over for the year now for me, except for one exam, Business Practice. It is the only one I have to try, and is the very last (Monday afternoon).

The weather here has suddenly turned from "like the kitchen sink" to "like the kitchen oven." 90° F in the shade this a.m.!

Your loving son
Alec

....

3 Ava Crescent
Toronto, Ont.,
Or R.R. #2 Lloydtown

July 11th 1943

Darling Mummy

I am terribly sorry I haven't written for so long, and you must be wondering what has happened to me. Well, for the last three weeks or so I have been at the farm. The weather has been superb, except for rain about once a week, which is very good.

This last week we have been at Mr. McAllister's farm, helping to bring in the hay. We have had jobs such as building the load, driving horses etc. and we have had a really good time.

Aunt Mavis was at Muskoka for the week on holidays.

You will probably want to know what the garden is like, so I'll tell you. Looking at it from the road, you see the house, with a rock garden in front, to the left flower beds along the fence, with hollyhocks, flocks [phlox], delphiniums etc. in them. To the right you would see a beautiful lawn sloping down a hill, and a lovely rose garden with a background of sweet peas. This successfully screens a large hole full of, or half full of weeds, grass, old cartons, scraps etc., which used to be the old log cabin still further to the right of the vegetable garden.... [diagram of the garden layout, beside which is written "entirely from memory"]

Behind the house is the perennial bed with a background of a willow, or willows. Still further behind is the tent, where Dave and I sleep. It is a wonderful pavilion affair, with a blue roof and white walls. We have the company of fireflies at night time, and this morning we found a wren, flying around the roof inside the tent!

The stream is as cold as ever this year, and we think it a bit deeper. We are trying to teach Jeremy to swim, but he seems to imagine crawfish are all over the bottom of the stream, so the opposition from that sector is rather stiff.

Dave has been admitted into UTS and has been having a lot of extra French lessons as he is behind in the subject. Forest Hill is not as far ahead in French as UTS is.

I have told you before of Katherine Cherry and Roddy, haven't I. Do you remember that weekend in the country last winter, just after my mumps, with Miss James, Katherine was there then too. Well, the Cherrys bought a horse, and called it Ben. It was quite a nice horse they thought, and even when it bolted with the wagon they kept their faith in it. However, last week they were out in the democrat[19] when a horse came at [and] *bit the*

---

19 A democrat wagon, antiquated term for a light flatbed farm wagon or ranch wagon that has two or more seats and is usually drawn by one or two horses.

back of Ben's leg. Ben immediately ran loose, throwing everyone out except Katherine, one wheel came off and the horse ran helter-skelter into Nobleton with one wheel off and Katherine desperately trying to hold on, so they have now sold the horse.

Well, my love to everybody and hoping to see you by September.

Yours lovingly

Alec

....

July 18th 1943

Darling Mummy

The letter enclosed [from 11 July 1943] *is one that I forgot to post, that I wrote last Sunday.*

I'm in a state of suspended animation about going back home right now. Tonight I am going into the city to get my fingerprints taken, and I expect to be back in England by the middle of August. Everything is very hush-hush, so I can't tell you much. I don't know what day I'm going, in fact, I doubt that even the authorities know much about it themselves.

Yesterday I got your letter of June 26th. I wasn't able to get my own papers back to send to you, but I sent my report, which you have probably got.

Business Practice was my worst subject, but all that was, was banking, postal rates, and utilities etc., which is not the same as England (except for banking). Banking was my good point luckily, which is in my opinion the most important part of Business Practice. Our teacher was Irish, and emphasized thrift! I quote, "Thrift is the Essence of Life," unquote.

This week has been quite wet, so we have been weeding every morning except for Monday and Saturday. Dave and I went to Mr. McAllister's to work.

The view I am getting from the tent door is wonderful, it keeps on putting me off my letter. I can see dark green poplars against the white clouds with rifts of blue in them, while nearer still is the back part of the lawn, and the house, white with green shutters. Quite a rhapsody of colour. There is practically every shade of green in the view.

In your letter you said that people were inviting me to the country all the time. Please don't break my [your?] neck over the holidays for me. I will have a wonderful time in the city, with you coming home at night from work. I can look after the flat while you are working—make beds, sweep rooms etc. and everything would be very nice and cosy. After all, I'm at school nine months out of twelve.

Well, I hope I'll be seeing you soon,

Yours hopefully,
Alec

CHAPTER 11
JULY TO AUGUST 1943:
RETURN TO ENGLAND

On 27 July, Uncle Harold and I, accompanied by another war guest who had been staying in Toronto, Master Edwin Fripp Clark, boarded the night train from Toronto to New York. Just before midnight we were woken up by an immigration official, as the train crossed the border at Buffalo. The incident is recorded on a form, "Imm. 106 (12/11/41)," "U.S. DEPARTMENT OF JUSTICE, Immigration and Naturalization Service, Buffalo District: *ITINERARY OF ALIEN IN TRANSIT*...Means of exit. (Here give name of vessel, train, bus or other means of transportation by which you are to travel.)" Presumably Uncle Harold had to explain at this point that we did not know the name of the vessel on which we were to sail.

This form recorded the fact that I was in transit from Toronto, Ont., to England with a proposed departure of July 31, "BOAT NAME UNKNOWN" and stated my itinerary as: "LEAVE TORONTO CAN. 7-27-43 BY TRAIN THROUGH THE U.S. BY TRAIN ARRIVE NEW YORK 7-28-43. LEAVE NEW YORK BY BOAT ABOUT 7-31-43 FOR ENGLAND." I was required to sign this document, over the following: "NOTE: Under present regulations, the holder of this form is required to pass through the continental United States in continuous transit, remaining in the United States no longer than necessary for such continuous transit. No deviation or delay in the transit journey will be permitted without the consent of the Secretary of State or the Attorney General."

At the bottom of the form is the handwritten entry "Admitted Buffalo 7-27-43—TRANSIT 5 days," and this was signed by "Nelson R. Clyde, U.S. IS."

Several documents had been prepared before we left Toronto, and they indicate the preparations Uncle Harold and Aunt Mavis had been making for the previous three weeks. We carried a list of the clothes and other items (including my Scout uniforms, various toys, school books, a hockey puck and a cricket bat), packed in my trunk.

NOTICE TO PROSPECTIVE TRAVELLERS TO DESTINATIONS OTHER THAN UNITED STATES AND NEWFOUNDLAND

Prospective travellers proposing to leave Canada by sea or air other than the United States and Newfoundland should, sufficiently in advance of their proposed departure, submit at a postal censorship office for examination all articles, documents, pictorial representations, photographs, gramophone records or any other articles whatsoever recording information, so that they may after examination be returned to them for carriage in a sealed package. This package, on embarkation, will be handed with the seal unbroken to the Security Central Officer for delivery by him to an officer of the ship or aircraft upon which the traveller proposes to travel for re-delivery to the passenger after departure.

Prospective travellers are warned that failure to observe these instructions may involve the surrender of any articles of the kind and entail their detention until after the departure of the ship or aircraft.

Security Control Officers will determine whether the outgoing passenger is carrying any articles not enclosed in the sealed package which requires censorship examination and, if he is, these will be submitted to the local censorship examiner.

Postal Censorship Offices are located in the following cities:

Charlottetown	Niagara Falls	Halifax
North Bay	Saint John	Winnipeg
Moncton	Regina	Quebec
Moose Jaw	Montreal	Saskatoon
Ottawa	Calgary	Toronto
Edmonton	London	Vancouver
Windsor	Victoria	Hamilton

At the bottom of the form, Uncle Harold added the following note:

Alex[1]:

I have talked to the local postal censor and as a result have eliminated from your luggage your snapshot album and your stamp collection. The censor does not think there will be any question about your school books. The stamp collection and the snapshot album can go over to you after the war.

H. Fry
Guardian

In the following letter, Uncle Harold addressed administrative requirements of the British Admiralty for what was to be the most exciting part of my return home: passage on a warship.

---

1 *This is addressed to me, but Harold Fry was the only one to spell my name as "Alex."*

Miss Helen P. Ryan,
Rogers Majestic Limited,
622 Fleet Street,
TORONTO, Ontario.

July 10th, 1943

Dear Miss Ryan

Re: W. Alexander B. Douglas

Referring to our conversation of yesterday and your letter of the 7th, I have pleasure in advising as follows:

- *I enclose certificate signed by me undertaking to absolve the Admiralty in connection with the transportation of Alex Douglas to Great Britain.*
- *Alex's luggage will consist of a trunk, a large suitcase, a small suitcase, the contents of which will consist of clothing and miscellaneous personal effects, books, games, and possibly a few small gifts, camera, steamer rug, sheets, towels, soap etc. Depending on the facilities for transportation, etc., between here and the embarkation port, the trunk, of course, could go by express to Great Britain. Alex will have a list of the important items making up his luggage.*
- *Alex will have not more than $30.00 American funds, or £7 sterling in his possession at the time of embarkation.*
- *Herein is a certificate signed by me covering Alex's ability as a swimmer. As a matter of fact, he holds one of the junior life saving certificates.*

We are presently occupied with the Department of External Affairs and the Immigration Department of Mines and Resources at Ottawa in connection with the passport and Exit Permit. On receipt of them we shall get in touch with the United States Consulate here to secure the necessary transit visa. We note that such a visa will obviate the necessity of the Admiralty

Representative at Washington securing an Exit Permit there.

If there is any further information you require, I hope you will let me know.

Yours very truly,
Harold Fry

....

Finally, there was a letter of introduction that also laid down the arrangements for my arrival in the United Kingdom.

Fry and Company
25 King Street West
Toronto

July 24th, 1945

TO WHOM IT MAY CONCERN

This letter will introduce Master W. Alexander B. Douglas. He has been a "War Guest" of Canada for the past three years under the guardianship of Mr. And Mrs. Harold Fry, 3 Ava Crescent, Toronto, Ontario. Master Douglas is returning home to Great Britain (via the United States) and will proceed as directly as possible, on arrival there, to his mother, Mrs. Hector Douglas, 77 Marylebone High Street, London, England.[2] Mrs. Douglas should be informed, as soon as possible (after his arrival in England) by telegram or telephone so that she may make arrangements to meet him at the London station. If it should happen that Mrs. Douglas should not be at home, on his arrival, he has been advised to communicate with my relatives, Mr. and Mrs. J. Leonard Thompson, "Riverside," Vicarage Lane, Laleham-on-Thames, Middlesex, England (telephone London directory).

Master Douglas is travelling with Master E. Fripp Clark, who

---

2 *My mother moved because she wanted more independence. She rented rooms on Marylebone High Street to friends. I recall that she was on the fourth or fifth floor, and there was a pub on street level below her, which was popular with Canadian soldiers.*

is also returning to Great Britain, and both boys have been instructed to co-operate with each other in connection with all matters pertaining to their arrival in Great Britain.

Yours very truly
Harold Fry

Mildred Dilling met us in New York, and there followed a day of great activity and fun. Aunt Mildred was her usual ebullient self, and insisted on taking me shopping for a present to take to my mother, while Uncle Harold delivered me safely to the British naval authorities.

We joined the ship at the Brooklyn Navy Yard on 29 July (three years to the day since Paul and Lilian Kingston had brought me safely to New York in the Cunard-White Star Line's MV *Britannic*), and found to my unutterable delight it was the auxiliary aircraft carrier HMS *Pursuer*, just having completed her conversion from a merchant ship to a "Woolworth Carrier,"[3] at Charleston, South Carolina. For the next fifteen days we would be members of the wardroom mess in *Pursuer.* We came on board at tea time, ("the first spot of tea I had had in three years" I said in the report we were asked to write before leaving the ship), and were taken in hand by the Air Staff Officer, Lieutenant Commander A.S. Marshall—our "temporary guardian." Since the ship was carrying a cargo of Republic P-47 Thunderbolts to the U.K., and there was no aircrew on board, Lt. Cdr. Marshall's duties were not heavy, and presumably he had time to spare for our welfare, not that we were much of a burden. Besides Edwin Clark, the other returning boys were Gerald Selous, Justin Lowinsky, Peter Fox and John Moore. We ranged in age from ten years old to sixteen. Gerry Selous, the oldest, was the son of the British Trade Commissioner in Vancouver and was said to be related—possibly

---

3 A Royal Navy term for a type of small, slow escort aircraft carrier of the time.

215

a great nephew—to F.C. Selous, the famous African big-game hunter, and one of the pioneers of Southern Rhodesia. Gerry had lived in Monte Carlo, where his father had held a diplomatic post before the war, and was perfectly fluent in French. He had Norman features: a prominent and straight nose on a rather saturnine face. I remember these details well, perhaps because he was a "character," and because we saw each other once more the next summer. We tried to tease him by calling him "Sealouse," to which he responded with instant indignation, even anger. His Monte Carlo background came to be useful at the end of our journey, as will be seen. Edwin Clark, who lived in Berkhamsted, proved to be very compatible but not so memorable. The others in our group, with whom I soon lost touch after arriving home, are not at all vivid in my memory.

We were given a routine and certain ground rules as soon as we came on board: "0700 Get up, 0730 clear of bathrooms [for] breakfast. 1200 lunch. 1530 Tea—1900 Supper. 2200—Pipe Down. [We] were only allowed on fore well deck of boat besides quarters and wardroom. Hangar deck was out of bounds—so was flight deck …."[4] We were shown the hangar deck, and the fighter aircraft closely packed for delivery to the U.K., a most impressive sight. What my diary did not note was the presence of fifty Free French sailors, with whom we were forbidden to fraternize. Whether we were told this immediately or later in the passage I am not certain, but it was a rule strictly enforced. Our accommodation, however, was luxurious beyond any expectations. Because the ship carried no aircrew—and that is presumably why there was room for passengers like us—we were in the aircrew quarters, where the bunks were fitted with enormously comfortable mattresses. Each cabin had a capacious desk, where I sat to write my diary. The steward assigned to us, to make up our bunks and offer us sage advice about the ship and the sea in general, was from the merchant marine (how this was possible I am not sure, but the ship

---

4   Excerpted from Alec's letter to his mother of 6 August 1943.

was carrying quite a number and variety of personnel for return to England) and told us he had had several ships sunk under him already. Consequently, he was a real mother hen, ensuring that we were ready for any emergency, and tense as a kitten whenever an announcement came over the ship's broadcast system.

The ship left her berth at 8:40 a.m. on Friday, 30 July, and joined the convoy in the Hudson River. According to my diary there were about sixty ships in the convoy, a fast 10-knot convoy. Because the ship and her cargo had unusual value, we were stationed in the centre of the centre column, and because we were in no way able to carry out ship's duties, we boys were placed under firm restrictions. The diary continues:

[We] were allowed onto gunnels around flight deck but still not on flight deck .... Made good progress. Lunch at same time [1200] Justin Lowinski feeling a little giddy. Had a practice "Action Stations." Our action station [in the] meteorological office. Met Scotch sailor there. Later on had "Emergency Stations." Justin went to cabin a little before this. Tea at 1530, supper 1900 as usual.[5] Weather hazy as a rule, good sun—bad visibility. Had escort of a couple of destroyers and a corvette. One destroyer was a four-stacker lend lease ship. The other was too far away to identify. Piped down 2200.

July 31st 1943

Woken up by Boatswain's pipe at 0645—Waky-Waky-Waky etc. Good breakfast. Beautiful day, quite a breeze, clear visibility for about fifteen miles. Met more sailors. Saw how to work detectors and Erlikons.

---

5   *I switched to writing the time in military style while on the ship.*

Being allowed up to the oerlikon platforms taught us a good deal more than how to work those 20-millimetre guns. The men I met that day were Newfoundlanders, and they exposed me, for the very first time in my life, to the famous four-letter word that sailors love to use. We also found out from these seamen that the ship's company consisted largely of men who had just come off course in the U.S., or had just finished their time in cells, so there was an unusually large proportion of "skates" (habitual offenders against King's Regulations and Instructions for the Royal Navy) on board, and only a nucleus of the crew that would eventually take the ship into action. They told us as well, and the ships' officers confirmed it, that the ship's trials off Charleston had been something of a fiasco because, on the first salvo from the single and rather ancient four-inch pedestal gun on the quarterdeck, large amounts of welding broke loose and the ship had to go back in for major repairs before being allowed to sail. And whether it was on this or a later occasion, our young eyes tended to see flotsam and jetsam floating by before the sailors we were talking to saw it. They reacted with alarm until assuring themselves the objects were not periscopes. Our presence on the upper deck on such occasions, therefore, made people—particularly, I gather, the captain—nervous, and we received firm orders not to go anywhere but the meteorological office during Action Stations.

Aug 1st 1943

Church in morning. Saw sloop oiling from tanker in convoy. Weather very nice—water was smooth as glass, P.O. Hicks said .... In afternoon some guns were practicing in convoy. Couldn't see where they were however. Darned good rummy game going on now, leave diary till later ....

I lost the game of rummy and went to bed disconsolate half an hour after pipe down. The next day followed a similar pattern. There were some distant unexplained explosions, and we boys began to fill our time with interminable monopoly games. Our temporary guardian inserted a new activity into our routine, PT at 0715, something that we noticed the French matelots [sailors] were also doing on the aft well deck. The only real excitement in the next few days was the destroyer HMS *Griffin* coming alongside for some unknown purpose on August 5. We had run into fog and rain. That day I wrote a letter to Mother, writing "On Active Service" in lieu of a stamp on the envelope: something to boast about!

Somewhere in the Atlantic
R.N. c/o G.P.O. London

Aug. 6th 1943

Dear Mother,

I am in a warship on the Atlantic right now, and the main purpose of this letter is to tell you that I ought to be home very soon now. We are in quite a large convoy, and having a wonderful time.

We are making quite a few friends in the ship's company, and everyone is very friendly.

There are quite a few fellows in the merchant marine on board.

Besides me, there are five boys coming over, Edwin Clark, Gerald Selous, Justin Lowinsky, Peter Fox, and John Moore. We have three cabins. Edwin is with me, Gerald with Justin and Peter with John. The cabins are just below the officers' mess. We are fitted out very comfortably and have a very good routine.... PT at 0715 is quite an effort you know. Well, that's all I'll say just now.

Yours lovingly
Alec

That day there was an intriguing change to our usual stately progress in the middle of the formation. In the forenoon, *Pursuer* suddenly increased to fifteen knots and took station on the starboard wing, then detached with seven other ships under the escort of two corvettes, but remained in visual contact with the main convoy. We of course received no explanation of these manoeuvres, nor so far as we knew did the ship's company, and in the evening we returned to our *Monopoly* tournament. The next day, Saturday, we had to tidy up our cabins for captain's rounds, (another new experience, but we were not required to be on hand for the inspection), and there for some reason my diary comes to an end. Perhaps it went astray, since it was written on flimsy sheets from a notepad. Its final statement reads: "then I went up on deck for a while." The daily routine would not have changed over the following five days, except that no doubt sighting the coast of Northern Ireland was a heart-stopping moment. On the other hand, we may have been below playing *Monopoly*.

We arrived in Belfast on 12 August, and were handed our mess bills:

Received from Master W.A.B. Douglas the sum of Two Pounds fifteen shillings in payment of Mess Bill on board H.M.S. "Pursuer"

Messing for 15 days at 3/6 a day	2.12. 6
Laundry (Bed Linen etc.)	2. 6
	2. 15. -

A.J. Young
Pay. Lieut. Commander RNR
ACCOUNTANT OFFICER

The last thing we were asked to do in *Pursuer* was to write up our impressions of the ship. My effort was hardly sparkling, but it does provide a sort of closing statement about the experience:

My Impressions of HMS Pursuer

Our temporary guardian, Lieutenant Commander Marshall, has asked us to write an essay regarding our impressions of HMS *Pursuer*. The writing quality of this essay is not of the best, so I beg of you to forgive me if it is rather boring.

When I first boarded the ship I was rather surprised. I had not expected an aircraft carrier to be the ship I was to go home on. The atmosphere on the ship seemed to be very cordial, and I was quite satisfied, in fact very pleased.

My first meal in this ship was very appropriate for an English ship—the first spot of tea I had had for three years.

I was overjoyed at hearing the English language, although some ratings had picked up a bit of Yankee slang.

As I advanced into the ship, I came upon certain evidence that the ship was built in the United States, such as brass plates testifying that the shipbuilders who built this ship always had and always would build the finest ships in the world. Another point was the welding. English ships generally have more riveting than welding. I do not know whether English ships have brass plates in view or not.

Before I had been on the ship very long, I found that the stewards proved most useful in supplying us with essential information, running errands in the canteen for us and making beds for us (the latter remark may seem quite unorthodox, but it was quite a change for us). Talking of beds, ours are the most comfortable I have slept in for a long time. I sincerely thank whoever was responsible for providing our sleeping quarters.

I also thank the officers and crew of HMS *Pursuer* for their kindness and helpfulness on the journey over, especially whoever was responsible for giving us permission to come on the HMS *Pursuer.*

I am sure that after a refit, this ship will again come to sea, to help win the fight for freedom.

I hope that the cargo of the ship will also prove very useful in helping us toward victory.

Good luck and good sailing!

Disembarking from *Pursuer,* just like joining it, was ridiculously easy, especially in comparison with our experience three years before on MV *Britannic.* No doubt the captain was glad to be rid of us! In no time we found ourselves on the ferry from Larne, in Northern Ireland, to Stranrauer, in Scotland, where we arrived in time to take the night train to King's Cross Station, London. This provided us with a new adventure.

When we reached our compartment, which as in all British trains of the day had bench seats facing each other, enough for about eight passengers, we found a WAAF (Women's Auxiliary Air Force) member occupying a corner seat. As we sat down, Gerry Selous immediately started "chatting up" the young lady, who snubbed him "good and proper," so he said something like "ta ta chaps—see you later" and disappeared down the train. We settled in for the night, sleeping soundly as youngsters can even in uncomfortable conditions, and awoke as the train was approaching London about seven in the morning. Gerry appeared as the train was pulling into the station, having been up all night playing craps with the Free French matelots, waving £50 in notes that he had won from them during the night. We were suitably impressed and wide-eyed as we came into King's Cross. On the platform was Mother, all smiles (no tears this time), and all she said was, "The same flower on a longer stalk!"

The stockings Mildred Dilling had persuaded me to buy, to bring back with me for Mother because they were so scarce in England, turned out to be rose-coloured net stockings. Mother wore them with pride wherever she went, and drew disapproving stares from women who saw us walking arm in arm on the London streets. She made me feel, as always, more like a brother than a son, and happily took me to meet not only the family, but all the friends she had made in London over the previous three years. I had resisted her suggestion in July of visiting friends in the country when I came home. As I'd written, "I will have a wonderful time in the city, with you coming home at night from work. I can look after the flat while you are working, make beds, sweep rooms etc. and everything will be very nice. After all, I'm at school nine months out of twelve ..." It was a perfect transition from Canada to England, and as August drew to a close the beginning of a new school year at Christ's Hospital made the transition complete.

A request to Mother in September 1943 by the BBC for me take part in a broadcast about my "views on life in Canada," and a suggestion that I join the "Junior Brains Trust," which was broadcast monthly in the North American Service, was met with an adamant refusal by the headmaster of Christ's Hospital, Mr. H.L.O. Flecker. The woman arranging these broadcasts then offered the extraordinary suggestion that I should "come round and see us as soon as possible and also ... get round his Headmaster!" Anyone who knew Mr. Flecker knew how hopeless a cause that would have been. I was well and truly back in the British public school system, and would remain there for nearly four years to come. In that time, of course, our lives would once again undergo great changes,[6] and my three years in Canada would open entirely new horizons, but for the time being, Mother and I were back to just being a pair of Londoners.

---

6 *Mother would marry Walter Gilling in March 1945, and follow him to Canada late in 1946. I would follow them on leaving Christ's Hospital in April 1947.*

CHAPTER 12
1943 TO 1947: TRANSITION FROM A WAR GUEST TO A CANADIAN

Returning to England, apart from the very happy reunion with my mother, would in the end turn out to be a temporary affair. In less than a year my mother would marry the Canadian army chaplain Walter Gilling, and in 1947 I would join them in Canada. In the meantime, there were interesting comparisons and contrasts with the experiences of the previous three years, and they deserve to be described.

When I went back to Christ's Hospital for the Michaelmas term of 1943, it was a much less tearful occasion than in 1938. The contrast with Forest Hill Village School, however, was extraordinary, and is worth some comment. In the first place, a school uniform was required. The wartime uniform for junior boys, consisting of a nondescript tweed jacket and short trousers, with grey flannel shirt and tie, just about exhausted my clothing ration coupons. There was a lot of harmless teasing about my so-called North American accent, but in other respects it was as though I had never been away. As in 1940, when Forest Hill Village School ended up simply assigning war guests to classes according to average age, Christ's Hospital had difficulty assessing my level of schooling. As I had been without Latin or Greek in Canada, and was well behind in science and maths, I ended up in Lower Erasmus, the lowest form of lower fourth.

Fig. 6: Alec Douglas at school, 1944.

Our teachers bore little resemblance to those who had taught us in Canada. "Dido" Hyde, called out to replace young teachers who had joined the armed forces, was a brilliant mathematician: he had been a Cambridge wrangler.[1] He was very ancient, very short-sighted, very deaf, and had halitosis. His classroom was at ground level, and in one particularly cruel prank we tampered with the test he had set us on the blackboard. By changing one or two numbers on the board before he came in to the classroom, the answers we arrived at, although all the same, seemed to be wrong. He would take one paper after another, scribble on it furiously, then gradually realise that all the wrong answers were the same. He would turn around to gaze at the blackboard, shake his head and revise his marking. It never seemed to occur to him, or perhaps he realised but did not intend to admit it, that we would have had the temerity to change what he had written. He was conscientious, and tried to give us individual attention, but when he leaned over your desk, (his halitosis making his presence painfully evident) and found you were reaching the wrong answer he would thunder "all wrong, boy, all wrong," and with a blunt HB pencil would scrub out, violently, what you had written, usually tearing the page in the process. I did not acquire a great deal of capability under his tutelage. The next year the school, breaking long tradition, brought in some women teachers. Miss Jarvis, who later married one of our science teachers, replaced "Dido" Hyde, and the transformation was miraculous. I actually enjoyed arithmetic under her guidance, and would do reasonably well in School Certificate.[2]

Another teacher who stands out in my memory was Lionel Carey, who taught us English and history. His interpretation of the

---

1 At the University of Cambridge in England, a "wrangler" is a student who gains first-class honours in the third year of the University's undergraduate degree in mathematics. The highest-scoring student is the Senior Wrangler, the second highest is the Second Wrangler, and so on. https://en.wikipedia.org/wiki/Wrangler_%28University_of_Cambridge%29

2 *Hyde was a greatly respected teacher, but the level of class in which I was placed in 1943 contained most of the poor maths students. Described by William Armistead as a man with a "never failing sense of humour … he was strict and inculcated in his pupils a respect for honest and accurate work." Clifford Jones, The Sea and the Sky: The History of the Royal Mathematical School of Christ's Hospital (published privately by Clifford Jones, 2015), 261.*

Civil War—it was about states' rights, he said, and *not* about Negro emancipation—is perhaps the most significant impression he left us with. Our teachers at Forest Hill Village School never displayed such vivid points of view. Mr. Carey was in the Victorian tradition, and the very model of a modern British Tory. He exposed us to Tennyson and Matthew Arnold, making us memorize long passages of Malory's *Le Morte d'Arthur* ("The old world changeth, yielding place to new, and God fulfils himself in many ways"), and poems such as "Break, Break, Break" by Tennyson ("Break, break, break, on thy cold gray stones O Sea ..."). We had a tendency to doze off during his monologues, and this invariably resulted in a run around the quad, for as many times as he considered appropriate to the offence.[3]

Science was a mystery. Chemistry (taught by Mr. Sills— "Kappa" Sills to us insensitive boys because he walked with a peculiar limp and was always bent over, possibly the result of polio, rather in the shape of the letter K) and later by A.H. Buck, became for me an exercise in memorizing formulae. Biology was a relatively strong point, however. Major Kirby, who taught us biology one year, brought in baby rabbits and frogs to be dissected. I think he intended to teach by the so-called heuristic method, described by the great inventor and Christ's Hospital product Sir Barnes Wallace, but to my mind Major Kirby combined the heuristic method (if that was his purpose) with humiliation, explaining anatomy by having a boy stand up before us without his clothes on. (Major Kirby was also responsible for the Junior Training Corps Signals Platoon, which consisted of Classics Grecians[4]

---

3 Lionel Carey eventually became a headmaster in another school. See Barclay Hankin, *In This Place, 1927–2004: Memories of Christ's Hospital* ([privately published?], 2005), Appendix B.

4 The military training program at Christ's Hospital was a Contingent of the Junior Division of the British Army's Officer Training Corps. Students in the senior class at Christ's Hospital were nicknamed "Grecians," while the second-most senior class were named "Deputy Grecians." "Classics" denoted the students who pursued the traditional "Latin" course of study at the school, in contrast to the "modern" or "mathematical" course of study. *The Quarterly Army List*: April 1944, Part 2 (London: His Majesty's Stationery Office, 1944), 2477a :"Christ's Hospital," *Encyclopedia Britannica*, 11th edition (Cambridge: Cambridge University Press, 1911), vol. 6, 296.

who would communicate in Latin and Greek, thus befuddling Canadian army units exercising in the neighbourhood.) I cannot imagine such eccentricities in our Canadian public and high school teachers in those days.[5]

Scripture was a required subject. The Reverend W.C. Johns, one of several clerics on the school staff, and known to all as "Boggy" Johns (a nickname whose origin I never learned) required us to memorize bible passages, and when we got them wrong or forgot them would bring down a ruler smartly on the knuckles of the errant's hand. Beating knowledge into pupils, an eighteenth-century practice made famous in Christ's Hospital lore, was recalled by Samuel Taylor Coleridge in his description of the Reverend James Boyer, "a very severe master" whose epitaph was: "may all his faults be forgiven; and may he be wafted to bliss by little cherub boys, all head and wings, with no bottom to reproach his sublunary infirmities." It was still the practice of one or two of our masters, the most famous of whom was probably "Boomer" McNutt, who gave a Latin verb test every Friday, and as we were led to believe, administered one stroke of the cane for every mark below seven out of ten.

All in all, despite the vivid personalities and eccentricities of our teachers—and those mentioned here merely scratch the surface of that subject—academic life among those not marked out for greatness, or as yet not fired with ambition and passion for academic subjects, was pretty humdrum at Christ's Hospital. We did have variations of routine that made life more interesting. Art classes were compulsory and, so we were led to believe, particularly helpful to students in abstract fields like advanced mathematics. Some hidden talents came to light, but in my case, except for one encouraging remark from the art master (Mr. Guest) to the effect that a design I had drawn had "real spunk," this was not a field in which I made much progress. Manual training, another diversion,

---

5 "Uncle" Bill Kirby "wrapped gown around him on formal occasions. Biology, Signals Swimming, Singing. Made you think. Bees and mating frogs": see Barclay Hankin, *In This Place*, Appendix B.

placed us under the perfectionist demands of Major Harrup. For those of us who were a bit ham-fisted an interminable amount of time was spent getting corners exactly square and edges planed perfectly flat. Making cigar box violins at Forest Hill Village School had been more satisfying, if more frivolous.

Looking back, it is hard to remember how we made time for anything other than school work and compulsory sports. We would get out of bed at about 7 o'clock in the morning and have half an hour to wash, dress, make our beds and be on breakfast parade. (We marched to the dining hall for all meals, in ranks four abreast and preceded by a boy carrying the house flag. On entering the dining hall, we were given the order "form two-deep," to enable a relatively orderly entrance into the building.)

In winter we also had to spend the first few minutes of the morning standing at the end of our beds and blowing noses in unison, five times each. (Our unusual and innovative school doctor, Dr. Friend, initiated this as a preventive measure against the colds that invariably afflicted almost every boy in the school. It was not very effective but may have cleared the sinuses a bit). If we were late for parade we received the punishment of "double changes," in which we had to change from our full uniform to running shorts and shirt in two minutes. My constant over-optimism about the time remaining before parade resulted in frequent double changes. "Sleepy" became one of my less welcome nicknames as a result of this tardiness, but it also resulted in much healthy exercise. When three or more double changes were given in a week, you also had to use the period between morning classes and lunch (12:15 to 1 p.m.) to run around the avenue behind the Big School, about one mile, wearing rugger shorts and shirt, and ordinary black walking shoes.

After this brisk beginning to the day, and in winter it was almost always very brisk because the central heating did not radiate much warmth in our large dormitories, we had a large breakfast of lumpy and lukewarm porridge or boiled herring—

sometimes, as a special treat, we had kippers, bread and butter, and plenty of "kiff" (tea) to drink. If we wanted jam or marmalade, we had to buy it from the tuck shop and carry it in to dining hall. Following breakfast, we went to chapel. This was compulsory, and on Saturday entailed practicing the hymns for Sunday under the direction of our director of music, Dr. Lang, brother of Cosmo Gordon Lang, the Archbishop of Canterbury. Following chapel we went to classes until about 10 o'clock, then returned to our houses for morning PT—about twenty minutes of simple calisthenics on the lawn in front of the building—and a snack of milk from the school's dairy herd and biscuits from a bakery in Horsham. They were about as hard as hardtack, and made wonderful things to throw at each other and the walls, to see if they would break on contact. The second class of the day lasted until 12:15, when we could relax a bit in the common room (or be obliged to run round the mile) until lunch parade. For lunch we marched to the accompaniment of the school band, under the direction of Mr. Stagg, a retired Royal Marine bandsman who demanded high standards. The band always marched in to the quad, led by one of the few boys who had earned the role of drum major, and who took pride in how high they could toss the mace. We enjoyed all this pageantry: it sort of made up for the quality of the food.

There is no doubt that the school tried to provide us with a healthy, balanced diet: not necessarily palatable, but healthy nevertheless. The dietician, Miss Stevenson, was a Scot, a no-nonsense lady whom we regarded with some awe and about whom we had little that was complimentary to say. All our fish came from Scotland, or so we gathered from seeing the crates from Aberdeen on the school railway platform, with cats sniffing around them. It was mostly herring, either plain or smoked, in the form of kippers, although we must also have had finnan haddie, a cold-smoked haddock, every now and then. Mutton was almost a staple—possibly also from Scotland—and the famous dish we all loved to hate was "Housey Stew," which featured large chunks of mutton floating in grease. We used to sing a paean to this dish to the tune of the "Colonel Bogey March": "Housey makes a very good stew/ Housey is very good for you ..." et cetera. Early in the war, Dr. Friend, who was highly regarded in his profession, protested the rationing of bread for schoolboys. He went to see Lord Woolton, the Minister of Food in London (so we were told), and negotiated the same rations for boys as for coal miners. Thus, when we were hungry and had a few pence to spare from whatever pocket money we received, we would invade the school tuck shop behind the dining hall and buy entire loaves of whole-wheat bread, fresh from the bakery and often still warm, all or most of which we would devour on our way back to our houses. In winter, the early afternoon was taken up with sports, depending on the season—rugger was the principal team sport in the Michaelmas term—and we had track and field in order to pass standards, in running especially.

We were very lucky in our housemaster, Arthur Humphrey, a mathematician and a music lover. Arthur, who became a dear friend long after leaving school, was a gentle man. He avoided corporal punishment. Only once did I know of him caning a boy. Once a week, about half a dozen of us would be invited to Arthur's study to listen to classical music on his gramophone, which was fitted with thorn needles so as not to exert excessive wear on the records and because the sound may have been better than with steel needles. He was an accomplished cello player himself, and organized chamber music concerts with talented boys, among whom was the future principal conductor of the London Symphony Orchestra, Sir Colin Davis.

The Junior Training Corps occupied a good deal of our time and energy. There were weekly parades, and we had to prepare for "Certificate A," involving elementary infantry tactics and weapons knowledge. There were periodic field days when we put our training to use, and once every school year those who required it took "Certificate A." One of the "Certificate A" tests was to take a verbal message and pass it on to the next cadet some fields away, so that he could pass it on, and so forth. The message always got garbled. It did not help that the Canadian officer (from the 2nd Canadian Division, which was based in the area and charged with testing us) who gave me the message had a strong French-Canadian accent.

In the summer term of 1944, we were very conscious of the preparations for D-Day, and we heard flights of aircraft flying overhead continuously in May and June. On the morning of 6 June, the hymn at morning chapel was "The fight is o'er, the battle won, now is the victor's triumph won," and we sang with huge enthusiasm. There was a whole holiday, and a number of boys climbed up the school water tower, tossing rolls of toilet paper over the edge to look like victory streamers.

School holidays—Easter, summer, and Christmas—were a wonderful change of pace. They were long enough—four weeks at Christmas and Easter and six weeks in the summer—to really enjoy the change. In the summer holidays of 1944, Mother and I went camping in the Lake District. In fact, she sent me to stay at a farm in Cumberland, where I worked on the harvest with the labourers, for two or three weeks before her holidays began. When we returned to London in late August or early September, we heard rumours of a new German secret weapon and the train conductor pointed out a large crater near the train. On arriving home, I turned on the gas stove to make the usual cup of tea when the gas was suddenly sucked back into the pipes and we heard a loud if distant explosion. This, we were told, was one of the first V-2s that landed in London.

In early 1945, Walter Gilling ("Gaffer," as he was called by friends and family), who had been in Italy when I first got home and was now going to northwestern Europe as deputy principal chaplain to the First Canadian Army, arrived in England from his furlough in Canada (having been one of the few who had served five years overseas in 1944). I remember answering the door

Fig. 7: Alec Douglas, Phyllis Gilling, Lt. Col the Rev. W.J. Gilling, in Regent's Park, London, 1945.

when he arrived at our flat and introducing myself. Since all he had heard about me dated back to 1940, it was something of a shock to find a fifteen-year-old boy now about six feet in height (I think—I was no longer outgrowing my clothes as fast as I had been in Canada), rather than the eleven-year-old who had gone to Canada four years previously. My mother had warned him, but the actual sight may have given him pause.

Mother and Gaffer married on Maundy Thursday, 29 March 1945, at St Marylebone Parish Church. Gaffer had been given leave, but because it was Holy Week he could not as an Anglican priest marry on any other day of the week, and his leave expired before Easter week was over. For the very brief honeymoon that followed his return from northwestern Europe after VE Day, Mother— concerned that I would feel left out by the marriage—told me I was very welcome to bring a friend with me to stay in London

Fig. 8: At Christ's Hospital, 1945, with the author's mother and his best friend, the late Brian Hogben.

during this period. Consequently, Brian Hogben (then my best friend at school) came back to London to share the honeymoon, after we spent a week with his family in Heathfield, East Sussex. Because Gaffer and I were very similar in size, Mother would lend me his jackets and trousers to wear, something that he accepted with astonishing tolerance. He had brought back with him from Holland a case of apricot brandy, "liberated" by his batman, supposedly from a collaborationist's house, and one night after Mother and Gaffer had retired, Brian and I poured ourselves each a glass of this delicious liqueur—our first experience of alcoholic beverages.

Eventually, probably with the thought of my stepfather being an Anglican priest, I decided to be confirmed as an Anglican. The school chaplain, Father Hahn, prepared a number of us boys for confirmation, and I must say his guidance was very persuasive. His own history, which he told at least some of us about, was memorable.[6] He was a Roman Catholic priest and an army chaplain in the Great War, and what he saw on the Western Front destroyed his faith. He left the Church, but after much soul-searching came back, but into the fold of the Church of England. He was a dynamic and militant priest. On one occasion in chapel, he detected us singing "When shepherds washed their socks by night / All seated round a tub, a bar of Sunlight soap came down / And they began to scrub." He brought a complete stop to the service with a stentorian roar of "STOP." After we had sung the carol properly, he got up in the pulpit and preached on blasphemy. I was confirmed by the Bishop of Chichester in 1944.

The end of the war in Europe, VE Day, was the cause of much rejoicing. Once again, some characters climbed up the water tower and let loose numerous rolls of toilet paper as streamers (it

---

6 *Father Hahn kept in touch after the war, counseling me when I became severely ill in 1953, and he encouraged me to remain the navy when I was considering whether to resign. I have heard in recent years that he returned to the Roman Catholic church, moved to Canada, and eventually took his own life.*

Fig. 9: Alec Douglas, his mother, and a dog, c. 1945.

Fig. 10: Cadet Alec Douglas, c. 1946.

was a better use of that awful paper than what it was supposed to be used for), and we had a service of thanksgiving.

In the fall of 1945, having passed School Certificate (the Oxford and Cambridge exam with matriculation exemption), the school allowed me to continue on as a probationary Deputy Grecian, specializing in history under the supervision and care of the Honourable David "Daddy" Roberts. For the next year and a half, I had the benefit of this man's wise and entertaining counsel. He had the habit, when reading the weekly essay we had to prepare for him, of expressing huge delight or interest in something we had written, placing his forefinger on the side of his nose and uttering a long "Ah-ha-a-a."[7] Because the objective now was

---

7   "Wonderful storyteller with infectious chuckle. Courteous in criticism. History Grecs adored him ..." Barclay Hankin, *In This Place*, Appendix B.

entry to Oxford or Cambridge, with either an exhibition or scholarship, we had to concentrate on one field of history and hone our knowledge in other areas—particularly languages (it would be necessary to undergo a "sight unseen" translation of a passage in German and one in Latin) and general knowledge.

At the end of each Easter term, the school had an Oxford or Cambridge don come down to set sample exams. My first effort was, if not lamentable, certainly unsatisfactory, owing mostly to my writing style. Candidates for these exams had to demonstrate adequate mastery of either medieval or modern history, and Christ's Hospital prepared us in medieval history. My results in this were adequate, but my three-hour essay did not impress the examiner at all. In the post-mortem, the headmaster would interview each of us, and he suggested to me that I find a historian with an excellent writing style on which to model my writing. I told him I was reading James Joyce, *A Portrait of the Artist as a Young Man*. "Oh," he said, "the Irish." He advised me to seek better models, and recommended Gibbon's *The History of the Decline and Fall of the Roman Empire*, with which, he said, he put himself to sleep every night. H.L.O. Flecker never seemed to me to have a sense of humour, and he evidently did not see the irony of this remark. "Daddy" Roberts simply said I would no doubt be a "late developer," like many of his previous students.

In the summer of 1946, my parents arranged for me to go to an Institut de Jeunes Gens in St. Prex, Switzerland, for three weeks in order to learn French. Mother and Gaffer had travelled to Switzerland earlier that year, partly to see where Gaffer's father had spent two years at Mürren, during the First World War on a prisoner of war exchange. During their travels they had met Dr. Hans Walter, the proprietor of the Institut Walter, and were evidently persuaded by him that this would be a good experience for me. It was indeed.

Routine at the Institut was fairly strict: we were only supposed to converse in French, but all the other boys wanted to practise their English and we broke the rules constantly. There were morning classes every day in French grammar and vocabulary. We rose at about 7 a.m., did PT before breakfast, and spent the afternoons in sports, tennis, and rowing for the most part. Hans's son, Stanley Walter, was a most impressive chap to have as an instructor, both in French and in athletic endeavours. He was, we were told, a diamond sculls athlete who was trained at Boston College before the war and participated in the Olympics. (Years later at a dinner at the Swiss Embassy in Ottawa in 1978, I mentioned my stay at the Institut to the ambassador. He told me Stanley Walter had later been lost, killed by bandits, during an expedition to the Nile, but I have never been able to determine the truth of this story). In the evenings we relaxed, rode bikes into town and gorged on Swiss pastries filled with chocolate and cream: unbelievable luxuries after English wartime fare.

There were two "holidays" during the three weeks we were there. The first consisted of rowing in a "yole," the term used to describe a quad sculling shell, from St. Prex to Geneva with one night camping en route. It was healthy and uneventful, except for the mosquitoes at night. We slept in a boathouse, in sleeping bags, in Geneva. The second holiday was a bicycle tour from St. Prex to Lugano, crossing the Furka and St. Gotthard passes. This was a fantastic adventure.

After this wonderful holiday, I took the train to Paris, arriving the day before my mother, who was to meet me at the hotel in the Place de la Madeleine, right opposite the famous church. When she arrived the next day, she first listened to my French, and told me I had a Russian accent. Next, she asked me how much money I had. After the Metro fare from the station, all I had left was a few francs, which shocked and dismayed my mother, and she immediately had me relegated to a room in the attic. Then she got about finding a solution. To her amazement the bank account in Paris that had been established when she was a fashion buyer before the war was still extant, so we were saved. But in showing me Paris, she also determined to show me proper frugality. The only restaurants we went to were those used by the working class. We would not have wine with our meals, but Vichy water. However, when we went to a restaurant in Montmartre, the Vichy water we ordered arrived in a bottle that had sediment floating in the liquid—quite evidently just hauled out of the River Seine—so she broke down and ordered *vin ordinaire*. Mum's favourite person in Paris was her milliner, a wonderful, feisty little woman who greeted me as *"mon petit cochon,"* and announced that I would have to go to the Folies Bergère. We went, and sat in the front row of the Dress Circle. Madame kept asking me if I liked the lovely ladies. I did.

We went home to London poor but very happy. It had been a terrific summer holiday for me, and I think Mother had a lot of pleasure in showing her "wee lamb" (her pet name for me) something of the experiences she had had as a girl growing up between the wars. Even if I did have a Russian accent.

....

Gaffer, after contemplating seriously the possibility of accepting a parish in England, decided to return to Canada to rejoin the Diocese of Toronto. I believe Archbishop Derwyn Owen influenced his decision, and late in 1946 he returned to Canada to become rector of St. Luke's Church, Peterborough. (Before the war he had been a curate at St. John's, Peterborough, after ordination, and then at St. Simon's, Toronto, and eventually had gone to Trinity College, Toronto as chaplain). Mother was to follow late in the year, and I had to make up my mind whether I wanted to stay in England, sit for an exhibition or scholarship to Oxford or Cambridge, or follow my parents to Canada to attend university there. It did not take me long to decide on Canada, and Mother immediately began finding out what I needed to enter Trinity College, Toronto, in view of Gaffer's previous connection with the place. It turned out that my Oxford and Cambridge School Certificate with matriculation exemption was sufficient for entrance to any Canadian university except Toronto. In order to qualify, the University told my mother I would need another maths and another science subject. She, examining the curriculum, informed the registrar that he was wrong, and that two languages would do just as well. She was right, so I had to work up French and Latin sufficiently to pass Ontario Grade 13 exams in those two subjects. That meant, in addition to my history preparation, I would have to get extra tutoring from two Christ's Hospital teachers, the Reverend "Boggy" Johns and Mr. Blamire-Brown. When the latter saw the examples of Ontario Grade 13 Latin exams, he commented, "Oh, rather like our provincial exams," referring to entrance exams to universities other than Oxford or Cambridge.

The school leaving service, where we were presented with a Christ's Hospital bible and prayer book, was at the end of the Easter term in 1947. The Cunard White Star liner RMS *Aquitania* sailed from England on 3 April 1947, and a week later we arrived in Halifax, Nova Scotia. Canada was now to be my country. In due course, strongly influenced by the 1943 promise to serve in the Royal Navy when old enough, I joined the university naval training division, and in 1950, my last year at Trinity College, transferred to the Royal Canadian Navy.

even. I played patience till then and then ...

...ooked to see what kind of a day it was and ...

...it marvelous. There was only the slight...

...n the sea and a small swell. I went out on ...

...nd was greatly surprised to see a school a...

...LES! They were about 200 yds to the ster...

...ame right out of the water on its belly. Some ...

...wards said it reminded them of the ...

...τ,

...t with wales and calm dies."

...ighted a fishing fleet later on, of about ...

...s. Me and Michael Faber went to the bow ...

...if we could see better, and we certainly ...

...After that we had breakfast and I had five ...

...s. After that I made friends with a

adian steward. He lived in London, a ferm
o from Forest Hill Village. He went to se
onto too. After a bit of talking he said he
ng to 'feed the Lions'. By that he meant he w
ive the petty officers their lunch.   I fou
were going to sight land at 1 p.m. Whethe
true or not I don't know. I decided to go s wi

o'clock but found out that I had g
of it. Then I wrote my letter for the day
It was 12 o'clock when I finished. Any t
aken at noon, It started being foggy
gain. The foghorn was blown every minu
a lunch and did not have any tea either.
to much till after dinner except play ten
h two very nice Siamese girls. After dinner
ncent, The first turn was Bazzoni a famo
inist playing a few tunes. The best one was
ria by Schubert. Don you know it? I
ne Noel Coward singing a few songs. He

Taking Responsibility for Children edited by Samantha Brennan and Robert Noggle • 2007 • xxii + 188 pp. • ISBN 978-1-55458-015-6

Home Words: Discourses of Children's Literature in Canada edited by Mavis Reimer • 2008 • xx + 280 pp. • illus. • ISBN 978-1-55458-016-3

Depicting Canada's Children edited by Loren Lerner • 2009 • xxvi + 442 pp. • illus. •ISBN 978-1-55458-050-7

Babies for the Nation: The Medicalization of Motherhood in Quebec, 1910–1970 by Denyse Baillargeon, translated by W. Donald Wilson • 2009 • xiv + 328 pp. • illus. • ISBN 978-1-5548-058-3

The One Best Way? Breastfeeding History, Politics, and Policy in Canada by Tasnim Nathoo and Aleck Ostry • 2009 • xvi + 262 pp. • illus. • ISBN 978-1-55458-147-4

Fostering Nation? Canada Confronts Its History of Childhood Disadvantage by Veronica Strong-Boag • 2011 • x + 302 pp. • ISBN 978-1-55458-337-9

Cold War Comforts: Maternalism, Child Safety, and Global Insecurity, 1945–1975 by Tarah Brookfield • 2012 • xiv + 292 pp. • illus. • ISBN 978-1-55458-623-3

Ontario Boys: Masculinity and the Idea of Boyhood in Postwar Ontario, 1945–1960 by Christopher Greig • 2014 • xxviii + 184 pp. • ISBN 978-1-55458-900-5

A Brief History of Women in Quebec by Denyse Baillargeon, translated by W. Donald Wilson • 2014 • xii + 272 pp. • ISBN 978-1-55458-950-0

With Children and Youth: Emerging Theories and Practices in Child and Youth Care Work edited by Kiaras Gharabaghi, Hans A. Skott-Myhre, and Mark Krueger • 2014 • xiv + 222 pp. • ISBN 978-1-55458-966-1

Abuse or Punishment? Violence Towards Children in Quebec Families, 1850–1969 by Marie-Aimée Cliche, translated by W. Donald Wilson • 2014 • xii + 396 pp. • ISBN 978-1-77712-063-0

Girls, Texts, Cultures edited by Clare Bradford and Mavis Reimer • 2015 • x + 334 pp. • ISBN 978-1-77112-020-3

Engendering Transnational Voices: Studies in Families, Work and Identities edited by Guida Man and Rina Cohen • 2015 • xii + 344 pp. • ISBN 978-1-77112-112-5

Growing Up in Armyville: Canada's Military Families during the Afghanistan Mission by Deborah Harrison and Patrizia Albanese • 2016 • xii + 250 pp. • ISBN 978-1-77112-234-4

The Challenge of Children's Rights for Canada, Second Edition by Katherine Covell, R. Brian Howe, and J.C. Blokhuis • 2018 • x + 248 pp. • ISBN 978-1-77112-355-6

A Question of Commitment: The Status of Children in Canada, Second Edition, edited by Thomas Waldock • 2020 • xiv + 364 pp. • ISBN 978-1-177112-405-8

Boom Kids: Growing Up in the Calgary Suburbs, 1950–70 by James A. Onusko • 2021 • viii + 250 pp. • ISBN 978-1-77112-498-0

A War Guest in Canada by W.A.B. Douglas • 2023 • xxii + 242 pp. • ISBN 978-1-77112-368-6